Teaching Climate

Welcome to the Anthropocene. Since the start of the Industrial Revolution, human-caused climate change has impacted the globe with the burning of fossil fuels. The debate in classrooms and the political realm should not be whether climate change is happening or how much it places human civilization at risk but over how societies and individuals should respond. This interdisciplinary book offers an in-depth examination of the history of the Earth's climate and how historians and citizens can influence contemporary climate debate and activism.

The author explains climate history and climate science and makes this important subject matter accessible to a general audience. Chapter topics include examining the Earth's geological past, the impact of climate on human evolution, the impact of climate on earlier civilizations, climate activism, and the need for international cooperation. Presenting climate history, human history, and climate science in a readable format and featuring resources for students, this book is meant for use by teachers in high school elective or an introductory college course setting.

Alan J. Singer is a teacher educator at Hofstra University, Hempstead, NY, a former New York City high school teacher, and a life-long political activist starting with the anti-war and Civil Rights movements of the 1960s.

Teaching Climate History
There is No Planet B

Alan J. Singer

Routledge
Taylor & Francis Group

NEW YORK AND LONDON

First published 2022
by Routledge
605 Third Avenue, New York, NY 10158

and by Routledge
2 Park Square, Milton Park, Abingdon, Oxon, OX14 4RN

Routledge is an imprint of the Taylor & Francis Group, an informa business

Library of Congress Cataloging-in-Publication Data
Names: Singer, Alan J., author.
Title: Teaching climate history : there is no Planet B / Alan J. Singer.
Description: New York, NY : Routledge, 2022. | Includes
    bibliographical references and index.
Identifiers: LCCN 2021031615 (print) | LCCN 2021031616
    (ebook) | ISBN 9781032061344 (hardback) |
    ISBN 9781032061320 (paperback) | ISBN 9781003200864
    (ebook)
Subjects: LCSH: Climatology—History—Study and teaching. |
Climatic changes—History—Study and teaching. | Nature—
    Effect of human beings on—Study and teaching. | Human
    ecology—Study and teaching.
Classification: LCC QC855 .S56 2022 (print) | LCC QC855
    (ebook) | DDC 551.6—dc23
LC record available at https://lccn.loc.gov/2021031615
LC ebook record available at https://lccn.loc.gov/2021031616

ISBN: 978-1-032-06134-4 (hbk)
ISBN: 978-1-032-06132-0 (pbk)
ISBN: 978-1-003-20086-4 (ebk)

DOI: 10.4324/9781003200864

Typeset in Galliard
by Apex CoVantage, LLC

Contents

vi *Contents*

Acknowledgments

I am deeply indebted to authors Elizabeth Kolbert, Eugene Linden, Brian Fagan, Jared Diamond, and Naomi Klein, whose books shaped my ideas. Their work should be widely read; consider this book their introduction to new audiences. Some of the lesson materials were originally developed by teachers and Hofstra alumni Dean Bacigalupo, Kristen Bradle, and Jessica Hermann for an article in the New York and New Jersey Councils for the Social Studies journal *Teaching Social Studies* (V. 20/N. 2). Bradle, Hermann, and Bacigalupo created "Integrating Climate History into the Global History Curriculum" as a resource to assist educators who are teaching the high school Global History and Geography curriculum.

I want to thank colleague Brett Bennington, chair of the Hofstra University Department of Geology, Environment, and Sustainability, whose video presentation on Greta Thunberg's *No One is Too Small to Make a Difference* (Penguin 2019) clearly explains the causes and implication of the greenhouse effect, students in my "Why Study History?" classes who held me to a rigorous academic standard and insisted that I support claims with evidence and present them in ways that are accessible to an audience of non-specialists, and students in my graduate seminars who debated climate change history and assisted with editing the text, including Dennis Belen-Morales, Tara Burk, Tom Clancy, Alexa Corben, Christopher Cucinotta, Alexis Farina, Emma Farrell, Thomas Ferrante, Karla Freire, Barney Giannone, Madison Hamada, Sarah Johnson, Robert Kleiman, Douglas Lensing, Crystal Ortiz, Christina Paccadolmi, Daniel Petschauer, Anthony Richard, Michael Scott, Brandon Swartz, Elizabeth Tyree, and Debra Willetts. Science buddies including Arthur Camins, Amy Catalano, and Janice Koch pointed me in the right direction on key topics. As always I was aided and supported by Hofstra colleagues Dean Bacigalupo, Janice Chopyk, Sean Fanelli, Andrea Libresco, David Morris, Pablo Muriel, Eustace Thompson, and Stacy Zalewski and my life partner Felicia Hirata. Any errors are my own.

This book is dedicated to young people around the world fighting for climate awareness and to reverse climate change. I pledge to donate any author's earnings to their cause.

Introduction

There is an African American spiritual of resistance, "O Mary Don't You Weep," that dates back to slavery days. In a verse that references the Judeo-Christian biblical book of Genesis (6:5), the Hebrew God regrets having created humanity because of its "wickedness" and decides to send flood waters that will "wipe from the face of the earth the human race" and all species of animals, birds, and "creatures that move along the ground." God then relented a bit and instructed Noah, a "righteous man," to build an ark so his family and a male and female representatives of each species could survive to repopulate the planet.

After the flood receded (9:9–17), God told Noah, at least according to the song, that fire, not floodwaters, would be used if God decided to destroy humankind again. African American author James Baldwin made the phrase "The Fire Next Time" the title of a 1963 collection of essays on race in America (New York: Dial). As those living through the third decade of the 21st century already know, the Earth and humankind now face both fire and flood waters as a result of global warming–induced climate change.

In January 2021, Copernicus, the European Climate Change Service, announced that 2020 tied 2016 as the warmest year at least since 1880 when accurate modern temperature record keeping began. September, October, and November 2020 each set records for high average temperature. The previous six years, 2015 through 2020, were the six warmest years on record, and the decade 2011–2020 was the warmest decade. During 2020, the largest "temperature deviation from the 1981–2010 average" was in the Earth's Arctic region, including northern Siberia. CO_2 concentration in the atmosphere continued to rise in 2020 despite the global economic downturn caused by the COVID-19 pandemic (https://climate.copernicus.

eu/2020-warmest-year-record-europe-globally-2020-ties-2016-warmest-year-recorded).

This book began as a series of lessons in an introductory class "Why Study History" at Hofstra University. In response to concerns about global climate change, my section was an in-depth examination of the history of the Earth's climate and how historians and citizens can influence contemporary climate debate and activism.

At Hofstra University, I teach in both the History Department and the School of Education. During the course of the semester, I realized with urgency that our class and curriculum can be taught, should be taught, in both high school and college. For this book, I adapted mini-lectures so they can be the basis for classes on both levels. At the end of every chapter, there are ideas for teaching and additional material is posted on my website (https://alansinger.net). There is news about climate change almost every day. Chapters focus on broader historical and contemporary issues, while teaching documents are largely drawn from current events while I was writing the book.

The debate in classrooms and the political realm should not be whether climate change is happening or how much it places human civilization at risk but over how societies and individuals should respond. Climate change is real, and it is threatening. In this book, I see myself as a translator who explains climate history and climate science (climatology) so it is accessible to a general audience. My audience is primarily teachers who have the daunting task of preparing their students to be climate activists, but the chapters in this book, the Teaching Documents and questions, and the online activities and edited material are designed so they can be introduced into secondary school and college classrooms. This book is a snapshot in time; new evidence and new proposals are constantly emerging. For engaged readers, it should be a starting point in the study of climate history. As a climate activist, I hope the book also finds its way to the general public. If you think it is of value, please recommend it.

I try not to be too technical in my writing, but my students recommended I include some vocabulary at the start.

Climate Vocabulary

Anthropocene: The current geological age marked by human influence on climate the and environment.

cap and trade and carbon tax: These are related proposals to eliminate excess greenhouse gases by making it economically advantageous for companies to reduce pollution. Governments set an allowable carbon dioxide emission limit and tax polluters that breach the cap while allowing companies to purchase "pollution credits" from businesses that are below their limit. If you are a sports fan, the carbon tax sounds a lot like baseball's luxury tax on teams with high payrolls, while cap and trade sounds more like basketball teams trading player contracts to create cap space to sign new players.

carbon budget: The total amount of carbon dioxide that can safely be emitted into the atmosphere on an annual basis or over a longer period of time without triggering severe global warming and a climate catastrophe.

carbon capture: Advocates for carbon capture as at least a partial solution to prevent climate change propose using technology to trap carbon dioxide emissions from factories, power plants, and vehicles before it enters the atmosphere and either reuse it or store it, usually underground. A useful comparison is catalytic convertors that filter automotive exhaust.

carbon footprint: The total national carbon footprint is the amount of carbon dioxide a country annually releases into the atmosphere. It can also be presented as a per capita carbon footprint. China has the largest carbon footprint, but the United States has the largest per capita carbon footprint.

climate: Long-term averages for weather, including temperature, precipitation, and wind velocity. Weather is what happens on a daily basis. On its website, the National Oceanic and Atmospheric Administration sums it up this way: "Climate is what you expect, weather is what you get."

climate sensitivity: Climate sensitivity is the amount of global warming measured when the concentration of carbon dioxide in the atmosphere reaches twice preindustrial levels. Prior to 1750, carbon dioxide in the atmosphere was about 280 parts per million (ppm). Scientists expect it to reach 560 ppm around 2050.

climatology: The scientific specialty for the study of climate.

El Niño and La Niña: Alternating phenomenon of the Pacific Ocean Southern Oscillation current that influence regional and global climate.

extractivism: A form of capitalism based on extracting wealth from the Earth without regard for the consequences.

geoengineering: A technological approach for limiting the impact of climate change.

greenhouse effect: Retention of solar energy as heat in the Earth's atmosphere because of the presence of carbon dioxide and other greenhouse gases.

Gulf Stream: The North Atlantic Ocean current that brings warmer Caribbean water and temperatures to western Europe.

jet stream: Atmospheric wind currents that influence regional climate.

Kyoto Protocol (1997): An international treaty in which signing nations agreed to voluntarily reduce greenhouse gas emissions.

Milankovich cycles: Earth orbit and rotation patterns that influence climate.

Paris Climate Agreement (2015): Agreement in which signing nations agreed to set goals to reduce greenhouse gas emissions that were supposed to be binding, but there was no provision for enforcement.

1 "Our House Is on Fire"

I am sensitive to the sun, and because of the type of skin I have, I can easily get a harsher sunburn than most other people. Some people avoid certain foods because they have negative reactions to them; they may develop a rash or have uncomfortable digestion problems. Similarly, Planet Earth is sensitive to things that that affect its biosphere, the realm inhabited by all living things. Too much carbon dioxide in the atmosphere, currently being added by the burning of fossil fuels, is causing the average global temperature to rise. This is leading to a cascading series of changes that alter ocean and atmospheric currents, introduce new climate patterns, force human migration, and threaten the survival of several species.

Scientists measure the impact of the Earth's climate sensitivity in different ways. CO_2 concentrations in the atmosphere are increasing gradually but steadily, continually changing climate in a *transient climate response*. The long-term impact of increased CO_2 concentrations in the atmosphere, *Earth system sensitivity*, includes melting ice sheets, rising sea levels, and new vegetation patterns. These changes can trigger other broader climate changes until the CO_2 concentration in the atmosphere stabilizes and *equilibrium climate sensitivity* is reached. Eventually that will happen. The problem is whether human civilization will be able to survive until a new environmental balance is reached – or whether civilization will collapse (Hausfather, 2018a).

While responsible science understands the Earth's climate sensitivity problem and the threat of increased greenhouse gases in the atmosphere to human civilization, there are powerful influencers that either deny or minimize the human impact on climate change. The problem confronting the world is not science; it is politics. To win the political battle requires a deep understanding of both the science and history of the Earth's climate.

In a September 2020 broadcast, Fox News commentator Tucker Carlson claimed that global warming was not responsible for the record-setting wildfires devastating the U.S. Pacific coast states during summer 2020. Philip Duffy, executive director of the Woodwell Climate Research Center, responded that climate change doesn't cause the fires, but "It causes them to get big" and "drives the intensity." In an interview, Daniel Swain, a U.C.L.A. climate scientist who accused Carlson of misrepresenting his views in the broadcast,

DOI: 10.4324/9781003200864-1

explained that climate change is "changing the character of wildfires irrespective of ignition sources. There are so many ways to start a fire" (Schwartz, 2020; Arango and Baker, 2020).

Scorching summer temperatures in California during 2020 produced dry conditions that transformed forests already strewn with dead trees from years of drought, into tinderboxes, ready to burst into flames with virtually any cause. By one estimate, there were over 150 million dead trees in California forests. Roy Wright, a former official at the Federal Emergency Management Agency (FEMA) described what was happening in California as "apocalyptic" (Fuller and Flavelle, 2020: A1).

Six of the twenty largest wildfires in modern California history occurred in 2020. In one day in September 2020, multiple mega-fires were burning more than three million acres of forest, and millions of Californians were exposed to smoky and toxic air. At the same time, hundreds of thousands of people were evacuated from fire threatened areas in Oregon and Washington. These fires are so intense they are now capable of generating tornado winds. They cause or contribute to rolling electricity blackouts during triple-digit heat waves, dangerous chemicals entering ground water and aqua-filters, and insurance companies canceling homeownership policies. The state's governor, Gavin Newsom, addressed the rest of the country. "If you are in denial about climate change, come to California" (Struzik, 2020; Fuller and Flavelle, 2020: A1)

Greta Thunberg's insisted in her January 2019 speech at the World Economic Forum in Davos, Switzerland that "our house is on fire" is not just a metaphor. In 2020, there were out-of-control wildfires in the American west, Australia, Indonesia, Amazonia, and Siberia. The U.S. National Interagency Fire Center reported that in the United States, almost 60,000 wildfires in 2020 burned through over 10.2 million acres of forest, almost double the acreage that burned during the 2019 fire season. Many were started by lightning strikes, which have also increased in number as the Earth warms. During the 2019–2020 Australian summer, bushfires burned over 45 million acres of land. Unprecedented heat waves led to vast fires in Arctic regions of Siberia burning peat lands and boreal conifer forests that released a record 244 megatons or 5 billion pounds of carbon dioxide. Portugal and South Korea also set fire records in recent years. About 25% of the Pantanal wetland covering parts of Brazil, Paraguay, and Bolivia burned in wildfires that were worsened by climate change. Scientists believe that Scandinavian forests and forests in the northeast region of the United States will soon be at risk (NIFC; Antonova, 2020; Witze, 2020, Einhorn, 2020).

Since 1980, the United States and the American people experienced almost 250 weather and climate disasters. The cumulative economic cost for these events exceeds $1.6 trillion. Between 2016 and 2018, the annual average number of billion-dollar disasters was more than double the long-term average. Despite the 2015 Paris Climate Agreement, the world is now on track to become 3°C (5.4°F) hotter by the end of the 21st century. Even a 2°C (3.6°F) increase in average temperature would mean sea levels rising nearly 2 feet; annual coastal flood would displace 30 million people; 37% of the Earth's population would face a severe heat wave at least every five years; 200 million people would be exposed to severe drought; almost 400 million people would suffer from water scarcity; and crop yields and global per-capita gross domestic product (GDP) would fall sharply (Smith, 2019; Holden, 2020).

Climatologists and geographers always located New York City in the "humid continental" climate zone. As a result of climate change, they now reclassify the city as humid subtropical. The humid subtropical climate zone classification requires that summer day and night temperatures average above 72°F and winter months average above 27°F. Despite occasional cold snaps, after winter 2019–2020, New York had met these criteria for the previous five years. I miss snow, but don't mind the milder winters. The problem is scorching summers. The last week of July 2020, the Temperature/Humidity Index for New York City hovered around 100°F, and it was almost impossible to stay outside (Collins, 2020: MB1).

By 2021, major international businesses came to recognize and take into account the impact climate change will have on local communities and the global economy. Swiss Re, one of the largest suppliers of backup insurance to other insurance companies, issued a report estimating that by 2050, climate change will lead to an annual decline in the global economy by about $23 trillion or between 11% and 14%. The hardest hit areas in their prediction would be countries in south and east Asia, including India, the Philippines, Malaysia, and Thailand (Flavelle, 2021a: B3).

At Davos, Greta Thunberg warned that according to the Intergovernmental Panel on Climate Change, humanity was less than 12 years away from a tipping point when it would no longer be able to undo ecological mistakes. A year later in January 2020, Zimbabwe, in south central Africa, faced famine because of water shortages. Ethiopia was struck with a locust plague facilitated by warming Indian Ocean temperatures. Insect infestations were invading new climate zones and destroying coffee plants in Central America. The cities of Sydney, Australia, and Valparaiso, Chile, over 7,000 apart and separated by the Pacific Ocean, were surrounded by fires. Both cities are located near 30 degrees latitude in the Earth's Southern Hemisphere during their summer (Singer, 2020).

Greta Thunberg concluded her Davos speech by saying, "Adults keep saying: 'We owe it to the young people to give them hope.' But I don't want your hope. I don't want you to be hopeful. I want you to panic. I want you to feel the fear I feel every day. And then I want you to act. I want you to act as you would in a crisis. I want you to act as if our house is on fire. Because it is" (Thunberg, 2019).

Greta's words are not the only words of warning. Former U.S. Congressional Representative and civil rights activist John Lewis warned in 2011, during debate over legislation to protect the environment, "When we take our air, waters and land for granted; when we show a simple lack of respect for nature and our environment, we unmake God's good creation. Humanity is the most important endangered species under threat from climate change and yet we flood our ecology with poisons and pollution" (Ali, 2020).

Carbon Budget

In her speech at the World Economic Forum, Greta Thunberg introduced the term *carbon budget*, previously a very technical term, into general discussion of climate change. Greta commented, "People are not aware that there is such a thing as a carbon budget, and just how incredibly small that remaining carbon budget is. And that needs to change today. No other current challenge can match the importance of establishing a wide public awareness and understanding of our rapidly-disappearing carbon budget that should and must become a new global currency and the very heart of future and present economics" (Thunberg, 2019: 21).

The carbon budget is the amount of carbon dioxide that can be emitted into the atmosphere by the burning of fossil fuels without causing cataclysmic and possibly irreversible climate change. Climate scientists determine the carbon budget by measuring global carbon dioxide emissions and its accumulation in the atmosphere, oceans, and other bodies of water and on land and projecting its impact on average world temperature (Friedlingstein et al., 2020: 3269–3340). Generally, they argue that when atmospheric greenhouse gases raise the average global temperature by 1.5°C (2.7°F), the Earth will reach a point of no return. Based on their calculations, some scientists argue that human societies may have already exceeded the carbon budget, while more conservative estimates place the tipping point in the 2030s (Hausfather, 2018b). In her speech, Greta Thunberg argued, "We are less than 12 years away from not being able to undo our mistakes" (17).

Teaching Documents

Greta Thunberg's 2019 World Economic Forum Address (Excerpts)

Source: http://opentranscripts.org/transcript/greta-thunberg-world-economic-forum-2019/

Questions

1. Why does Greta Thunberg argue, "Our house is on fire"?
2. Why does Greta Thunberg means when she insist the problem is either "black or white"?
3. Why does Great Thunberg call for climate activism?
4. Are you willing to join Greta Thunberg as a climate activist? Explain.

  1. "Our house is on fire. I am here to say our house is on fire. According to the IPCC, we are less than 12 years away from not being able to

undo our mistakes. In that time, unprecedented changes in all aspects of society need to have taken place, including a reduction of our CO_2 emissions by at least 50%. . . . We are facing a disaster of unspoken sufferings for enormous amounts of people. And now is not the time for speaking politely or focusing on what we can or cannot say. Now is the time to speak clearly."

2. "Solving the climate crisis is the greatest and most complex challenge that *Homo sapiens* have ever faced. The main solution, however, is so simple that even a small child can understand it. We have to stop our emissions of greenhouse gases. And either we do that or we don't. You say nothing in life is black or white, but that is a lie. A very dangerous lie. Either we prevent a 1.5° of warming or we don't. Either we avoid setting off that irreversible chain reaction beyond human control or we don't. Either we choose to go on as a civilization or we don't. That is as black or white as it gets. There are no gray areas when it comes to survival."

3. "Some say that we should not engage in activism. Instead we should leave everything to our politicians and just vote for change instead. But what do we do when there is no political will? What do we do when the politics needed are nowhere in sight? Here in Davos, just like everywhere else, everyone is talking about money. It seems that money and growth are our only main concerns. And since the climate crisis is a crisis that has never once been treated as a crisis, people are simply not aware of the full consequences on our everyday life."

4. "No other current challenge can match the importance of establishing a wide public awareness and understanding of our rapidly disappearing carbon budget that should and must become a new global currency and the very heart of future and present economics. We are now at a time in history where everyone with any insight of the climate crisis that threatens our civilization and the entire biosphere must speak out in clear language, no matter how uncomfortable and unprofitable that may be."

5. "Adults keep saying, 'We owe it to the young people to give them hope.' But I don't want your hope. I don't want you to be hopeful. I want you to panic. I want you to feel the fear I feel every day. And then I want you to act. I want you to act as you would in a crisis. I want you to act as if the house was on fire. Because it is."

Additional Teaching Documents at https://alansinger.net: World on Fire

2 Responsibility of the Historian as Public Intellectual

In an article posted on *History News Network*, David Carlin, who works on climate change for the United Nations Environment Program's Finance Initiative and leads a global project to help banks understand and assess the risks and opportunities brought about by climate change, discussed the history of both climate change and climate change denialism. According to Carlin, if you depend on media coverage, "you could be forgiven for thinking that climate change is a sudden crisis." Headlines like "Climate Change Is Accelerating, Bringing World 'Dangerously Close' to Irreversible Change" in *The New York Times* and "Climate Change is Reaching a Tipping Point" in the *Financial Times of London* reveal far more about current public and political "discourse than anything new in climate science" (Carlin, 2020). I believe a responsibility of historians as public intellectuals is to document the history of climate science, to explain what we know and how and when we knew it, and to expose companies and political groups that try to obfuscate what is happening to the planet.

The greenhouse effect on global climate was first explained by scientists starting in the early 19th century. Pioneering research was conducted by Horace Bénédict de Saussure of Geneva, Jean-Baptiste Joseph Fourier and Claude Pouillet in France, John Tyndall in Ireland, Eunice Foote of the United States, and Svante Arrhenius in Sweden. De Saussure, considered the father of modern meteorology, developed a device where sunlight heated the air in a glass-lined vase, demonstrating what would later be called the greenhouse effect. Fourier, a mathematician and physicist, was Napoleon Bonaparte's science adviser and participated in France's ill-fated 1798 effort to conquer Egypt. As a scientist, he developed a theory of heat transfer and arrived at the conclusion that the Earth should be significantly colder because of its distance from the sun. He concluded that the Earth's atmosphere acted as an insulator and was responsible for retaining solar energy and keeping the planet habitable. Based on his work, Fourier proposed that human activities could have an impact on the Earth's temperature. Pouillet added to an emerging understanding of the role the Earth's atmosphere played in stabilizing temperature, theorizing that water vapor and carbon dioxide in the atmosphere helped to retain solar energy. Tyndall later demonstrated that carbon dioxide and methane absorbed

DOI: 10.4324/9781003200864-2

infrared radiation. Foote conducted early experiments that demonstrated the greenhouse effect. In the 1890s, Sweden's Svante Arrhenius discovered the connection between atmospheric CO_2 and climate. Arrhenius was probably the first scientist to directly tie the industrial burning of coal and the release of carbon dioxide into the atmosphere with rising temperatures (Carlin, 2020).

Since the end of World War II, scientists have greatly expanded our understanding of the impact of the Industrial Revolution and greenhouse gas emissions on climate. They include discoveries about the limited capacity of the Earth's oceans to absorb CO_2 and the accumulation of CO_2 in the atmosphere. On May 1, 1965, *The New York Times* science writer Walter Sullivan reported on a speech by Dr. Philip Abelson, editor of the journal *Science*, in which Abelson explained how humanity had already altered the Earth's climate by introducing excess carbon dioxide and other greenhouse gases into the atmosphere, which contributed to a general warming trend from 1900 to 1950 (Sullivan, 1965: 1). In 1975, Wallace Broecker, a geochemist at Columbia University, accurately predicted the level of global warming that would impact the Earth's climate by 2015 (Broecker, 1975: 460–463).

Five years later, in 1979, the National Academy of Sciences (N.A.S.) established an Ad Hoc Study Group on Carbon Dioxide and Climate headed by meteorologist Jule Charney of the Massachusetts Institute of Technology. The NAS committee's report declared, "We now have incontrovertible evidence that the atmosphere is indeed changing and that we ourselves contribute to that change. Atmospheric concentrations of carbon dioxide are steadily increasing, and these changes are linked with man's use of fossil fuels and exploitation of the land" (vii). The study group issued a dire warning: "We have tried but have been unable to find any overlooked or underestimated physical effects that could reduce the currently estimated global warmings due to a doubling of atmospheric CO_2 to negligible proportions or reverse them altogether. However, we believe it quite possible that the capacity of the intermediate waters of the oceans to absorb heat could delay the estimated warming by several decades. It appears that the warming will eventually occur, and the associated regional climatic changes so important to the assessment of socioeconomic consequences may well be significant, but unfortunately the latter cannot yet be adequately projected" (3). The study group believed its conclusions would be "comforting to scientists," but they would be "disturbing to policymakers" (viii).

1988 was another landmark year as scientists continued to push for recognition of the threat to humanity posed by climate change. James Hansen, who led NASA's Goddard Institute for Space Studies (GISS), testified before the U.S. Senate Energy and Natural Resources Committee, explaining that NASA was 99% certain that observed temperature changes were not natural variation. "The evidence is pretty strong that the greenhouse effect is here" (Shabecoff, 1988: A1).

In 1988, the United Nations Environment Programme (UNEP) and the World Meteorological Organization (WMO) created the Intergovernmental

Panel on Climate Change (IPCC) to study the physical science of climate change and the numerous effects of the changes. The First Assessment Report (FAR) in 1990 stated, "Emissions resulting from human activities are substantially increasing the atmospheric concentrations of the greenhouse gases." Since then, the dangers have only grown closer and clearer with each report. New reports not only forecast hazards but describe the present chaos too. As the 2018 Special Report (SR15) explained, "We are already seeing the consequences of 1°C of global warming through more extreme weather, rising sea levels and diminishing Arctic sea ice, among other changes."

The governmental response in the United States to the threat of climate change has been erratic at best. In November 1965, the Environmental Pollution Panel of the President's Science Advisory Committee issued a report on climate change that included a section on atmospheric carbon dioxide concentrations. The report presented the scientific conclusion that "with fair assurance that at the present time, fossil fuels are the only source of CO_2 being added to the ocean-atmosphere-biosphere system." The report warned that by 2000, climate change could lead to melting ice caps, rising sea levels, and ocean acidity. According to Carlin, the report was accurate except for one detail. "Humanity increased its emissions faster" than the scientific panel predicted (Nuccitelli, 2015).

I can find no record of any kind of official response to the 1965 climate report by anyone in the Johnson Administration. However, during the Nixon Administration, policymakers did recognize the scientific evidence for climate change. Daniel Patrick Moynihan, the Assistant to the President for Domestic Policy, wrote a 1969 memorandum explaining the greenhouse gas effect and "instability through the burning of fossil fuels" where he referenced the report (Moynihan, 1969). In the memorandum, Moynihan reported:

> It is now pretty clearly agreed that the Co2 content will rise 25% by 2000. This could increase the average temperature near the earth's surface by 7 degrees Fahrenheit. This in turn could raise the level of the sea by 10 feet. Goodbye New York. Goodbye Washington, for that matter. We have no data on Seattle. . . . I would think this is a subject that the Administration ought to get involved with. It is a natural for NATO.

NATO, responding to a U.S. initiative, established the Committee on the Challenges of Modern Society (CCMS) and in 1970, President Nixon established the Environmental Protection Agency (EPA). Unfortunately, in the 1980s, the Reagan Administration rolled back environmental regulations, eviscerating the EPA and ignoring evidence of acid rain, ozone depletion, and climate change.

In 1992, the United Nations issued a Convention on Climate Change following an Earth Summit in Rio de Janeiro, Brazil. The Convention, eventually ratified by 154 governments, sought to stabilize greenhouse gas concentrations in the atmosphere at levels that would prevent major climate change.

In a follow up, Convention signatories met in Kyoto, Japan, in 1997, where they agreed on legally binding limitations on the use of fossil fuels that would reduce carbon dioxide emissions to 1990 levels. While the United States was a major participant in developing the 1997 Kyoto Protocol and President Bill Clinton signed the agreement, the United States Senate refused to ratify it, and Clinton's successor, George W. H. Bush, renounced the agreement. The major objection was the claim that it would hamstring the U.S. economy while giving underdeveloped countries a free rein to pollute (Sanger, 2001: A1). From 2009 to 2021, there was a similar pattern of recognition and regression as the Trump Administration reversed many of the environmental protections put in place during the Obama presidency, including U.S. participation in the Paris Climate Agreement (2015), only to have them restored by his successor. Interestingly, widespread Republican Party opposition to the climate agreements may have served to introduce the impact of climate change to a much broader audience and certainly energized environmental organizations (Dewar and Sullivan, 1997: A37).

David Carlin argues that scientists have "understood the potential for human-caused (anthropogenic) global warming for decades. Only the fog of political and corporate denialism has obscured the long-held scientific consensus from the general public." The obfuscation campaign is similar to the 1960s campaign by tobacco companies claiming that smoking does not cause cancer. Making these connections available to a broad audience is the job of the historian as public intellectual. In an October 1956 *Esquire* magazine essay, "A Case of Voluntary Ignorance," British writer and philosopher Aldous Huxley argued, "That men do not learn very much from the lessons of history is the most important of all the lessons that history has to teach" (Huxley, 1956: 47). Historians have a crucial role to play in public debate examining the Industrial Revolution of the 19th century and explaining the history of climate science and climate change in the second half of the 20th century. With the impending consequences of climate change, humanity cannot afford for Huxley to be right.

Teaching Documents

Restoring the Quality of Our Environment (1965)

Source: John Tukey, chair, Environmental Pollution Panel President's Science Advisory Committee, White House, November 5, 1965, 112–131.

Questions

1. According to the presidential report, what does the data "clearly and conclusively" demonstrate?
2. What do the scientists conclude?

3.   What is the general tone of the presidential report?
4.   In your opinion, should the report have triggered a greater governmental response? Explain.

"Within a few short centuries, we are returning to the air a significant part of the carbon that was slowly extracted by plants and buried in the sediments during half a billion years. Not all of this added carbon dioxide will remain in the air. Part of it will be dissolved in the oceans, and part will be taken up by the biosphere, chiefly in trees and other terrestrial plants, and in the dead plant litter called humus. The part that remains in the atmosphere may have a significant effect on climate: carbon dioxide is nearly transparent to visible light, but it is a strong absorber and back radiator of infrared radiation . . .; consequently, an increase of atmospheric carbon dioxide could act, much like the glass in a greenhouse, to raise the temperature of the lower air."

(113)

"The date show, clearly and conclusively, that from 1958 through 1963 the carbon dioxide content of the atmosphere increase by 1.36 percent. The increase from year to year was quite regular, close to the average annual value of 0.23 percent. By comparing the measured increase in the know quantity of carbon dioxide produced by fossil fuel combustion . . . we see that almost exactly half of the fossil fuel CO_2 apparently remained in the atmosphere."

(116)

"We can conclude with fair assurance that at the present time, fossil fuels are the only source of CO_2 being added to the ocean-atmosphere-biosphere system. If this held true throughout the last hundred years, the quantity of CO2 in the air at the beginning of the present decade was about 7% higher than in the middle of the last century."

(119)

We are fairly certain that fossil fuel combustion has been the only source of CO_2 coming into the atmosphere during the last few years, when accurate measurements of atmospheric carbon dioxide content have been available. Carbon dioxide may have been produced by other sources during earlier times but it is not now possible to make a quantitative estimate.

(124)

"Through his worldwide industrial civilization, Man is unwittingly conducting a vast geophysical experiment. Within a few generations he is burning the fossil fuels that slowly accumulated in the earth over the past 500 million years. . . . The climate changes that may be produced by the increased CO2 content could be deleterious from the point of view of human beings. The possibilities of deliberately bringing about counter-vailing climatic changes therefore need to be thoroughly explored."

(126–127)

Greenhouse Effect and Global Climate Change (1988)

Testimony by Dr. James Hansen, Director, NASA Goddard Institute for Space Studies

U.S. Senate Committee on Energy and Natural Resources, June 23, 1988

Source:https://pulitzercenter.org/sites/default/files/june_23_1988_senate_hearing_1.pdf

Questions

1. What "three main conclusions" does Dr. Hansen present to the Senate committee?
2. Why does Dr. Hansen address the probability of chance?
3. What is the general tone of Dr. Hansen's Senate testimony? Cite two examples that support your answer.
4. In your opinion, should Dr. Hansen's testimony have triggered a greater governmental response? Explain.

(A) "I would like to draw three main conclusions. Number one, the earth is warmer in 1988 than at any time in the history of instrumental measurements. Number two, the global warming is now large enough that we can ascribe with a high degree of confidence a cause and effect relationship to the greenhouse effect. And number three, our computer climate simulations indicate that the greenhouse effect is already large enough to begin to affect the probability of extreme events such as summer heat waves. . . . The present temperature is the highest in the period of record. The rate of warming in the past 25 years . . . is the highest on record. The four warmest years . . . have all been in the 1980s. And 1988 so far is so much warmer than 1987, that barring a remarkable and improbable cooling, 1988 will be the warmest year on the record."

(B) "Causal association requires first that the warming be larger than natural climate variability and, second, that the magnitude and nature of the warming be consistent with the greenhouse mechanism . . . The observed warming during the past 30 years . . . is almost 0.4 degrees Centigrade by 1987 relative to climatology, which is defined as the 30 year mean, 1950 to 1980 and, in fact, the warming is more than 0.4 degrees Centigrade in 1988. The probability of a chance warming of that magnitude is about 1 percent. So, with 99 percent confidence we can state that the warming during this time period is a real warming trend. . . . Altogether the evidence that the earth is warming by an amount which is too large to be a chance fluctuation and the

similarity of the warming to that expected from the greenhouse effect
represents a very strong case. In my opinion, that the greenhouse
effect has been detected, and it is changing our climate now."

(C) "I would like to address the question of whether the greenhouse
effect is already large enough to affect the probability of extreme
events, such as summer heat waves. . . . [W]e have used the temperature changes computed in our global climate model to estimate the
impact of the greenhouse effect on the frequency of hot summers in
Washington, D.C. and Omaha, Nebraska. A hot summer is defined
as the hottest one-third of the summers in the 1950 to 1980 period,
which is the period the Weather Bureau uses for defining climatology. So, in that period the probability of having a hot summer was
33 percent, but by the 1990s, you can see that the greenhouse effect
has increased the probability of a hot summer to somewhere between
55 and 70 percent in Washington according to our climate model
simulations. . . . [I]n the late 1980's and in the 1990's we notice a
clear tendency in our model for greater than average warming in the
southeast United States and the midwest. In our model this result
seems to arise because the Atlantic Ocean off the coast of the United
States warms more slowly than the land. This leads to high pressure
along the east coast and circulation of warm air north into the midwest or the southeast. There is only a tendency for this phenomenon.
It is certainly an imperfect tool at this time. However, we conclude
that there is evidence that the greenhouse effect increases the likelihood of heat wave drought situations in the southeast and midwest
United States even though we cannot blame a specific drought on the
greenhouse effect."

Additional Teaching Documents at https://alansinger.net:
- Stanford University Report for the American Petroleum Institute (1968)
- Memorandum, Daniel Moynihan to John Ehrlichman, September 17, 1969

3   Tipping Points

In *The Tipping Point: How Little Things Can Make a Big Difference* (2000), Malcolm Gladwell, defines a tipping point as "the moment of critical mass, the threshold, the boiling point" (12). Systems, societies, even human relationships, exist in stasis or equilibrium, but internal tensions build up, or external forces intervene, and then BOOM!

As a historian, I identify the tipping point as the point of no return when even if you are not aware, there is no going back. When the American Continental Congress voted for independence from Great Britain on July 2, 1776, they knew there was no turning back. In response to the decision, Benjamin Franklin is supposed to have said, "We must all hang together, or we shall all hang separately." But the actual tipping point was probably over a year earlier on April 19, 1775, when fighting started in Massachusetts at the Battles of Lexington and Concord.

Gladwell's *Tipping Point* focused on the social phenomenon of how something becomes a trend. If Gladwell were writing the book today, he would probably explore the role of social media influencers and how something goes viral on the Internet. A sociological study published in 2008 discussed tipping points in the rapid segregation of once interracial communities and schools in a number of American cities. Researchers found that as long as the minority population, meaning Black, Latino, or Asian, of a neighborhood was under 15%, it maintained a racial balance, and schools were integrated. Once the minority population passed that "tipping point," whites either began to sell their homes and move out and/or younger white families opted not to move in (Card, Mas, and Rothstein, 2008).

In history, tipping points are generally harder to identify than in contemporary studies, usually because there are multiple underlying causes so there might not be an actual individual, discernable tipping point. The Roman empire probably lingered for over 200 years from the death of Emperor Constantine in 337 AD until the tottering giant collapsed after the 535 AD eruption of the Krakatoa volcano in Indonesia undermined global food supplies. I have seen the blame for the collapse of Rome placed on a monetary crisis in 249 AD; the adoption of Christianity as a state religion in 312 AD; a huge Germanic migration circa 376 AD, when they were pushed out of the Russian

DOI: 10.4324/9781003200864-3

steppes by the Huns; and the sacking of Rome by the Germanic Ostrogoths in 546 and 549.

Civil engineers must take into account tipping points during the design and construction of buildings and bridges. Lay people, me included, think of steel structures as permanent, but they aren't. Every metal, including steel, has an ultimate tensile strength, the maximum stress it can sustain before microscopic fracturing, which can cause a sudden break. Structural steel is susceptible to strain aging, which makes it more brittle. The 2007 collapse of the Interstate 35W highway bridge across the Mississippi River in Minneapolis, Minnesota, was the result of steel reaching its "tipping point" in metal stress and fatigue (Przywara, 2011).

In science, tipping points can be established via experiments. According to NASA, a spacecraft leaving the surface of Earth must be going 7 miles per second, or 25,000 mph, to enter orbit without falling back to the Earth. In biology, species are at risk of extinction when the breeding population falls below a certain number. In chemistry, a supersaturated solution is a liquid with dissolved material, such as a salt, that has reached a concentration at which the addition of a fractional amount more releases all of the material. Earthquakes occur when pent up tension finally causes underground rock to break along a fault line and shift. During the COVID-19 pandemic, medical science discusses herd immunity, the point where a high enough percentage of the community is immune to a disease through vaccination or prior illness, making the spread of this disease from person to person unlikely.

To understand tipping points, think of an arm wrestling match between relatively equal opponents. For a long time, it looks like a standstill, as neither combatant is able to gain any ground. Then one of them suffers muscle fatigue, and the match quickly ends. Some teachers use the game of Jenga to illustrate a tipping point. Although the tower might be shaky, it stands until the removal of one last wooden block causes it to suddenly collapses. As with the Jenga block tower, once a tipping event starts, it is impossible to stop.

In climate, a tipping point is reached when, if the trend continues, the entire system changes, sometimes very dramatically. In the past, the Earth's climate has shifted back and forth multiple times from cooler periods with extensive glaciers to warmer eras when ice sheets are limited in range to higher latitudes and altitudes. If global warming continues, a tipping point could be reached at which it is impossible to reverse climate change. The melting of the Greenland and Antarctic ice sheets, shifts in ocean currents, deforestation, and the release of methane buried in the permafrost accelerate the shift toward a hothouse planet (Sheridan, 2018).

So far, the United Nations Intergovernmental Panel on Climate Change (IPCC) has refused to identify a point of no return, but its warnings have become increasingly dire. In 2002, it advised that a climate tipping point would most likely not be reached unless global warming exceeded 5°C above pre-industrial levels. A 2018 revision warned that a climate tipping point might be reached if average global temperature was only 1° and 2°C above pre-industrial levels. The next IPCC report is due in 2022 (Berwyn, 2019; Pachauri and Meyer, 2014; Hoegh-Guldberg et al., 2018).

In the 2015 Paris Climate Agreement, participating countries agreed to try to limit global warming to below 2°C. However, current pledges to reduce greenhouse gas emissions will not achieve that goal, even if they are actually implemented (United Nations, 2015). A 2018 study published in *Proceedings of the National Academy of Sciences* by an international team of scientists concluded, the "Earth System may be approaching a planetary threshold that could lock in a continuing rapid pathway toward much hotter conditions – Hothouse Earth. This pathway would be propelled by strong, intrinsic, biogeophysical feedbacks difficult to influence by human actions, a pathway that could not be reversed, steered, or substantially slowed" (Lenton et al., 2019; Steffen et al., 2018).

As the Earth and climate research heat up, scientists in different fields have contributed to our understanding of the risks posed by climate change and its immediacy. The journal *Nature* reported on an experiment by environmental scientists at Barro Colorado Island in Panama. Carbon is naturally stored in soil, where it is the food supply for bacteria and fungi that release carbon dioxide into the atmosphere. The scientists used electric current to heat soil in a tropical rainforest by about 6°F to mimic the higher temperature levels anticipated as the planet warms. They discovered that microbes in soil are more active at warmer temperatures. Because of this, hotter soil released 55% more carbon dioxide than soil in the same area that was not artificially heated. If the experiment becomes the climate norm in the future, carbon dioxide released from warmer soil could be the trigger that plunges the planet into catastrophic climate change. The team, led by Dr. Andrew Nottingham of the University of Edinburgh, estimates that if all the soil covering the Earth reacted in the same way, the amount of carbon dioxide released into the atmosphere by 2100 would be six times greater than the annual human contribution from burning fossil fuels (Popkin, 2020: D3; Nottingham et al., 2020). If they are correct, this would be an enormous climate disaster.

Permafrost, permanently frozen ground in the Northern Hemisphere, contains vast amounts of carbon accumulated from dead plants and animals over the course of thousands of years. Estimates suggest that permafrost could hold twice as much carbon as there currently is in the Earth's atmosphere. Rotten organic material is exposed as permafrost thaws. A broad thaw caused by global warming would release the stored carbon into the atmosphere as carbon dioxide and methane, another greenhouse gas. The release would trigger even greater planetary warming and more thawing. To understand the process, leave frozen chicken on the kitchen counter. You will soon have a puddle of water, and eventually the chicken will start to smell as it decomposes.

Climate affects different regions of the Earth differently. Warming in regions above the Arctic Circle in Siberia, Alaska, and Canada has increased twice as fast as in other areas of the planet. The temperature in the Eastern Siberia town of Verkhoyansk reached 38°C (100°F) in June 2020. It was the hottest Arctic Circle temperature ever recorded (Schädel, 2020; BBC, 2020).

Another potential climate trigger for climate change is the CO_2 dissolved in the Earth's oceans. The Pacific, Atlantic, Indian, and Arctic Oceans cover over 70% of the Earth's surface and absorb about 30% of the carbon dioxide created by burning fossil fuels. According to oceanographers, as oceans warm as a result of climate change, they will release CO_2 into the atmosphere, amplifying the greenhouse effect. There are two primary reasons that rising temperatures cause the oceans to release carbon dioxide. Melting Arctic and Antarctic ice caps release cold water into the oceans, which increases ocean turbulence and dredges up deep ocean waters that are rich in CO_2. Also, the process of warming forces a liquid to release gas. As an experiment, gradually warm a bottle of soda before opening it and watch the gas and foam pour out. Scientific models projecting climate change have tried to predict how long the oceans have to be heated before they belch CO_2. It might not happen for 200 years. But the trigger point, the point of no return, will most likely be much sooner, unless humanity acts (Zukerman, 2011; NASA, 2020).

Professor Bret Bennington's Primer on Climate Change

My Hofstra University colleague, geology professor Brett Bennington, prepared a video (www.youtube.com/watch?v=1z9JEPLca24) on the science of climate change that I find easily accessible to a general audience. Brett makes a series of key points that I will summarize here, but the best thing is to watch his illustrated presentation. If anyone from TED Talks is reading this, sign Brett up now.

Brett starts by describing the Goldilocks Zone for planets orbiting a star, the orbital distance where it is neither too hot nor too cold for life to emerge and survive. The Earth's orbit is right in the middle of the Goldilocks Zone, but Venus and Mars, a little farther in and a little farther out, could potentially have water in its liquid state and support life. None of the planets generates its own energy; they all depend on the Sun and either trap or reflect back into space solar light and heat. The problem for Venus and Mars is their atmospheres. The Venetian atmosphere is almost entirely made up of carbon dioxide, the basic greenhouse gas, so it traps solar radiation and the planet becomes incredibly hot, even hotter than Mercury, which is closer to the Sun. The average surface temperature of Venus is about 450°C (840°F). Any water that ever formed is long boiled off. Mars has the opposite problem: Its average surface temperature is –60°C (–80°F). Water on Mars, if it exists at all, would be frozen. Most of the Martian atmosphere is also carbon dioxide, but in this case the atmosphere is so thin that solar energy that reaches Mars is just bounced back into space.

Carbon dioxide in the atmosphere, the major cause of climate change, is also what makes the Earth habitable. Life on Earth seems to work best when the average temperature is about 14°C (57°F) and a small amount of CO_2 in the atmosphere, about 0.04%, is what makes this temperature possible.

Most of the energy from the Sun arrives at the earth as visible light. The light passes through the Earth's atmosphere and strikes the Earth's surface. This causes the Earth to warm and transforms the solar energy into heat that would be radiated back out into space, if it were not for a small amount of greenhouse gases in the atmosphere, mostly in the form of carbon dioxide, that keep some of the heat locked in and the Earth's temperature within the habitable range.

Photosynthesis, the process by which plants turn carbon dioxide in the atmosphere into the carbon that they use to grow while exhaling oxygen that animals, including humans, need to breathe, keeps the amount of CO_2 in balance and the Earth's temperature on an even keel. But vegetation eventually dies because of age, combustion, or decay, and much of the carbon from earlier eras is now stored in the Earth's crust in the form of coal and oil. When wood from cut-down trees, or coal and oil, fossil fuels, are burned, the stored carbon combines with oxygen and is released into the atmosphere as carbon dioxide.

Because of the burning of fossil fuels since the start of the Industrial Revolution, in factories, homes, and cars, the photosynthesis–CO_2 balance has been disrupted as larger and larger amounts of greenhouse gases have been emitted into the atmosphere, especially since the end of World War II in 1945. In the late 1950s, which is within my life span, the global average atmospheric carbon dioxide was below 320 parts per million. In April 2020, atmospheric carbon dioxide approached 420 parts per million, an increase of almost 25%. The added CO_2 in the atmosphere means that more solar heat is trapped, the Earth gets warmer, and climate changes.

In the video, Brett introduces two important concepts, feedback loops and thresholds or tipping points. As the Earth warms, more carbon dioxide is released into the atmosphere, from carbon stored as decayed vegetation in the Earth's far north and as the oceans discharge dissolved carbon dioxide. The added greenhouse gasses in the atmosphere cause even greater warming, which releases additional carbon dioxide that warms the planet even more. Ice caps melt and less heat and light are reflected back into space. Cause–effect–amplified cause–amplified effect.

Eventually, so much CO_2 would have been released into the atmosphere that the Earth's climate would be fundamentally altered challenging food and water supplies. Brett does not think it is likely that human societies will reverse global warming, but he believes the warming can be slowed down with immediate, cooperative, concerted action, allowing human civilization enough time to adapt to new climate norms.

Teaching Documents

Nine Potential Climate Tipping Points

> **Source:** Robert McSweeney, 2020, October 2. "Nine 'tipping points' that could be triggered by climate change," *Carbon Brief.* www.carbonbrief.org/explainer-nine-tipping-points-that-could-be-triggered-by-climate-change
>
> **Question:** The author identifies nine potential climate tipping points. If you were a climatologist, which potential tipping point or points would you monitor most closely? Why?

1. "Shutdown of the Atlantic Meridional Overturning Circulation. The Atlantic Gulf Stream current brings warm water and weather to Europe and makes Northern Europe habitable. Release of cold fresh water into the Atlantic Ocean from the melting of the Greenland ice cap could shift Atlantic currents. This current has weakened by about 15% since the mid-20th century."
2. "Disintegration of the West Antarctic ice sheet. This ice sheet holds enough ice to raise global sea levels by over 10 feet, dramatically affecting coastlines around the world."
3. "Amazon rainforest dieback. Evaporation from the Amazon rainforest is responsible for generating a significant portion of the Earth's cloud cover and rain."
4. "West African monsoon shift. Monsoons bring rainfall to West Africa and the Sahel. A shift in rain patterns would destroy agriculture and make this area uninhabitable."
5. "Melting permafrost. Permanently frozen ground in the Northern Hemisphere holds vast amounts of carbon from dead plants and animals that accumulated over thousands of years and stored carbon dioxide and methane. Permafrost may contain twice as much carbon as there currently is in the Earth's atmosphere."
6. "Coral reef die-off could interrupt the global food chain."
7. "Indian monsoon shift. India, with a population of 1.3 billion people, receives around 70% of its annual rainfall from seasonal monsoons. A shift in monsoon rains would devastate India, Bangladesh, and South East Asia."
8. "Disintegration of the Greenland ice sheet. The Greenland ice sheet is the second largest on Earth. It holds enough water to raise global sea levels by 24 feet. Melting of the Greenland ice sheet is already accelerating."
9. "Boreal forest shift. Boreal forests are found in the cold climates of the northern hemisphere high latitudes and account for a third of the Earth's forests. The trees in Boreal forests may store more than a third of the terrestrial carbon."

(Nottingham et al., 2020)

Additional Teaching Documents at https://alansinger.net:
- Trajectories of the Earth System in the Anthropocene
- Hotter Tropical Soils Emit More Carbon Dioxide
- Warmer Oceans Release CO_2 Faster Than Thought
- Acting Rapidly to Deploy Readily Available Methane Mitigation Measures

4   Great Climate Migration

If the world should have learned anything from the coronavirus pandemic, it is that walls don't stop viruses. Reinforcing national boundaries is also not likely to stop climate change refugees as rising seas flood coastal areas, potentially uprooting 100 million people in Bangladesh; as scorching heat waves force sub-Sahara Africans to make the dangerous trip to Europe; and as Central Americans, whose farms have become unsustainable, try to enter the United States through the southern border. People leave home because they have no alternative (Szczepanski, Sedlar, and Shalant, 2018; Lustgarten, 2020).

In a *New York Times Magazine* report in July 2020, Abrahm Lustgarten, a senior environmental reporter for *ProPublica*, documented what he describes as the Great Climate Migration as people fled and will continue to flee famine conditions caused by climate change. In regions of Guatemala, droughts followed by flooding rains, have repeatedly destroyed the primary food crop, maize, and the country's principal export crop, coffee. An estimated half of the children in rural Guatemala are chronically hungry. Many of the children have weakened bones and stunted growth. It is anticipated that conditions will only worsen. Rainfall is expected to decrease by 60% in decades to come, and semi-arid areas may ultimately turn into deserts, forcing people to abandon traditional villages and try to enter the United States, El Norte. El Salvador is located in the same climate zone as Guatemala and has similar conditions and problems. A coffee blight that was worsened by climate change wiped out 70% of El Salvador's crop in 2012. According to a United Nations food-security organization, drought and unpredictable storms since then have contributed to a "progressive deterioration" of life in El Salvador, with roughly 15% of its population fleeing to the United States. Lustgarten predicts that Mexico, where one in six families relies on farming and almost 50% of the country lives in poverty, will be the next country in the region severely impacted by climate change as water availability per capita is sharply reduced and crop yields decline. Mexican migration to the United States is expected to climb as millions of people are displaced during prolonged droughts.

Since the initial discovery of agriculture about 12,000 years ago, human civilization has largely existed within a narrow climate zone that supports food production. Research published by the U.S. National Academy of Sciences

DOI: 10.4324/9781003200864-4

predicts that because of climate shifts, 20% of the Earth's land will be a desert-like hot zone by 2070. Between one and three billion people will either be struggling to survive in regions that can no longer feed them or forced to somehow find new homes (Xu et al., 2020).

Groundswell, a 2018 World Bank report focusing on Sub-Sahara Africa, South Asia, and Latin America, predicts that by 2050, almost 150 million people will be forced by climate change to relocate within their own countries' borders, largely migrating from devastated agricultural regions to over-populated urban slums. The study's authors anticipate that the trend will then accelerate. Another scientific study predicts that by 2100, the combination of high temperature, above 35°C (95°F), and high humidity in densely populated regions of Asia that are now home to about 20% of the world's population, including parts of India and Eastern China, will exceed the "upper limit on human survivability" and "result in death even for the fittest of humans" after a few hours of exposure (Rigaud et al., 2018: xix; Im, Pal, and Eltahir, 2017).

Global warming is also responsible for rising sea levels that threaten regions and coastal nations, forcing people to migrate. Bangladesh is caught in a climate vise. Himalayan glaciers are disappearing, reducing fresh water streaming into rivers, while salt water from a rising Indian Ocean is pushing inland. The resulting salinity intrusion is destroying rice fields and increasing food insecurity, forcing people to abandon rural communities and relocate in urban slums. Adults are forced to look for work in sweatshop factories and as domestic help, while their children pick through garbage in waste dumps. In a massive labor migration, millions of men have left Bangladesh to resettle as guest workers in the Middle East and Europe. By 2050, high tides will flood much of Vietnam, including the Mekong Delta, where 18 million people live, heavily populated parts of China, Thailand, southern Iraq, and the Nile Delta in Egypt. These areas, as well as many coastal regions of the United States, will become uninhabitable. New estimates suggest that 150 million people will be displaced globally by rising sea levels within the next few decades, with as many as 300 million people displaced by all facets of climate change (Szczepanski, Sedlar, and Shalant, 2018; Rigaud et al., 2018: 155; Lustgarten, 2020). It is not clear where these people will be able to resettle.

Climate change indirectly forces migration as it exacerbates tensions between and within affected countries and people flee from conflict zones. In June 2007, United Nations Secretary General Ban Ki-moon described the civil war in the southern Sudanese region known as Darfur as the world's first climate change conflict (Notaras, 2009). According to Ban Ki-moon:

> Almost invariably, we discuss Darfur in a convenient military and political shorthand—an ethnic conflict pitting Arab militias against black rebels and farmers. Look to its roots, though, and you discover a more complex dynamic. Amid the diverse social and political causes, the Darfur conflict began as an ecological crisis, arising at least in part from climate change.
>
> (Ban, 2007)

Ban's conclusions about the civil war in Sudan were supported in a Proceedings of the National Academy of Sciences (PNAS) journal article that found "strong historical linkages between civil war and temperature in Africa, with warmer years leading to significant increases in the likelihood of war. When combined with climate model projections of future temperature trends, this historical response to temperature suggests a roughly 54% increase in armed conflict incidence by 2030, or an additional 393,000 battle deaths if future wars are as deadly as recent wars. Our results suggest an urgent need to reform African governments' and foreign aid donors' policies to deal with rising temperatures." The Sahel region of Africa on the southern border of the Sahara Desert is increasingly subject to drought, rising temperatures, desertification, and civil war as groups are pitted against each other for survival. Armed conflict was reported in every one of the 11 countries in the region stretching from Mauritania and Senegal in the west to Sudan, Ethiopia, and Eritrea in the east during 2020 (Burke et al., 2009; Skretteber, n.d.; ACLED, 2021).

Climate change is at least partly responsible for the civil war in Syria, where a three-year long drought from 2007 to 2010 contributed to migration from farms to cities, ethnic tension, and popular discontent. Prolonged drought in the southern and eastern Mediterranean created similar conditions across the region and were probably a factor in Arab Spring uprisings in Egypt and Libya at the end of 2010 (Kelley et al., 2015; Werrell, Femia, and Slaughter, 2013).

The United States is not immune from either the impact of climate change or internal climate migration. Since 1980, the United States and the American people have experienced almost 250 weather and climate disasters with a cumulative economic cost exceeding $1.6 trillion. On August 29, 2005, Hurricane Katrina, which peaked over the Gulf of Mexico as a Category 5 storm with winds topping 157 mph, made landfall in Louisiana south of New Orleans. A million people were forced to evacuate, there were over 1,800 reported deaths, and 80% of the city was flooded. The Red Cross reported that two weeks after the hurricane, almost 400,000 people were still living in shelters, hotels, and other people's homes scattered across more than 30 states. According to the New Orleans *Times-Picayune*, 10 years after Katrina, the population of New Orleans was 20% less than recorded in the 2000 federal census (NOAA, 2021a; Grier, 2005; NOLA, 2015).

Teaching Documents

Climate Culprit in Darfur

> By Ban Ki-moon, United Nation Secretary-General, June 14, 2007
> Source: Ban. K. 2007, June 16. "A climate culprit in Darfur," *United Nations.*
> www.un.org/sg/en/content/sg/articles/2007-06-16/climate-culprit-darfur

Question: Why does Ban Ki-moon argue that the underlying cause of the civil war in Darfur and other armed conflicts in Africa was related to climate change?

"Almost invariably, we discuss Darfur in a convenient military and political shorthand—an ethnic conflict pitting Arab militias against black rebels and farmers. Look to its roots, though, and you discover a more complex dynamic. Amid the diverse social and political causes, the Darfur conflict began as an ecological crisis, arising at least in part from climate change. Two decades ago, the rains in southern Sudan began to fail. According to U.N. statistics, average precipitation has declined some 40 percent since the early 1980s. Scientists at first considered this to be an unfortunate quirk of nature. But subsequent investigation found that it coincided with a rise in temperatures of the Indian Ocean, disrupting seasonal monsoons. This suggests that the drying of sub-Saharan Africa derives, to some degree, from man-made global warming. It is no accident that the violence in Darfur erupted during the drought. Until then, Arab nomadic herders had lived amicably with settled farmers. A recent *Atlantic Monthly* article by Stephan Faris describes how black farmers would welcome herders as they crisscrossed the land, grazing their camels and sharing wells. But once the rains stopped, farmers fenced their land for fear it would be ruined by the passing herds. For the first time in memory, there was no longer enough food and water for all. Fighting broke out. By 2003, it evolved into the full-fledged tragedy we witness today. . . . The stakes go well beyond Darfur. Jeffrey Sachs, the Columbia University economist and one of my senior advisers, notes that the violence in Somalia grows from a similarly volatile mix of food and water insecurity. So do the troubles in Ivory Coast and Burkina Faso."

Additional Teaching Documents at https://alansinger.net:
- Civil War in Africa
- Syrian Civil War and Drought
- Deadly Heat Waves
- Future of the Human Climate Niche
- Human Survivability
- An Interconnected World

5 Earth's Past Climates

To know what direction the global environment is headed, we have to know where it was in the past. The Earth has kept records that we can read if we know how and look carefully. One of my all-time favorite disaster movies is *The Day After Tomorrow* (2004). Dennis Quaid plays Jack Hall, a paleoclimatologist whose team is drilling ice cores on the Larsen Ice Shelf in Antarctica when he begins to realize that humanity faces a potential new ice age. His hypothesis is confirmed by scientists who are monitoring ocean currents in the North Atlantic. My favorite scene in the movie is when Hall arrives at the New York Public Library in Manhattan after a 200-mile ice-bound trek from Washington, DC, and saves his son and his son's friends. As his father walks into the room where they are clustered together and barely alive, the son, played by Jake Gyllenhaal, proclaims. "I knew he would come." That's every dad's best line.

The movie is supposedly based on *The Coming Global Superstorm* (1999), a "non-fiction" book written by fiction writers Art Bell and Whitley Streiber. While it is extremely unlikely that climate change will come as rapidly as the movie presents it, some parts of *The Day After Tomorrow* are scientifically accurate. Brian Fagan (2000) in his book on the *Little Ice Age* cites the research of Wallace Broecker to explain substantive and relatively rapid climate changes in the Earth's deeper past. Broecker (2010) credits, or rather blames, the orbit of the Earth and a shimmy in its axis for flipping the switch on ocean currents and redirecting the Great Ocean Conveyor Belt. Shifts in ocean currents as fresh water from melting polar ice caps pours into the oceans can reorganize climate on a global scale. Currently, warm equatorial water from the Caribbean flows clockwise on the ocean surface along the U.S. coast and then crosses the Atlantic Ocean to warm Western Europe. The ocean current gradually cools as it meets Arctic water and turns south to complete its circular cycle. Similar circular currents flow in all the oceans, clockwise in the north, counter-clockwise in the south. This system has operated relatively smoothly during the age of human civilization, the Holocene. But the currents can shift markedly toward the equatorial region because of glacial melt. In that case, global warming

DOI: 10.4324/9781003200864-5

would produce the next ice age in north temperate areas like Europe, the United States, and Canada.

Anything that has annual layers, including ocean coral, underground rock formations called stalagmites that are formed by minerals dissolved in liquids dripping from the ceiling of caves, trees, and some shelled sea creatures, records the climate conditions of the past. To go even further back in time, scientists dredge sediment cores from the bottom of the ocean and drill ice cores from the Arctic and Antarctic, which contain, in microscopic amounts, ash, dust, and bubbles of long-trapped gas. If there was a volcanic eruption in the 6th century, you can see the ash in the ice and ocean floor segments from that era. In another example of geological layering, scientists found a thin layer of iridium, a mineral that is extraordinarily rare on Earth, at the 65 million years ago level of rock that confirmed a meteor strike leading to the extinction of large dinosaurs. Small dinosaurs survived the mass extinction event, and their descendants are the birds (Gross, 2018).

At a March 2018 Smithsonian Earth's Temperature History Symposium, Gavin Schmidt, director of NASA's Goddard Institute for Space Studies, and Richard Alley, a geologist at Pennsylvania State University, explained how climate models based on climate in the past enable scientists to predict climate in the future. The main natural factors that shaped climate in the past are ashes thrust into the atmosphere by volcanic eruptions, where they reflect sunlight back into space; episodic shifts in the Earth's orbit and axial tilt that change the amount of sunlight that reaches different latitudes; circulation of ocean currents; the ebb and flow of sea ice caps; the position of continents; the relative size holes in the atmosphere's ozone layer, which allow ultraviolet light to reach the Earth's surface; and cosmic ray blasts from the sun; and deforestation. The Earth's orbit, affected by the gravitational pull of the other planets, seems to change like clockwork every 405,000 years and may have been responsible for a major climate shift about 50 million years ago. Greenhouse gases such as carbon dioxide and methane can also be the product of natural processes, although since the industrial era starting in the 19th century they are likely to be the by-product of human activity. The Earth records climate changes in ice cores, ocean sediment, rocks, and fossils (Gross, 2018).

An ice core is a cross-section of layers of compressed snow that melted and froze. Small airspaces in the snow and ice contain atmospheric gases. Paleoclimatologists can analyze the trapped air bubbles and calculate the ratio of different isotopes of oxygen in the water making up the ice to estimate the Earth's temperature for the past million years. They can even figure out how much it snowed in a particular year. Ice layers also trap dust, volcanic ash, and pollen circulated by the wind, providing clues to historical developments in other areas of the world. The shells of fossilized, once living, microorganisms and fossilized teeth from long extinct sea creatures help scientists push the climate calendar back over 500 million years. The mineral content of rocks provides climate evidence for even earlier geological epochs. For more recent time frames, trees, with annual growth rings, provide an accurate record of rainfall (Gross, 2018; Daley, 2019).

Volcanic eruptions are often responsible for elevated CO_2 concentrations and temperatures. Using evidence contained in a climate change calendar dating back hundreds of millions of years, paleo-climatologists have been able to explain periodic mass extinctions. About 450 million years ago, give or take a few million years either way, volcanic eruptions spewed carbon dioxide into the atmosphere and oceans, and an estimated 85% of marine species disappeared. Two hundred million years later, roughly 250 million years ago, at the end of the Permian Period, life on Earth almost died off again as over 95% of all marine species became extinct when the eruption of Siberian volcanoes produced chemical reactions that bonded atmospheric oxygen with carbon molecules, leading to intense warming and the deoxygenification of the oceans. About 55 million years ago, there was an era of extreme global warming caused by a doubling of atmospheric CO_2 that may also have been triggered by volcanic eruptions. The Earth's oceans turned acidic with lukewarm bathtub-like temperatures, and many life forms became extinct.

During the span of human history, approximately 12,000 years, the Roman Republic was already unstable when a volcano erupted 6,000 miles away in the Aleutian Islands. In the midst of climate change induced famine and disease, a series of political assassinations led to the collapse of the Republic (between c. 44 and c. 27 BC) and the emergence of the Roman Empire. Plutarch, in the *Life of Antony*, wrote that the Roman army was forced to subsist on wild berries and roots, tree bark, and "animals never tasted before" (Plutarch, 1920: 175).

More recently, the eruption of Mount Tambora in April 1815 on the Indonesian island of Sumbawa may have been the most powerful volcanic eruption in human history. A mixture of sulfur dioxide and ash was ejected over 12 miles up into the stratosphere, where it circled the globe, causing three years of "volcanic winter"; it snowed in New York City in June. The eruption caused widespread crop failure and hunger and may have been responsible for a global cholera pandemic. Following Tambora, new weather patterns in Bengal, where cholera was endemic, contributed to the emergence of a new, highly contagious, strain that rapidly spread around the world (Hall, 2020: D4; Zimmer, 2018: D3; Gross, 2018; Kornei, 2020: D1; Dodwell, 2020; Wood, 2015: 88–89).

In the last 250 years of the Holocene, the age of human civilization, human action, rather than natural phenomena, is the primary cause of climate change. While the cause of climate change is different, patterns from past climate help paleo-climatologists create computerized models to predict the climate future. The primary lesson from the past is that climate change endangers any species that is narrowly adapted to its environment and that includes humans.

Ocean and Air Circulation

There is debate over why we see a spiral effect when water drains from a bathtub. In 2001, *Scientific American* interviewed a number of scientists to try to solve the mystery. The consensus answer was that in a controlled laboratory setting the Earth's rotation on its axis would determine the direction that water drains, clockwise in the Northern Hemisphere, counterclockwise south of the Equator. However, under normal circumstances, other factors, including a bathtub not being completely level or a slight irregularity, will have a greater impact. You can try it out at home in your bathtub. Scientists recommend you let the water remain in the tub overnight to settle any turbulence (*Scientific American*, 2001).

Understanding the global circulation of water and air is crucial as climatologists try to refine climate models so they can better explain and predict global warming and the impact of climate change on regions of the Earth. The impact of the Earth's rotation and uneven solar heating on the circulation of water in the oceans and air in the atmosphere is known as the Coriolis effect, and a shift in the patterns can be caused by and contribute to climate change. While the water and air currents are generated by solar heat, the direction of their circulation is influenced by the Earth's rotation (DeRoberts, 2019; NOAA, n.d.).

There are three independent "wind belts" circling the Earth in the Northern and Southern Hemispheres, Hadley (equatorial), Ferrel (temperate zones), and polar cells, although the tropical Hadley cell has the greatest impact on climate.

Hot air rises. The Hadley cell or circulation starts as warmer air near the Equator rises about 10 to 15 kilometers (six to nine miles) into the atmosphere and then flows north and south toward the poles. The warmer air then drifts downward in the Earth's sub-tropical climate zones that include all of northern and southern Africa; most of Australia, China, and India; and the southern half of the United States. Recent studies indicate that as the global climate warms, the Hadley cells are expanding farther north and south, and recent temperature change now places New York City in the sub-tropical climate zone. As the Hadley cells expand with climate change, they are also drying out regions, increasing the risk of drought (Witman, 2018). NASA analysis of satellite data suggests that with the expansion of the tropical and sub-tropical climate zones, high altitude clouds normally found in the Earth's mid-latitudes are shifting closer toward the North and South poles. Clouds reflect solar radiation, which might cool the polar regions slightly while leaving the temperate regions, where people live, warmer (Gray, 2016).

Ocean currents are also influenced by the rotation of the Earth and heat transfer. The two most important currents because of their influence on regional climate are the Gulf Stream in the North Atlantic, which brings warmer weather to western and central Europe, making them habitable, and the South Pacific Gyre. There is a significant surface temperature and elevation difference between the western and eastern Pacific Ocean; western Pacific water off of the coast of Asia is 8° to 10°C (14°–18°F) warmer than eastern Pacific of the coast of South America. The differences in temperature generate the counter-clockwise Pacific Southern Oscillation current. Cooler water originating in the Antarctic flows north along the coast of South America toward the Equator; a flow known as the Humboldt Current. At the Equator, the current turns westward toward Asia, gradually warming. For reasons that are not completely understood, the temperature shift in the South Pacific is not consistent. On an irregular basis, every two to seven years, there are relative warmer phases known as El Niño and cooler phases known as La Niña. During an El Niño, warmer water reverses direction and heads back to South America rather than toward Asia. Changes in the temperature of the South Pacific Ocean current affects lower atmospheric winds, creating what is called the Southern Oscillation, and heavily influences fish populations and weather conditions across the globe. La Niña events bring colder winters to North America, more Atlantic hurricanes, and an intensified cyclone season in Southeast Asia and Eastern Australia. An El Niño causes increased rainfall and a higher risk of flooding in the southern United States but drought conditions in Central America and large areas of Africa and Asia (Lindsey, 2016). In 1998, an El Niño event led to the death of thousands of people in Latin America and China from floods, food shortages, and riots in Indonesia and caused $100 billion in damage. There is speculation that El Niño events might have contributed to food shortages that precipitated the French Revolution and failed invasions of Russia by Napoleon in 1812 and Nazi Germany in 1941. An El Niño event in 1877–1878 led to failure of Indian Ocean monsoon rains, prolonged drought in India and China and the death of between 25 and 30 million people (Linden, 2006, 181–182; 196–197).

Teaching Documents

New Suspect in Cold Case Has Long, Deadly Record

By Shannon Hall, *The New York Times*, June 16, 2020, D: 4
www.nytimes.com/2020/06/10/science/global-warming-ordovician-extinction.html

Questions

1. When was the Late Ordovician mass extinction?
2. What happened to life on Earth?
3. What theory is being used to explain this catastrophic event?
4. What evidence supports this theory?

1. "Roughly 445 million years ago, around 85 percent of all marine species disappeared in a geologic flash known as the Late Ordovician mass extinction. But scientists have long debated this whodunit, in contrast to clearer explanations for Earth's other mass extinctions. 'The Ordovician one has always been a little bit of an oddball,' said Stephen Grasby of the Geological Survey of Canada. Now he and David Bond of the University of Hull in England say they have cracked the case. . . . Widespread volcanic eruptions unleashed enough carbon dioxide to heat up the planet and trigger two pulses of extinction separated by 1 million years, they report. If true, it places the first grand wipeout of life on Earth in good company: Many of the other major mass extinctions are also thought to be victims of global warming."

2. "Dr. Bond and Dr. Grasby reached their volcanic hypothesis after collecting Ordovician rocks from a small stream in southern Scotland. They then shipped those rocks to Vancouver, British Columbia, where the specimens were heated in a lab until they released large amounts of mercury—a telltale sign that volcanoes had rocked the epoch. The rocks also emitted molybdenum and uranium—geochemical proxies that suggest the oceans were deoxygenated at the time. Only warming so easily robs the oceans of oxygen, they say, asphyxiating the species that live there. Think of a bottle of cola. 'If it's been in the fridge, it stays nice and fizzy because the gas in that carbon dioxide stays in the liquid,' Dr. Bond said. 'But if you leave it on a sunny table outside and it gets really warm, then that gas quickly dissociates out of that liquid and you end up with a flat coke.'"

Additional Teaching Documents at https://alansinger.net:
- Earth's Orbital Shifts May Have Triggered Ancient Global Warming
- Earth's Near-Death Experience
- A Far-Off Volcano and the Roman Republic's End

6 Climate Change and Human Evolution

Note: In this chapter, I try to integrate my understanding of findings from paleontology, anthropology, evolutionary biology, and climate science into an explanation of the impact of climate change on human evolution and the expansion of human intelligence. *Hominid* and *hominin* are often used interchangeably, and they are here. Technically, *hominid* includes all primates and their extinct ancestors, while *hominin* is limited to humans and their ancestral lineage.

Humanity's ancestors branched off from the ancestors of other primates between 6 and 8 million years ago, and there have been many hominid species since then; some were the ancestors of modern humans; others were "cousins" whose lines died off. According to the Smithsonian National Museum of Natural History, *Homo sapiens*, modern forms but not quite us, first appeared in Africa during a period of intense climate change about 300,000 years ago. Biologically, modern human beings are the only surviving members of the larger *Homo* lineage. Our species probably emerged in Africa between 100,000 and 150,000 years ago (Smithsonian, 2020).

Over time, humanity's ancestor species evolved the ability to walk upright and to use their hands to manipulate and create tools and exhibited increasingly complex mental and social behavior. An enlarged brain enhanced survival through cooperation and the use of tools and the extended maturation of offspring promoted social bonding to protect their young. All of these evolutionary changes were probably stimulated by climate change and its impact on environments. Environmental change also contributed to the extinction of other branches of the hominid family tree.

Scientific research based on the study of wind-blown African soil that settled on the floor of the Indian Ocean and oxygen isotopes in the fossilized microscopic skeletons of single-cell oceanic organism that lived million of years ago allow us to track climate changes that took place eons ago. Variations in the concentration of different oxygen isotopes suggest that the periods of more

DOI: 10.4324/9781003200864-6

rapid hominid evolution coincided with periods of environmental fluctuation. Studies by Dr. Peter deMenocal, a paleoclimatologist at Columbia University, of deep-sea sediment show thicker layers of Africa's dust on the Indian Ocean floor, indicating drier continental conditions, corresponding to Ice Ages in the Northern Hemisphere (Stevens, 1993: C1; deMenocal, 2004).

Elisabeth S. Vrba of Yale University developed a "turnover pulse hypothesis" for evolutionary change largely based on her study of East African antelope (Bovidae) fossils. She proposed that catastrophic changes in climate could result in the rapid extinction of species and the emergence of new species including hominids. Her idea of turnover pulse was incorporated into the theory of punctuated equilibrium that postulates species remain stable for long periods of time and that evolutionary change occurs in relatively quick bursts (Vrba, 1993, 1995; Eldredge and Gould, 1972).

As East Africa cooled and warmed, dried or became wetter, changing landscapes and flora from forest to savannah grasslands altered food sources. Episodic but long-term climate alteration placed a premium on the ability of a species to adapt to environmental change and may be responsible for the emergence of intelligence. Species that could not adapt died off, including hominid species. The ability to adjust to a variety of different habitats, from the Arctic to the tropics, from rainforests to semi-arid zones, and from plains to mountains, has come to characterize humans (Vrba, 1993; Stevens, 1993: C1; Smithsonian, 2020).

A key question for scientists is "Why did humanity's hominid ancestors evolve larger brains and greater intelligence?" One difficulty in answering the question is that climatologists, evolutionary biologists, and anthropologists approach the question from different angles and end up with different interpretations. There is a tendency to see scientific discovery as the work of individual geniuses. Discoveries about the relationship between climate change and human evolution challenge this view, presenting the compounding of scientific knowledge as a collaborative venture (Wayman, 2011).

Most explanations for the evolution of human ancestors focus on an environmental shift in East Africa from forest to savannah. As forests receded, a tree-dwelling quadruped learned to forage as a biped on the plains where more intelligent individuals had a better chance of survival and passing along their genes to offspring. Over a number of generations, hominids evolved greater brain capacity and intelligence that enabled them to compete and survive in more open space. During an extended cold spell about 2.8 million years ago, there was a permanent shift in East Africa to grasslands. At that point, the fossil evidence shows pre-humans splitting into at least two branches. *Australopithecus robustus* specialized as a vegetarian and eventually became extinct. Genus *Homo*, which evolved into modern humans, adapted to survive in multiple habitats where it depended on a variety of foods. Another cold period, about a million years ago, coincided with the emergence of *Homo erectus*, the immediate ancestor of *Homo sapiens*. The sole survivor of the hominid line migrated out of Africa to colonize Europe and Asia (Stevens, 1993: C1).

Richard Potts, director of the Smithsonian Institute's Human Origins Program, argues that earlier work on human origins focused too much on intrinsic species adaptation once hominids had migrated onto the East African savannah rather than on environmental impacts and viewed environmental change as passive. However, correlating the hominid fossil record with environmental records suggests that hominids continued to evolve in response to climate change during prolonged periods of environmental variability that lasted tens of thousands of years. These climate changes altered the proportion of dense woodlands and open plains and placed a premium of the ability of hominids to live in different environments. *Australopithecus* fossil remains suggest that the species was well-adapted to these changes with human-like hip bones, knee joints, and feet that supported upright walking and running on the savannah and longer ape-like arms and fingers for arboreal climbing (Potts, 2012). The most famous *Australopithecus* skeletal remains, known by the nickname Lucy, were uncovered in Ethiopia in 1974.

Both the traditional view and Potts' variation stress the emergence of greater intelligence in response to climate and environmental change, although Potts sees it as a continuing phenomenon. Supporting the Potts thesis is that the first known stone tools date to around 2.6 million years ago. Potts believes making and using stone tools provided versatility as hominids adjusted to their surroundings and conferred a selective advantage in hunting and food preparation. He postulates that the ability of hominids to tolerate different environments made possible the migration of early hominids into Asia about 1.9 million years ago. Enlargement of the hominid brain accelerated over the past 800,000 years, a period with the greatest worldwide climate fluctuation. Larger brains made it possible for hominids to plan, process, and store information; survive challenges; and expand their populations into new climate zones (Smithsonian, 2020).

With increased intelligence, about 400,000 years ago and again about 280,000 years ago, hominids experienced waves of technological innovation as stone tools became more sophisticated. This was facilitated by more effective communication, more complex social interactions, and cultural diffusion with the formation of localized trade networks. The importance of expanded intelligence for survival of *Homo sapiens* in the past 100,000 years is supported by the extinction of the concurrent Neanderthal population. Modern human bands possessed specialized tools that enabled them to exploit a wider range of dietary resources and were able to communicate more effectively and take advantage of networks, advantages the Neanderthals did not possess as the two groups competed for survival under sometimes harsh environmental circumstances.

Stephen J. Gould of Harvard University and the American Museum of Natural History and anthropologists Konrad Fialkowski and Marvin Harris also recognize the migration from forest to savannah as the crucial step in hominid evolution but offer exaptation, a shift in the function of an inherited trait, as a different explanation for the emergence of human intelligence. Hominid bipedalism and movement onto the East Africa savannah preceded the rapid increase in human brain size by more than a million years. Australopithecus was small brained but stood fully erect. Gould dismissed the "brain-centered view of human evolution" as a "powerful cultural prejudice imposed upon nature" (Gould, 1980: 131).

They credit increased brain capacity to "nonadaptive side consequences" of other evolutionary adaptations to environmental change that later made increased intelligence possible. A structure like the hominid brain has "latent capacities." Although it evolved for "one thing, it can do others— and in this flexibility lies both the messiness and the hope of our lives" (Falk, 1990: 333–344; Gould, 1997; 1980: 57–58). Basically, the human brain developed to facilitate heat transfer, and increased intelligence was a side benefit.

Harris and Fialkowski present the case that "a bigger brain made it possible for erectus to run in the midday sun, at a time of day when most predators seek shade and water and refrain from the pursuit of game." Because excess body heat was dissipated through the skull, "the brain of erectus was less likely to break down while experiencing heat stress during distance running" that accompanied hunting. According to Harris, "Modern humans are far from being the swiftest runners in the animal kingdom." However, "when it comes to covering long distance, humans have the capacity to outrun every other animal." In support of this view, many modern human features, including hair location and the ability to perspire, are related to heat transfer and the maintenance of a stable body temperature. Humans are more intelligent than other mammals because of a brain that evolved for heat transfer, not for smarts (Harris, 1990: 52).

In addition, Fialkowski argues that hominid tool making and tool using cannot explain the beginning of brain enlargement. Australopithecines already had sufficient intelligence to make simple stone tools. During the expansion of hominid brain capacity during the Early Pleistocene (2.6 million to 781,000 years ago) and the Middle Pleistocene (Chibanian), which extended to about 126,000 years ago, there was no increased sophistication in stone tool design, or in corresponding periods when "stone tools show no comparable breakthrough in sophistication." For Fialkowski, only the "side-effect hypothesis" explains why hominid brain capacity and a concurrent increase in intelligence expanded beyond the minimum requirements needed to create simple tools (Fialkowski, 1986: 288).

Gould, a paleontologist and evolutionary biologist, explained neotony, the relatively simple evolutionary process that made the enlarged human brain and intellectual capacity possible. Neotony is the maintenance of prenatal growth rates after birth. Coupled with delayed maturation, it allows for the retention of juvenile features in modern humans such as an enlarged cranium, minimal body hair, and prolonged brain development. Neotony also explains the evolution of modern dogs from their wolf ancestors as wolf pup-like behavior is retained by adult dogs (Gould, 1980: 132; Walker, 2014).

The evidence that it was heat transfer, not intelligence, that led to an enlarged human brain does not negate Vrba's "turnover pulse hypothesis" that catastrophic climate change promoted early human evolution or later intellectual development, but it does make the connection more nuanced.

On its website, the Smithsonian National Museum of Natural History explains, "Humans today represent the one species that has survived from the diversity of hominin species. Despite their very close relationship with our species, and despite the fact that all of them possessed some combination of features that characterize humans today, these earlier species and their ways of life are now extinct. The question ahead is how well our sources of resilience as a species will succeed as our alterations of the landscape, atmosphere, and water interact with the tendency of Earth's environment to shift all on its own" (Smithsonian, 2020).

Teaching Documents

African Climate Change and Faunal Evolution During the Pliocene-Pleistocene

> by Peter deMenocal, *Earth and Planetary Science Letters*, 220 (1–2): 3–24.
> Source: www.sciencedirect.com/science/article/pii/S0012821X 04000032?via%3Dihub
> Note: Ma means millions of years ago. 2.8 Ma means 2.8 million years ago. ±0.2 Ma means the estimate may be off by 200,000 years in either direction.

Questions

1. What happened to African climate during the period of hominid evolution?
2. What evidence supports this interpretation?
3. What was the impact of climate on hominid evolution?
4. There is a tendency to see scientific discovery as the work of individual geniuses. How do discoveries about the relationship between climate change and human evolution challenge this view?

> "Environmental theories of African faunal evolution state that important evolutionary changes during the Pliocene–Pleistocene interval (the last ca. 5.3 million years) were mediated by changes in African climate or shifts in climate variability. Marine sediment sequences demonstrate that subtropical African climate periodically oscillated between markedly wetter and drier conditions, paced by earth orbital variations, with evidence for step-like (±0.2 Ma) increases in African climate variability and aridity near 2.8 Ma, 1.7 Ma, and 1.0 Ma, coincident with the onset and intensification of high-latitude glacial cycles. Analysis of the best dated and most complete African mammal fossil databases indicates African faunal assemblage

and, perhaps, speciation changes during the Pliocene–Pleistocene, suggesting more varied and open habitats at 2.9–2.4 Ma and after 1.8 Ma. These intervals correspond to key junctures in early hominid evolution, including the emergence of our genus *Homo*. Pliocene–Pleistocene shifts in African climate, vegetation, and faunal assemblages thus appear to be roughly contemporary, although detailed comparisons are hampered by sampling gaps, dating uncertainties, and preservational biases in the fossil record. Further study of possible relations between African faunal and climatic change will benefit from the accelerating pace of important new fossil discoveries, emerging molecular biomarker methods for reconstructing African paleovegetation changes, tephra correlations between terrestrial and marine sequences, as well as continuing collaborations between the paleoclimatic and paleoanthropological communities"

(deMenocal, 2004: 3).

7   Extreme Heat

In July 2005, my wife and I attended a teaching conference in Granada, Spain, and decided to make a side bus trip to Cordoba, which was famous for its medieval Old City with remnants of Islamic and Jewish culture. It was a 20-minute walk from the bus terminal to the Old City and another 15 minutes to our hotel. I carried a backpack, and she dragged her small-wheeled luggage. A large LED sign flashed the temperature as 43°C. My wife asked me what the "real" temperature was. I denied knowing because she would have killed me but quickly did the calculations in my head.

Converting Celsius to Fahrenheit is a relatively simple ratio problem. The Celsius temperature range is 100° from the point where water freezes to the point where water boils at sea level. The Fahrenheit temperature range is 180° from 32°F (freezing) to 212°F (boiling). The ratio is 100:180 = 5:9. 10°C equals 18 + 32 (32° is the Fahrenheit base line) or 50°F. Another way to do the conversion is to multiply the Celsius temperature by 1.8 and add 32.

That afternoon in Cordoba it was 109°F. We were both healthy and in our mid-50s, tried to walk in the shade, constantly drank water, repeatedly stopped in stores that were misting, and grabbed a *cerveza frio*. Even then we barely made it to our destination, and we had money and an international hotel with air conditioning to go to. That was in 2005. In July 2017, Cordoba recorded the highest temperature ever in Spain, 46.9C, almost 117°F (Busby, 2018).

Extreme heat temperatures keep hitting new records across the globe. According to the U.S. National Oceanic and Atmospheric Administration (NOAA) Weather Prediction Center, on Sunday August 16, 2020, the afternoon temperature at a village in Death Valley, California, hit 130°F or 54°C, the highest ever reliably recorded temperature on the planet. The extreme heat in California's Mojave Desert broke records previously set in Kuwait in 2016 (53.9°C) and Pakistan in 2017 (53.7°C). July 2020 was the hottest month ever in Phoenix, Arizona, until August 2020 broke the record with an average daily high temperature of 110.7°F. September 2020 was the hottest September ever, setting heat records in Europe, much of Asia, the western United States, and parts of Australia. In 2020, more than 20 U.S. cities, including Miami, Florida; Savannah, Georgia; Norfolk, Virginia; Kahului, Hawaii; Scranton, Pennsylvania; Hagerstown, Maryland; and Brownsville, Texas, set

DOI: 10.4324/9781003200864-7

or tied records for the hottest year on record. According the NOAA's Arctic Scorecard, the Arctic region, defined as the section of the Earth north of 60 degrees latitude, was transforming into a "warmer, less frozen, and biologically changed" climate zone (De Leon and Schwartz, 2020; Livingston, 2020; Di Liberto, 2020; Erdman, 2021; NOAA, 2020; Fountain, 2020: A13).

In July 2020, scientists at the University of New South Wales in Australia released a comprehensive worldwide assessment of heat waves since 1950. They found heat waves had an increased frequency and duration in virtually every region of the world. Their research introduced the concept of "cumulative heat," which measured the amount of heat generated during both individual heat waves and a region's heat wave season by adding together how much hotter each day was above the previous average for that day. Using this matric, Russia and the Mediterranean basin both totaled an additional 200°C (360°F) in 2017. Between 1980 and 2017, the Mediterranean basin added an additional 6.4 heat wave days every decade (Perkins-Kirkpatrick and Lewis, 2020; Stone, 2020).

While extreme heat events are occurring across the globe, their impact is "profoundly unequal," affecting some regions, countries, and people much more negatively. According to the National Observatory of Athens, in the 1980s there were fewer than 50 hot days per decade with temperatures over 37°C (99°F), but by 2007 to 2016, the number had had more than doubled to 120 hot days. During the summer, Afghani refugees living in Athens' urban slum known as Kolonos sleep on rooftops, shower at public beaches, and hawk wares on streets that lack shade trees. In southeastern Nigeria, weather-related hot temperatures are exacerbated by heat emanating by methane flares from oil wells. According to researchers, temperatures reach 12°C (22°F) higher in homes near the oil wells. The heat is so debilitating that healthy people can barely work three hours a day in their fields. In Guatemala, indigenous farmers watch as their maize and bean crops are desiccated by heat and drought. They are forced to compete for low-wage work on coffee plantations to supplement earnings or abandon their farms and move to urban barrios. Some attempt the long trek to the U.S. border with Mexico that they hope to cross as undocumented immigrants. Debt-ridden Dalit families, India's casteless poor, pass on their financial obligations to their children. Entire families, including children, are forced to do casual construction labor, usually hauling sand and bricks, in oppressive heat and humidity that human beings cannot tolerate for extended periods of time (Sengupta, 2020).

The injustice of climate change is multiplied by the fact that the world's poor have the lowest carbon footprint. They are not responsible for global warming but suffer its worst consequences. The average American produces about 17.6 tons of carbon dioxide a year, almost 10 times the carbon footprint of the average person living in India (Dennis, Mooney, and Kaplan, 2020).

Extreme heat also affects the poorest and most vulnerable populations in the United States, especially older Americans. A study published in March 2020 estimated that between 2010 and 2020, as many as 12,000 people died each year from heat-related ailments, 80% of whom were older than 60 years of age. In Houston, Texas, where the average temperature rose by more than 3.5°F between 1970 and 2020, sweat "pools" in the boots of Mexican American day laborers working outdoors in the hot and humid summer heat, and many suffer from heat exhaustion. Because of what is known as the "urban heat island" phenomenon, Brownsville, Brooklyn, one of the poorest neighborhoods in New York City, has average daytime temperatures about 2°F higher than the city average because there are few parks, and trees and asphalt pavement absorbs and hold onto the heat (Shindell et al., 2020; Mohajerani, Bakaric, and Jeffrey-Bailey, 2017; Sengupta, 2020).

Episodes of combined extreme heat coupled with humidity have more than doubled since 1979. During these episodes, people are at risk because their sweat does not evaporate as fast, so their bodies are unable to cool down and their internal temperature rises. According to the International Labour Office (ILO) in Geneva, Switzerland, heat stress, defined as heat in "excess of that which the body can tolerate without physiological impairment," is a "serious problem for a large proportion of the world's 1 billion agricultural workers and 66 million textile workers (many of whom have to work inside factories and workshops without air conditioning), and for workers employed . . . in refuse collection, emergency repair work, transport, tourism and sports" (ILO, 2019: 3).

The ILO estimates that "by 2030 the equivalent of more than 2 per cent of total working hours worldwide is projected to be lost every year, either because it is too hot to work or because workers have to work at a slower pace." They project economic losses from heat stress will increase to $2.4 trillion.

Of greater concern, heat stress is a major health risk. Temperatures exceeding 39°C (102°F) can be deadly. Heat-related illnesses "range from mild forms, such as heat rash, heat cramps and heat exhaustion, to potentially fatal heatstroke." When a person's body temperature rises above 38°C (100.4°F), they start to suffer physical and cognitive impairment. Above 40.6°C (105°F), body organs begin to fail, causing unconsciousness and potentially death (17). In the Sahel region of Africa, higher temperatures have caused increased mortality rates with children and older adults at greatest risk (33).

The ILO report findings include that "productivity losses caused by heat stress" will be concentrated in agriculture and construction and in "subregions with already precarious labour market conditions, such as high rates of vulnerable employment and working poverty." They believe extreme heat conditions will "widen existing gender gaps in the world of work . . . by making working conditions worse for the many women," especially pregnant women. Extreme heat conditions will also prompt internal migration from rural areas to already overcrowded cities and mass emigration to other countries where the climate and work conditions are less extreme (14).

Extreme heat waves are taxing electric power networks across the United States, causing an increased number of prolonged "blackouts." The number of power failures, many caused by air-conditioning overload, increased by 60%

between 2015 and 2020. Studies conducted of Atlanta, Detroit, and Phoenix estimate that at least two thirds of the residents of these cities could suffer heat exhaustion or heat stroke during a summertime power blackout. In Atlanta, 70% of the population would be at risk if indoor temperatures remained above 90°F (32°C), with poorer segments of the population at the greatest risk. In Phoenix, the entire population of the city, over 1.5 million people, would face dire health consequences (Flavelle, 2021b: A15; Stone et al., 2021).

There are serious questions that need to be considered by international organizations and government policy makers, as well as by citizens concerned with the impact of climate change and social justice.

1. To what extent is climate inequality a product of historic colonialism, imperialism, and racism?
2. Will climate change be addressed effectively by the industrialized developed world while its impact is still most drastically felt by people living in developing countries?
3. If capitalist industrialization produced the climate crisis, can it be relied on to end the climate crisis or does the very nature of capitalism based on short-term profit prevent decisive action?
4. Do nations with heavy carbon footprints have an obligation to open their doors to admit climate refugees?

Teaching Documents

Extreme Heat

Questions

1. What percentage of the world's population is projected to live in regions impacted by extreme heat?
2. Which areas of the world will be most severely affected?
3. How will extreme heat in these region impact on other parts of the world?
4. Why is the impact of extreme heat "profoundly unequal"?
5. What is the economic impact of extreme heat?

(A) Billions Could Live in Extreme Heat Zones Within Decades
By Henry Fountain, *New York Times*, May 5, 2020, A15
www.nytimes.com/2020/05/04/climate/heat-temperatures-climate-change.html

"As the climate continues to warm over the next half-century, up to one-third of the world's population is likely to live in areas that are considered unsuitably hot for humans, scientists said Monday. Currently fewer than 25 million people live in the world's hottest areas, which are mostly in the Sahara region in Africa with mean annual temperatures above about 84 degrees Fahrenheit, or 29 Celsius. But the researchers said that by 2070 such extreme heat could encompass a much larger part of Africa, as well as parts of India, the Middle East, South America, Southeast Asia and Australia. With the global population projected to rise to about 10 billion by 2070, that means as many as 3.5 billion people could inhabit those areas. . . . A 2018 World Bank study . . . estimated that climate change would force about 140 million people in Africa, South Asia and Central and South America to migrate within their own borders by 2050."

(B) Here's What Extreme Heat Looks Like: Profoundly Unequal
By Somini Sengupta, *The New York Times*, August 8, 2020
www.nytimes.com/interactive/2020/08/06/climate/climate-change-inequality-heat.html

"Nearly everywhere around the world, heat waves are more frequent and longer lasting than they were 70 years ago. But a hotter planet does not hurt equally. If you're poor and marginalized, you're likely to be much more vulnerable to extreme heat. You might be unable to afford an air-conditioner, and you might not even have electricity when you need it. You may have no choice but to work outdoors under a sun so blistering that first your knees feel weak and then delirium sets in. Or the heat might bring a drought so punishing that, no matter how hard you work under the sun, your corn withers and your children turn to you in hunger. It's not like you can just pack up and leave. So you plant your corn higher up the mountain. You bathe several times a day if you can afford the water. You powder your baby to prevent heat rash. You sleep outdoors when the power goes out, slapping mosquitoes. You sit in front of a fan by yourself, cursed by the twin dangers of isolation and heat. Extreme heat is not a future risk. It's now. It endangers human health, food production and the fate of entire economies. And it's worst for those at the bottom of the economic ladder in their societies"

(C) "Working on a warmer planet: The impact of heat stress on labour productivity and decent work," International Labour Office, 2019.

"Climate projections point towards an increase in the frequency and intensity of extreme weather events, and one result of this trend is the loss of jobs and productivity. The rise in global temperatures caused by climate change will also make the phenomenon of 'heat stress' more common. Heat stress refers to heat received in excess of that which the body can tolerate without suffering physiological impairment. Such excess heat increases workers' occupational risks and vulnerability; it can lead to heatstroke and, ultimately, even to death . . . Excessive heat during work creates occupational health risks; it restricts a worker's physical functions and capabilities, work capacity and productivity. Temperatures above 24–26°C are associated with reduced labour productivity. At 33–34°C, a worker operating at moderate work intensity loses 50 per cent of his or her work capacity . . . Heat stress is projected to reduce total working hours worldwide by 2.2 per cent and global GDP by US$2,400 billion in 2030."

(D) "Compound Climate and Infrastructure Events: How Electrical Grid Failure Alters Heat Wave Risk" by Stone B Jr. et al. *Environmental Science and Technology*, April 30, 2021.
https://pubs.acs.org/doi/pdf/10.1021/acs.est.1c00024

"The potential for critical infrastructure failures during extreme weather events is rising. Major electrical grid failure or "blackout" events in the United States, those with a duration of at least 1 h and impacting 50,000 or more utility customers, increased by more than 60% over the most recent 5 year reporting period. When such blackout events coincide in time with heat wave conditions, population exposures to extreme heat both outside and within buildings can reach dangerously high levels as mechanical air conditioning systems become inoperable. Here, we combine the Weather Research and Forecasting regional climate model with an advanced building energy model to simulate building-interior temperatures in response to concurrent heat wave and blackout conditions for more than 2.8 million residents across Atlanta, Georgia; Detroit, Michigan; and Phoenix, Arizona. Study results find simulated compound heat wave and grid failure events of recent intensity and duration to expose between 68 and 100% of the urban population to an elevated risk of heat exhaustion and/or heat stroke."

Additional Teaching Documents at https://alansinger.net:
- This year is on track to be Earth's warmest on record, beating 2016, NOAA says
- Increasing trends in regional heatwaves
- The Arctic Is Changing in Ways "Scarcely Imaginable Even a Generation Ago"
- Climate concerns as Siberia experiences record-breaking heat
- Glacier Breaks, Crushing Dams and Flooding Towns in India
- Potentially Fatal Combinations of Humidity and Heat Are Emerging Across the Globe

8 Four Billion Years of Climate History

The weather has always fascinated me and pretty much everyone else I know. Weather, unlike climate, affects us on a daily basis. When I was a boy growing up in New York City in the 1950s, six inches of snow meant school was closed. Hurrah! Of course my friends and I headed out to play in the snow.

Today there is a cable television channel dedicated to reporting the weather across the country and around the planet, and you can check local weather hour by hour on the Internet and get fairly accurate predictions for the next month, but that was not the case when I was young. My father used to listen to the New York radio station WCBS's morning *Jack Sterling Show*. The show had a live jazz quintet headed by the trombonist Tyree Glenn. During weather updates, Sterling would turn to Glenn, who would lead the band in a piece, something appropriate for the occasion. My favorite, during winter months, was "Baby, It's Cold Outside."

As a summer camp counselor in the early 1970s, I staffed our "Weather Guild." The kids, mostly middle school age, tracked precipitation, humidity, wind direction and velocity, and cloud formations and prepared a daily weather report for the camp. They were always looking for cirrostratus clouds, clouds high in the atmosphere that look a little like spun cotton candy. During the summer, cirrostratus clouds signal rain in 12 to 24 hours, important information if a group is planning an overnight hike. Our reports were not always completely accurate, and unexpected rain did at times slam us. On one hike, I had my group pack their sleeping bags and walk in the rain most of the night. Toward morning, when it stopped raining, we stripped off our wet clothes, hung them up to dry, and were able to cuddle down in our dry sleeping bags to stay warm and get some sleep.

Clouds tell an interesting story about climate as well as weather. Hans Neuberger, a meteorologist at the Pennsylvania State University, published a study of how changing climate was depicted in European and U.S. art by focusing on how painters presented clouds. Neuberger sorted through 12,000 paintings from eight countries and over 40 art museums that were created between 1400 and 1967. It seems like one of those relatively esoteric academic studies that professors loved to do, except Neuberger's study had real implications.

DOI: 10.4324/9781003200864-8

He found a slow but steady cloud increase in paintings between the beginning of the 15th century and the middle of the 16th century followed by a sudden increase in cloud cover from about 1550 until it declined after 1850. But Neuberger also discovered that pristine blues of the earlier centuries faded during the Industrial Revolution (Fagan, 2000: 201–202).

In *Weather: An Illustrated History* (2018), Andrew Revkin and Lisa Mechaley examine the Earth's climate history by focusing on 100 weather-related events. Brief chapters, organized chronologically, include the emergence of the Earth's atmosphere and water, mass extinctions, civilization in the Fertile Crescent, the spread of agriculture, the development of meteorology, the Little Ice Age, mapping wind and ocean currents, greenhouse gasses, and climate-related scientific advances. Among other startling revelations, we learn that about 4.3 billion years ago, there was a period when it probably rained for a million straight years, creating a water world, and about 2.9 billion years ago, the sky turned pink during the planet's first ice age because of high levels of methane in the atmosphere.

Revkin, the strategic advisor for environmental and science journalism at the National Geographic Society, and Mechaley, an educator at the Children's Environmental Literacy Foundation start the book with a simple statement, "To have weather, a planet must have an atmosphere" (1). I found it useful to divide the book into two sections, climate before and after the emergence of human civilization, with a demarcation line at about 12,000 years ago, the beginning of the anthropological period known as the Neolithic Era and the start of agriculture.

The Earth and its atmosphere formed together about 4.5 billion years ago. The latest scientific explanation is that the atmosphere materialized from gasses emitted from the interior of the planet because of pressure and heat or were generated by the Earth's collisions with asteroids. The released gasses were trapped by the gravitational pull of the core mass and became the atmosphere. Later greenhouse gasses were ejected into the atmosphere by volcanic eruptions. As our knowledge increases about the formation of the Earth, the likelihood that life in some form appeared on planets orbiting other stars also increases, which I find very exciting (Kolbert, 2021).

The Earth's weather and life forms evolved together and very slowly at first. Between 3.7 and 4.1 billion years ago, the first microscopic life forms appeared in the Earth's seas (5–6). One billion years later, cyanobacteria synthesized sugar from carbon dioxide and water. Free oxygen started to enter the atmosphere through a process we now know as photosynthesis. Oxygen levels remained far below modern levels until about 800 million years ago as climate fluctuated widely with episodic ice ages. Eventually, oxygen concentrations increased because algae living in the Earth's oceans emitted oxygen into the atmosphere. Plants started to colonize land areas about 470 million years ago, which increased oxygen levels in the atmosphere and made possible the emergence of oxygen-breathing land animals about 50 million years later (9–10).

Between 262 and 252 million years ago, two-mile thick lava covered much of the Earth's landmass as the result of massive volcanic eruptions, known as the Siberian Traps, in northwestern Asia, present-day China and Russian Siberia. Greenhouse gasses released by the volcanic eruptions raised average global temperature by 10°C (18°F). Oceans became acidic, and 90% of marine life and 75% of land life became extinct during a period of about 60,000 years in what is known as the Great Dying (11–12; Oskin, 2013).

Gradually, climate stabilized again and with it came the age of the dinosaur from approximately 252 to 66 million years ago. Another mass extinction, caused either by a series of massive volcanic eruptions or a large asteroid hit, or both, then led to another mass extinction, wiping out large dinosaurs, with birds and small mammals surviving (13–14).

About 56 million years ago, there was another period of intense warming, possibly stimulated by plate tectonics and the continued break up of the Pangaean supercontinent releasing methane into the atmosphere. Average global temperature again rose about 10°C (18°F) above today's levels. During this warming period, tropical plants and animals thrived at the Polar regions. Then between 50 and 32 million years ago, decreased carbon dioxide concentration in the atmosphere caused the Earth's climate to cool and ice sheets to form (15–16).

Biologically modern humans evolved on the savannahs of the Nile Rift Valley of East Africa between 150,000 and 100,000 years ago during a period of milder climate. These humans survived changing weather patterns and additional ice ages, and about 12,000 years ago, they figured out agriculture and started to live in permanent settlements. A relatively moist climate in the eastern Mediterranean region facilitated an agricultural surplus, state formation, and the emergence of early civilizations in the Tigris-Euphrates and Nile River valleys by about 5,300 BC (25–26).

Revkin and Mechaley argued that until the advent of agriculture and permanent settlements, climate was impacting on people but that the situation changed with the new human civilizations. Now people started to impact on climate as they burned and cleared forests to expand land available for agriculture, raising the level of carbon dioxide and methane in the atmosphere.

Agriculture led to the tracking of weather to time planting and harvesting and the development of calendars. Revkin and Mechaley believe systematic weather observation and prediction started independently in Greece and China during the 4th century BC. In ancient Greece, Aristotle discussed his observations on climate zones and the Earth's water of hydrologic cycle in *Meteorologica* (32). In China, early scientists developed a calendar and mapped seasons by measuring the length of the day (34). In 1088 AD, Shen Kuo, a Chinese scholar, discovered fossilized bamboo in areas that no longer supported its growth. He argued that this was evidence that the regional climate had changed over time. In *Dream Pool Essays*, Shen Kuo also offered explanations for the formation of rainbows and tornadoes and commented on the properties of lightning and the erosion of forests (36).

The rate of weather-related experimentation accelerated in the 17th century, especially in Europe. Galileo and his contemporaries in Italy developed the concept of temperature as something that can be measured (41–43). Other scientific advances include understanding rainbow formation (44–46), mapping wind and ocean currents (53–55), conducting lightning (57–58), and describing tornadoes (57–58). During the 19th century, scientists including Joseph Fourier of France, Eunice Foote of the United States, and James Tyndall of Ireland studied and explained the impact of greenhouse gasses on climate (83–84). In 1896, Svante Arrhenius of Sweden, based on intensive mathematical calculations, proposed the theory that changes in carbon dioxide concentrations in the atmosphere explain planetary warming and cooling (111–112). In the 1920s, Wasaburo Oishi, a Japanese meteorologist, used high-altitude balloons to "map" Jet Stream wind currents, although its impact on climate variability was not really understood for decades (137–138). The first *Farmer's Almanac* was published in 1792 (61–62), regular weather forecasts began in London in the 1860s, and the predecessor of the U.S. National Weather service started operating in 1870 (91). The last developments were done to facilitate shipping and military planning.

During the previous millennium, the 1,000-year period from 1001 AD until 2000 AD, human civilization continued to be shaped by climate. Between 1100 and 1300, a medieval warming period lead to population growth in Eurasia; however, growth was eventually stymied by a little ice age between roughly 1300 and 1850 that reduced crop yields, made parts of the Northern Hemisphere inhospitable, and may have been responsible for pandemics like the Bubonic Plague (37–38). Major eruptions of the volcano Krakatoa between Sumatra and Java in the Indonesian archipelago severely influenced climate around the world, at least temporarily, in 416, 535, 1680, and 1883. The 535 AD eruption may have hastened the collapse of the Roman Empire. The 1815 eruption of Mount Tambora, part of the same volcanic chain, led to a year without summer in the Northern Hemisphere in 1816. There was snow in New England in June. The blast sent tens of millions of tons of sulfurous, sun-blocking particles into the atmosphere, resulting in the worst famine in Europe during the 19th century and a cholera epidemic in India (71–72). The 1930s Dust Bowl in the American Great Plains was probably caused by a combination of prolonged drought and plowing by farmers that broke up the topsoil and left vulnerable to heavy winds (131–132).

In the final sections of *Weather: An Illustrated History*, Revkin and Mechaley chronicle the increasing realization, first by scientists and then by policy makers and the general public, of the threat of human-induced climate change and increasingly extreme weather.

Jet Stream and Dragon Storms

In March 2021, we witnessed how fragile the global infrastructure is and how vulnerable it will be to climate change. An enormous cargo vessel with a deck stacked nine high with containers filled with goods being shipped from China to Europe turned sideways in the Suez Canal, completely blocking one of the world's heavily traveled shipping lanes. The canal was shut to traffic for six days. Speculation was that the ship turned horizontal because of powerful desert winds, dragon storms, that treated the containers piled on deck like a sail. The winds were laden with desert sand that made visibility on the canal almost impossible, so the ships crew was unable to compensate. The windstorms, known by the Arabic name "khamsin," are an annual spring occurrence in the Eastern Sahara. In recent years, the storms are growing stronger, which is attributed to a deeper dip in the Northern Hemisphere polar Jet Stream, winds that circle the Earth in a "sine curve"–like pattern about 15 to 20 miles above sea level. The deeper dip brings colder Arctic air farther south. The same phenomenon in reverse, a higher peak in the Jet Stream, is believed to be responsible for record heat waves in Siberia. The higher peaks and deeper valleys of the Jet Stream "sine curve" are probably do to global warming (NOAA, 2020; Yee and Goodman, 2021: A9; Cornwall, 2020).

Teaching Documents

Uncovering the History of Weather

The research and writings of Aristotle, Shen Gua, and Eunice Foote helped build an understanding of weather and climate.

Questions

1. What is the "circular process" described by Aristotle?
2. What evidence did Shen Gua believe established changes in climate?
3. How did the work of Eunice Foote differ from the work of Aristotle and Shen Gua?
4. In your opinion, why did it take until the 20th century before an understanding of weather and climate were established in science?

A. Aristotle's Discussion of the Rain Cycle in Meteorologica. c. 350 BC

Source: http://classics.mit.edu/Aristotle/meteorology.1.i.html

"The exhalation of water is vapour: air condensing into water is cloud. Mist is what is left over when a cloud condenses into water, and is therefore rather a sign of fine weather than of rain; for mist might be called a barren cloud. So we get a circular process that follows the course of the sun. For according as the sun moves to this side or that, the moisture in this process rises or falls. We must think of it as a river flowing up and down in a circle and made up partly of air, partly of water. When the sun is near, the stream of vapour flows upwards; when it recedes, the stream of water flows down: and the order of sequence, at all events, in this process always remains the same. So if 'Oceanus' had some secret meaning in early writers, perhaps they may have meant this river that flows in a circle about the earth. So the moisture is always raised by the heat and descends to the earth again when it gets cold. These processes and, in some cases, their varieties are distinguished by special names. When the water falls in small drops it is called a drizzle; when the drops are larger it is rain."

B. Shen Gua's Observation of Petrified Bamboo (Dream Pool Essays c. 1080)

Source: Needham, J. (1959). *Science and Civilisation in China* v. III (Cambridge, UK: Cambridge University Press). https://environmentalhistory.org/ancient/middle-ages/

"In recent years there was a landslide on the bank of a large river in Yong-ning Guan near Yanzhou. The bank collapsed, opening a space of several dozens of feet, and under the ground a forest of bamboo shoots was thus revealed. It contained several hundred bamboo with their roots and trunks all complete, and all turned to stone. . . . Now bamboos do not grow in Yanzhou. These were several dozens of feet below the present surface of the ground, and we do not know in what dynasty they could possibly have grown. Perhaps in very ancient times the climate was different so that the place was low, damp, gloomy, and suitable for bamboos. On the Jin-hua Shan in Wuzhou there are stone pine-cones, and stones formed from peach kernels, stone bulrush roots, stone fishes, crabs, and so on, but as these are all (modern) native products of that place, people are not very surprised at them. But these petrified bamboos appeared under the ground so deep, though they are not produced in that place today. This is a very strange thing" (612–614 614).

C. Eunice Foote's Experiment With the Greenhouse Effect

Source: Foote, E. (1856, November). "Circumstances Affecting the Heat of the Sun's Rays," *The American Journal of Science and Arts* 22 (66): 383–384.

"My investigations have led for their object to determine the different circumstances that affect the thermal action of the rays of light that proceed from the sun. Several results have been obtained. . . . The action increases with the density of the air, and it diminishes as it becomes more rarified. The experiments were made with an air-pump and two cylindrical receivers of the same size, about four inches in diameter and thirty in length. In each were placed two thermometers, and the air was exhausted from one and condensed in the other. After both had acquired the same temperature they were placed in the sun, side by side, and while the action of the sun's rays rose to 110° in the condensed tube, it attained only 88° in the other. I had no means at hand of measuring the degree of condensation or rarefaction [diminution of density]. . . . This circumstance must affect the power of the sun's rays in different places, and contributes to produce their feeble action of the summits of lofty mountains."

Additional Teaching Documents at https://alansinger.net:
- The Javanese Book of Kings (Pustaka Raja)
- Great Irish Famine (1845–1852)
- Farming the Dust Bowl" (1930–1936)
- Surviving Hurricane Katrina, New Orleans, 1995

9 Mass Extinctions

I have been a big forest hiker since I was in college in the late 1960s when my friend Ken Silver and I spent a month during the summer camping in Northern California's Klamath National Forest unsuccessfully searching for Bigfoot. During the COVID-19 pandemic, my partner Felicia and I spent a lot of time practicing "shinrin-yoku," or forest bathing, a Japanese tradition of spiritual cleansing by just walking through the woods and appreciating simple beauty— "shibui" (Li, 2018).

My best hike ever was in August 2001when I joined a group on a ten-hour trek to view Burgess Shale fossils at the Walcott Quarry in Yoho National Park, about an hour east of Banff, Alberta. I was introduced to the Burgess Shale by Stephen Jay Gould's book, *Wonderful Life, The Burgess Shale and the Nature of Human History* (1989). *Wonderful Life* recounts the story behind twice discovered 525-million-year-old fossils from the Canadian Rockies, probably the oldest known imprints of soft body parts. The fossils were first uncovered in 1909 by C.D. Walcott at a slate quarry. The slate that was being turned into gravel to support track on the Canadian Pacific Railroad that was under construction (Gould, 64–69). Walcott's fossils and later finds from the site were stored at Harvard University in Cambridge, Massachusetts, at the Smithsonian Institution in Washington, DC, and at two Canadian museums and were largely forgotten about until 1973 when they were "rediscovered" by English paleontologist Simon Conway Morris. Morris later found similar Cambrian Period (roughly 541–485 million years ago) fossils in China and Greenland (Morris, 1998).

Because the Walcott Quarry is a UNESCO World Heritage site, it can only be visited as part of a small group guided hike, so you need to register online months in advance. My group had 15 participants plus the guide. The hikers included 12 PhDs, biologists, geologists, paleontologists, one historian (me), and three teenagers who came with their parents. I think everyone was amazed because as we walked, people just started to informally talk about their area of expertise. We all wondered when we would get to the site, but after about five hours, we simultaneously recognized the type of rock formations and knew we had arrived. The fossils were everywhere. No one made an effort to sneak any out, not because we were watching each other or the guide could call ahead

DOI: 10.4324/9781003200864-9

if anyone did anything suspicious but, I think, because there was a universal feeling that we were in scientific "holy place" that was not to be disturbed. It was like we were with Indiana Jones on one of his quests.

A website maintained by the Royal Ontario Museum is worth exploring to learn more about the fossils (https://burgess-shale.rom.on.ca/en/science/burgess-shale/03-fossils.php). Over 200,000 specimens have been recovered, including about 150 different species of plants, animals, algae, and bacteria. There are two theories about why these fossils survived for 500 million years relatively intact. One is that they were deep underwater in the ocean and were buried by sediment. The other explanation, which Gould and I prefer, is that they were in shallow water, trapped by an underwater avalanche, and dragged to great depths and buried below the level where organisms reside that cause decomposition. We go with the second explanation because the algae that the Burgess Shale organisms fed on depended on sunlight for photosynthesis and would have more likely been closer to the surface. The majority of the species found at the Walcott Quarry are like contemporary sponges and lived on the seabed. Less plentiful are sediment-dwelling organisms and organisms capable of free swimming. Gould argued that some of the fossils at the Walcott Quarry are from evolutionary branches with no longer existing body types that were wiped out by a mass extinction event. These animals disappeared, not because they were ill adapted for survival but because they were in the wrong place at the wrong time 488 million years ago during the Cambrian-Ordovician mass extinction (233–239).

A major theme in Gould's writing about paleontology is the contingent nature of history, the evolution of life was not predetermined, natural catastrophes frequently intervened leading to mass extinctions, and if scientists had the ability to rewind and play Earth's history again, the overwhelming likelihood is that events would turn out differently. In an epilogue in *Wonderful Life*, Gould discussed the ancient chordate *Pikaia gracilens*, whose remains were found in the Burgess Shale. Pikaia, as a chordate with a "stiff dorsal rod," is a member of the phylum, or branch of living things, that later includes all vertebrates with internal spinal columns. Human beings are part of the phylum Chordata. If some Pikaia had not survived the Cambrian-Ordovician mass extinction, there may never have evolved *Homo sapiens* (321–323).

Elizabeth Kolbert, a staff writer at *The New Yorker* magazine, won the Pulitzer Prize for her book *The Sixth Extinction: An Unnatural History* (2014). In *The Sixth Extinction*, Kolbert describes five mass extinctions on Earth during the past half a billion years. In each case, vast numbers of species disappeared, leading to a sharp contraction in biodiversity. Although Charles Darwin is widely quoted as believing in "survival of the fittest," these were clearly examples of survival of the luckiest. The sixth mass extinction, according to Kolbert, is currently taking place, and unlike the previous five, which were caused by extra-terrestrial or geophysical phenomena, the sixth extinction is the product of cataclysmic human environmental actions.

Much of *The Sixth Extinction* is a compelling call to action. Kolbert argues that "Right now we are deciding, without quite meaning to, which evolutionary pathways will remain open and which will forever be closed. No other creature has ever managed this, and it will, unfortunately, be our most enduring legacy" (268).

The first documented mass extinction of life on Earth, 440 million years ago, was the result of global warming brought on by the depletion of oxygen in the atmosphere caused by massive volcanic activity. The Ordovician–Silurian Extinction probably killed off 60% to 70% of all species on Earth. The Devonian Extinction, 365 million years ago, may have been the result of a series of pulses, or multiple causes, over the course of 20 million years. It eliminated at least 70% of the Earth's life forms. The Permian-Triassic Extinction, 250 million years ago, was the Earth's largest, wiping out between 90% and 96% of all sea species and 70% of land-based ones, including insects. Potential causes include one or more large meteor impacts, massive volcanic eruptions, or climate change brought about by large releases of underwater methane. The Triassic-Jurassic Extinction, 210 million years ago, caused 70% to 75% of all species to become extinct. The most widely supported explanation for that extinction event is volcanic eruptions. The best-known mass extinction event to the general public and every six-year-old child who lives dinosaurs was the Cretaceous-Tertiary Extinction, 65 million years ago. It was triggered by the collision of a large asteroid with the Earth; the impact area was the Yucatan Peninsula and the Gulf of Mexico. Seventy-five percent of species became extinct, including large dinosaurs. Species of small mammals and dinosaurs, now known as birds, survived the Cretaceous-Tertiary Extinction, not because they were the fittest but because they were the smallest. If it had not been for the confluence of an asteroid strike and massive volcanic eruptions, dinosaurs would still dominate the planet, and humans would never have evolved.

Extinction is a relatively new scientific idea, first conceptualized by a late 18th century French scholar, Georges Cuvier. Up until that point, for most Europeans and European Americans, the only extinction event was Noah's flood, and in that case, God saved two members of each species so they could replicate and multiply. When mastodon bones were first uncovered, naturalist believed they were bones of an elephant or hippopotamus. In 1796, at a public session of the French National Institute, Cuvier, who collected fossils himself, introduced the idea that they were the skeletal remains of lost species from "a world previous to ours" (Kolbert, 2014: 24–25; Cuvier, 1796: 22).

Kolbert describes how warmer oceans evaporate more water vapor into the warmer air, which holds more moisture. As the moisture-laden air hits landmasses, it releases larger downpours that cause more frequent flooding and mudslides. You may have noticed that you are sweating more recently. That is because there has been a 4% increase in global humidity during the past three decades. Warmer air and water have also made possible the migration of viruses, bacteria, disease-carrying species like mosquitoes and ticks, and pest species from equatorial regions into densely populated areas like New York City that were previously considered temperate zones.

As a journalist, Elizabeth Kolbert draws on the work of scores of researchers in multiple disciplines, including geologists, botanists, and marine biologists. To illustrate her points, *The Sixth Extinction* introduces readers to a dozen species either extinct or facing extinction, including the Panamanian golden frog, staghorn coral, the great auk, and the Sumatran rhino. Estimates vary, but between 20% and 50% of plant and animal species are expected to disappear by the end of the 21st century. Coral reefs will probably be the first entire ecosystem to disappear in the sixth global extinction.

In a review of Kolbert's book, Al Gore (2014), former U.S. vice president and environmental activist, argues people have psychological difficulty grappling with mass extinction and the idea that living things can disappear forever. Gore believes this is at least part of the reason humanity continues to permit the world's atmosphere and oceans to be used as open sewers. More than 90 million tons of gaseous waste is ejected into the atmosphere on a daily basis, with about a third absorbed by the oceans. Even with the oceans acting as a sponge, fossil fuel pollution released into the "atmosphere traps as much extra heat energy every 24 hours as would be released by the explosion of 400,000 Hiroshima-class nuclear bombs." Gore believes "history is full of examples" of humanity's "capacity to overcome even the most difficult challenges whenever a controversy is finally resolved into a choice between what is clearly right and what is clearly wrong. The anomalies Kolbert identifies are too glaring to ignore. She makes an irrefutable case that what we are doing to cause a sixth mass extinction is clearly wrong. And she makes it clear that doing what is right means accelerating our transition to a more sustainable world" (Gore, 2014: BR1).

In Gore's own work, he is generally hopeful about the future and I think in the review he overstates Kolbert's hopefulness (Gore, 2006). In *Under a White Sky: The Nature of the Future*, (2021), a book that Kolbert describes as a sequel to *The Sixth Extinction*, she examines human efforts to intervene in natural systems, with both positive and negative impacts. In an interview with *Inside Climate News*, Kolbert was asked if the book was "hopeful or a cautionary tale" (Weisbrod, 2021). Her response was equivocal.

> "Ah, you have really gotten to the heart of the matter. I definitely leave that to you, dear reader. I think you can read the book and say, yes I'm more hopeful than when I started, there's a lot of really smart people working on these problems and they have some really ingenious answers. I think that would be a really valid response. And I think you can read the book and say, 'I'm terrified. I'm even more terrified than when I started the book.' Both I think are really reasonable responses to what's going on."

In my reading of Kolbert's books and of the Earth's history of mass extinctions, I lean toward the terror part.

Teaching Documents

Burning Fossil Fuels Helped Drive Earth's Largest Mass Extinction

By Lucas Joel, *New York Times*, December 1, 2020, D2
Source: www.nytimes.com/2020/11/18/science/extinction-global-warming.html

Questions

1. Why is the Permian-Triassic mass extinction known as the "Great Dying"?
2. What caused the Permian-Triassic mass extinction?
3. Why is the Permian-Triassic mass extinction used to explain today's climate threat?
4. How do the two events differ?

1. "Paleontologists call it the Permian-Triassic mass extinction, but it has another name: 'the Great Dying.' It happened about 252 million years ago, and, over the course of just tens of thousands of years, 96 percent of all life in the oceans and, perhaps, roughly 70 percent of all land life vanished forever. The smoking gun was ancient volcanism in what is today Siberia, where volcanoes disgorged enough magma and lava over about a million years to cover an amount of land equivalent to a third or even half of the surface area of the United States. But volcanism on its own didn't cause the extinction. The Great Dying was fueled . . . by extensive oil and coal deposits that the Siberian magma blazed through, leading to combustion that released greenhouse gases like carbon dioxide and methane. "There was lots of oil, coal and carbonates formed before the extinction underground near the Siberian volcanism," said Kunio Kaiho, a geochemist at Tohoku University in Sendai, Japan."

2. "The findings solidify the Great Dying as one of the best examples that we have from Earth's history of what a changing climate can do to life on our planet. Dr. Kaiho and his team retrieved samples from rock deposits in south China and northern Italy that formed around the time of the extinction, and they detected spikes of a molecule called coronene. That substance, Dr. Kaiho explained, is produced only when fossil fuels combust at extremely high temperatures—like those you might find in magma . . . [T]he team's findings are backed up by a Nature Geoscience study . . . that presents chemical evidence for the acidification of the oceans after the fossil fuel combustion and greenhouse gas release. As the planet warmed, the oceans absorbed more and more carbon dioxide. This caused waters to acidify to the point that organisms like corals would have dissolved. . . . Hana Jurikova, a biogeochemist at the University of St. Andrews in Scotland . . . and her team discovered spikes of the element boron—a

proxy for acidity levels—in fossil brachiopod shells found in rocks in Italy that stretch across the extinction boundary."

3. While you may be tempted to draw an analogy between the Great Dying and today's warming climate, there are significant differences. For one, the greenhouse gases emitted during the Permian-Triassic events were far greater than anything humans have produced. Also, the volcanoes released carbon dioxide 252 million years ago at a rate much slower than humans emit it today. "The amount of carbon released to the atmosphere per year from the Siberian traps, it was still 14 times lower than the rate we have at the moment," Dr. Jurikova said. "So, the amount of carbon we're burning per year at the moment is much higher than during the largest extinction. I mean, that's incredible, right?"

10 "Clocking" Climate Change

At the American Museum of Natural History in New York City, there is a 16-foot-diameter slab taken from a 1,400-year-old California Giant Sequoia tree. Loggers harvested the tree in 1891 when it was over 300 feet tall. In Yosemite National Park, Giant Sequoia trees can survive for over 3,000 years, but they are not the trees with the greatest longevity. That record is held by bristlecone pines that can live for over 4,500. At the museum, directly across from the Sequoia, is a display with much smaller and older specimens. These trees are all "climate clocks." Every tree ring represents one year of growth, and the widths of the rings signal rainfall in the area where they were growing. An extended number of narrow rings means a period of prolonged drought. Uneven rings indicate intense winds coming from one direction. Fire damage suggests a tree was damaged during a warm, dry period.

In the mid-1980s, I spent two weeks at the Crown Canyon archeological site near Mesa Verde National Park in Colorado. At Crow Canyon, I joined in uncovering and studying artifacts of the Anasazi who lived in the four corners region of the American Southwest where Colorado, Utah, Arizona, and New Mexico meet. One of the activities was comparing the grain patterns in preserved charcoal from fireplaces we found in abandoned campsites with the tree rings in older trees in the area. The comparisons established that the charcoal came from trees cut down for firewood in the early 14th century, a period of intense drying in the region that led to entire communities migrating along the San Juan River south into what is now New Mexico.

Even with the tree-ring "climate clock," questions remain among historical anthropologists whether drought conditions were severe enough to force tens of thousands of agricultural Anasazi to migrate. Some researchers blame the collapse of their communities on internecine warfare and religious divisions. We know that human remains indicate the Anasazi were experiencing malnutrition, reduced life spans, and higher infant mortality rates when they abandoned the Crow Canyon area, and evidence from tree rings and pollen shows that the Anasazi may have been prevented from moving to higher elevations with moister fields by global cooling. The Anasazi farmers appear to have been caught in a climate vise. At the lower elevations where they traditionally lived, conditions were now too dry to grow enough food to support

DOI: 10.4324/9781003200864-10

their communities, while at higher elevations, conditions were too cold and growing seasons too short. Climate change, decreasing food resources, and intensified competition for food and water were probably the causes of warfare between villages (Johnson, 1996: C1).

Historians and climate scientists use a variety of tools to measure climate in the past, including tree rings, ice cores, ocean and lake sediment, historical accounts, agricultural production documents, and economic indicators such as tax and tithe records. Economic historians have traced grain and wine prices in Europe back for centuries. In times of scarcity, supplies were low, and hoarding drove up prices. Ship captains and shipping companies, concerned about icebergs and frozen rivers and ports, kept detailed records of icing. The most detailed and precise climate histories come from ice core drilling in Greenland and Antarctica. They record changes in climate over the past 800,000 years (Davies, 2020).

In *The Winds of Change: Climate, Weather, and the Destruction of Civilizations* (2006), Eugene Linden, a weather and climate reporter for a number of prominent publications, including *Time* magazine, examined the impact of climate change on human history starting with human evolution in the East African Rift Valley. Linden discussed a number of the Earth's regions and time periods, including the Mesopotamian Fertile Crescent and the Yucatan and Central America where the Maya civilization prospered and then collapsed, carrying his study into the modern era. Linden found that civilizations repeatedly grew prosperous, and populations increased during extended periods of accommodating climate and then collapsed when climates changed and they could no longer support their now larger populations or were plunged into wars over increasingly scarce resources.

Linden organized *The Winds of Change* into six parts. The first part examined the role climate change played in the collapse of the Mayan and Akkadian civilizations and the disappearance of Norse settlements in Greenland. Parts two and three explore the link between climate, geography, and human evolution as changes in climate eliminated initial geographic advantages. Part four looked at the connection between periodic Pacific El Niño-Southern Oscillation events caused by the circulation of ocean currents and severe 19th century droughts and famines in India, China, Southern Africa, Brazil, Indonesia, and the Philippines. Contemporary societies with larger populations are especially vulnerable to the effects of an El Niño on agricultural production. An El Niño episode in 1997 and 1998 caused severe drought in Indonesia, scorched rice fields, caused massive forest fires that sickened millions of people, and brought down the Suharto government (Goldstein, 2016).

Part five takes a close look at the North Atlantic Gulf Stream (also known as Atlantic Meridional Overturning Circulation or AMOC), an ocean conveyor belt that transports warmer water from the Caribbean to North America and Europe, making them habitable. He also critiqued public skepticism and policy maker refusal to accept the science of climate change. Unfortunately, while the book was written 15 years ago, before much awareness of the potential of a climate catastrophe, governments in the United States, Brazil, China, and Russia and major corporations, especially from the fossil fuel industry, continued to question scientific authority.

The power of the Gulf Stream was first recognized in 1513 by Spanish explorer Juan Ponce de León. De León reported that northward flowing ocean currents off the coast of Florida pushed his ships backward with such force that they were able to counter the winds propelling his ships south. In the 18th century, British sailors estimated that because of the Gulf Stream, the trip from North America to England could be several weeks shorter than a return voyage. American inventor and diplomat Benjamin Franklin published the first map of the Gulf Stream in 1770 based on information he received from ship's captains on changes in the behavior of whales, water temperature, bubbles on the water's surface, and the water's color (Zimmerman, 2013).

The Gulf Stream is such a strong ocean current that it carries 30 times more water by volume than all of the Earth's rivers combined. Students are generally amazed when they realize London in the United Kingdom is on the same line of latitude as southern Alaska (51.5 degrees) and that Stockholm, Sweden, is farther north than large sections of the Canadian province of Labrador (59.3 degrees). Tropical waters in the Gulf Stream provide Scandinavia with the heat equivalent of 78,000 times more energy than other sources. If the Gulf Stream was pushed south by fresh cold water pouring into the Atlantic Ocean from a melting Greenland ice cap, London, Stockholm, and much of Europe could be transformed into a frozen wasteland (Velasquez-Manoff and White, 2021).

In part six, Linden peers into a dire future of increasingly traumatic climate events like Hurricane Katrina unless countries, companies, and economies act quickly and radically to change. His hope is that modern societies, unlike past civilizations, can make the necessary changes and survive.

The deeper Linden delved into climate change, the more alarmed he became. In 1996, scientists detected an increase in the velocity of "ice streams." These streams transport glacial ice from the interior of Antarctica to its coast. The scientists realized that they were looking at a self-triggering effect. As glaciers diminished, salt water from the open ocean would seep back under the ice and cause it to float. This would raise the sea level around the world, flooding low-lying areas of Florida, Bangladesh, and Indonesia and displacing hundreds of millions of people. A scientist with NASA's Jet Propulsion Laboratory published a study confirming that the Antarctica ice sheet, which had been stable during the entire course of recorded human history, was in a state of "irreversible decline."

The stimulus for Linden's book, Hurricane Katrina in 2005, was the most destructive storm to strike the United States and the costliest, causing over a hundred billion dollars in damage. According to the National Oceanic and Atmospheric Administration (NOAA), Katrina formed as a tropical storm southeast of the Bahamas and north of Cuba, about 400 miles from Miami, Florida, on August 23, 2005. When it reached southern Florida two days later, Katrina was a moderate Category 1 hurricane with winds just over 75 mph. It did little damage and Florida, and by the time it reached the Gulf of Mexico, wind speed had dropped, and it was no longer classified as a hurricane. However, by August 28, after gathering strength from the warmer Gulf waters, Katrina was a Category 5 hurricane with winds of 175 mph (Knabb, Rhome, and Brown, 2005).

Hurricanes, which are the world's costliest natural disasters, are intensifying because of climate change. Eighty-five percent of all hurricane damage is caused by Category 3, 4, and 5 storms. A hurricane with 150-mph wind speed has the potential to do 250 times the damage of a hurricane with 75-mph winds. As the Earth's climate warms, there has been a substantial regional and global increase in the proportion of the strongest hurricanes—Category 4 and 5 storms. Wind is not the only problem. Scientists project that the amount of total rainfall will increase by about 15% by the end of the 21st century, leading to even more disastrous flooding (NOAA).

The Earth's "climate clocks" keep ticking, and the alarm has already gone off. If humanity does not wake up soon to the risks, it may be too late to respond.

A Different Kind of Climate Clock

There is a large digital clock on the face of a building overlooking Union Square in New York City. For Climate Week 2020, it was reset as a countdown clock with the years, days, hours, minutes, and seconds until the Earth reaches a deadline when it may be too late to reverse climate change. Based on calculations by the Berlin-based Mercator Research Institute on Global Commons and Climate Change, the countdown clock was set at 7 years, 103 days, 15 hours, 40 minutes, and 7 seconds. But there is some possibility for optimism. On Sunday, April 18, 2021, Union Square countdown clock switched to a new digital display showing the percentage of the Earth's energy produced from renewal sources – 12.23% and slowly increasing (Moynihan, 2020: C3; Moynihan, 2021: C6).

The Mercator Research Institute also has its own countdown clock on its webpage. I checked it on April 20, 2021, at 9 AM EDT. It projected that the Earth only had about 6 years, 8 months, 11 days, and 3 hours left before it exhausts its carbon budget and climate change is irreversible (www.mcc-berlin.net/en/research/co2-budget.html).

Teaching Documents

What Does the Future Hold?

Sources: www.unep.org/emissions-gap-report-2020
www.nytimes.com/2020/12/09/climate/paris-agreement-anniversary-united-nations.html

Questions

1. What concerns were raised in the United Nations Environment Programme Emissions Gap Report?
2. Which nations bear the greatest responsibility for these conditions?
3. What positive signs are reported?

The 11th annual edition of the United Nations Environment Programme Emissions Gap Report was produced while the COVID-19 crisis dominated the news. The economic disruption caused by the COVID-19 virus briefly slowed, but did not eliminate, the "historic and ever-increasing burden of human activity on the Earth's climate. This burden is observable in the continuing rise in extreme weather events, including wildfires and hurricanes, and in the melting of glaciers and ice at both poles" (UNEP, 2021: iv). Greenhouse gas emissions grew by over 12% between 2010 and 2019, with a sharp rise in 2019. The year 2020 set new climate records, but unfortunately, they will only stand until new records are set.

The world is dangerously behind schedule in slowing catastrophic climate change. Its richest people and nations must make major changes in their lifestyles if climate disaster can be averted. The wealthiest 1% of the global population produces more than twice the greenhouse gas emissions than the poorest 50% of the population – combined.

One sign of hope is that the countries that produce the most greenhouse gases have promised to reduce their emissions to net zero by midcentury, meaning that they would eliminate as much greenhouse gas from the atmosphere as they emit. China, Great Britain, Japan, and Korea have each announced newer, more stringent climate targets. The United Nations is pressuring other countries to approve similarly ambitious climate targets. If these promises are met, it is possible to world will be able limit temperature rise sufficiently to avoid the worst climate disaster scenarios.

Another positive sign is that more of the world's electricity, which came almost entirely from burning toxic fossil fuels in the past, is coming from renewable sources. The price of solar power is falling far faster than expected, carmakers are producing more electric vehicles, and some large investment companies are moving money out of fossil fuel companies.

Additional Teaching Documents at https://alansinger.net:
- How Drought, Deforestation, and Desertification Transform Civilizations
- 2020: A Record Season for Hurricanes
- Emergency From Climate Change on Two Coasts
- Things We Know About Climate Change and Hurricanes
- Developer Eyes Wetlands That Helped Stop Flooding During Sandy
- The Gulf Stream

11 Disease Carried by Mosquitoes or Hidden in the Ice

Throughout history, humans have existed side by side with bacteria and viruses. A joke, sometimes not very funny, is that bacteria and viruses, with their genetic simplicity, are the pinnacle of evolution, and humans only exist as their host. As we learned from the COVID-19 pandemic, bacteria and viruses can cause serious illness and death and be highly disruptive of economies and daily life (Patta, 2021). One medical concern is that some have become invasive species in new areas as the result of climate change.

During summer 2020, health officials in Connecticut issued a warning that people with open sores who were swimming at Long Island Sound beaches risked serious illness. At least five people were hospitalized after being infected by the pathogenic bacteria *Vibrio vulnificus.* This bacteria is usually present in warmer water farther south on the Atlantic coast, but as climate change is warming the oceans, the bacteria migrated farther north (Brodsky, 2020).

V. vulnificus is not the only virus that is extending its range as climate warms. The Zika and West Nile viruses are spread in the human population via mosquito bites, and the areas dealing with mosquito infestations are expanding both because of warming temperatures and stagnant water breeding pools in locales where they were not previously a problem. The Zika virus is primarily transmitted by *Aedes* mosquitoes, which are mainly found in tropical and subtropical regions. Infection with the virus is most dangerous when a woman is pregnant. It can cause miscarriages, premature births, and microcephaly, an abnormally small head in newborns. The same mosquito also transmits other tropical diseases, including dengue, chikungunya, and yellow fever (WHO, 2018; CDC, 2020a, 2020b).

West Nile virus is carried by at least 65 different species of mosquito and is the leading cause of mosquito-borne viral diseases in the United States. While only 20% of the people infected with the virus develop significant symptoms and the fatality rate is extremely low, there are currently no vaccines to prevent illnesses caused by the West Nile virus or medications to help treat the diseases (Colpitts et al., 2012; Pope, 2019).

Malaria, which is caused by five different bacterial parasites, is the deadliest of the mosquito-borne diseases. In 2019, there were more than 200 million cases worldwide and over 400,000 deaths. While Malaria is still relatively rare in northern latitudes, that could change with global warming. Increases in

DOI: 10.4324/9781003200864-11

temperature, rain, and humidity will aid the proliferation of malaria-carrying mosquitoes, and bacteria carried by mosquitoes are expected to mature faster, increasing the rate of mutation, transmission, and illness. Some studies suggest that global warming will stimulate the evolution of new mosquito species, further inhibiting eradication programs and accelerating the spread of diseases (Fernando, Wickremasinghe, and Wickremasinghe, 2012; Tang et al., 2018).

At the same time that viruses and bacteria are moving north from the tropics, they may be moving south from the Arctic Circle, where they have been frozen in permafrost that is now melting. In August 2016, at least 20 people were hospitalized in northern Siberia, and a 12-year-old boy died after being infected by anthrax. The outbreak was probably caused by the defrosting of a reindeer carcass that were frozen for over 75 years when over a million reindeer died from anthrax in the early 20th century (Fox-Skelly, 2017).

According to the Centers for Disease Control and Prevention, anthrax is a serious infectious disease caused by *Bacillus anthracis*. Although it is generally rare among humans, people can get sick from anthrax if they come in contact with infected animals and breathe in spores. People also become infected if they eat food or drink water that is contaminated. Anthrax infection can be treated with prompt the administration of antibiotics, but untreated it is so deadly that powdered spores have been used as a terrorist weapon (Fox-Skelly, 2017; CDC, 2020c).

Anthrax probably originated in Egypt and Mesopotamia and is the disease called cattle murrain in the ten Egyptian plagues described in the Judeo-Christian Book of Exodus and the Jewish Passover Seder. Anthrax appears in *The Iliad* by Homer, written around 700 BC, and in poems by Virgil, who lived in Rome from 70 to 19 BC. At the start of *The Iliad*, Homer "described a 'burning wind of plague' that attacked 'pack animals first, and dogs, but soldiers too.'" In Virgil's poem "Georgics," animal carcasses were abandoned in their stalls where they were "rotting with putrid foulness." In 1770 in Saint-Domingue (modern Haiti), about 15,000 people, many who were enslaved Africans, died from a form of intestinal anthrax after eating meat from infected animals (Gugliotta, 2001).

The hardiness of anthrax spores and their lingering virulence make anthrax a preferred weapon in modern biological warfare. During World War I, Germany tried to infect reindeer in Norway that were being used to smuggle supplies to British and French forces. These anthrax spores were analyzed by scientists in 1998 and found to still be capable of causing infection. During World War II, the military on both sides had biological warfare programs that included using anthrax as a weapon against their enemy. After the war, it took 36 years for the British to decontaminate the soil of island they used for anthrax testing. In 1979, an anthrax leak from a Soviet Union biological weapons plant killed over 60 people. One reason for the 1991 Persian Gulf War was fear that Iraq had accumulated thousands of gallons of weaponized anthrax bacteria (Gugliotta, 2001).

During 2020, the permafrost region of Siberia set high temperature records. In May, temperatures were 10°C (18°) higher than average. In June, one

Siberian town recorded a temperature of 38°C (100.4°F), probably a record temperature for the Arctic region during the past 140 years when accurate records are available. Smallpox, caused by infection with the *Variola* virus, was eradicated as a human scourge in the 1970s, so people are no longer vaccinated, but with global warming, it can return. In the 1890s, a smallpox epidemic swept through Siberia, and victims were buried in permafrost that is now being exposed. An estimated 50 million people died during the 1918 flu pandemic. Genetic material from that flu virus was recovered from now unfrozen mass graves in Alaska (Gramling, 2020; Fox-Skelly, 2017).

With higher temperatures, more and deeper permafrost melts. The deeper permafrost can house bacteria frozen as much as a million years ago, long before humans emerged as a species, so people have no preexisting immunity. In 2007, scientists revived bacteria that may have been frozen in the Antarctica ice cap 8 million years ago. Viruses have also been revived from Siberian permafrost that were frozen for at least 30,000 years, and once unfrozen, they become infectious again. Bacteria and viruses that once plagued now extinct hominid species like the Neanderthals could reemerge and infect modern humans, meaning us.

Environmental Racism

Environmental pollution and climate change place American minorities, African Americans, Latinos, and Indigenous people at the greatest risk. Almost 75 million people of color, approximately 60%, live in counties with a failing grade for ozone or particle pollution that cause asthma and other breathing difficulties. The year 2019 was the Earth's second hottest year on record. African Americans living on urban heat islands where bricks, concrete, and asphalt absorb and hold onto heat are disproportionately exposed to extreme heat that causes illness and premature death. A Chicago-area ZIP code with the greatest flood risk is in Englewood, near the South Side, where almost 95% of residents are African American. Pregnant women exposed to high temperatures or air pollution are more likely to have children who are premature, underweight, or stillborn, and African American mothers and babies are harmed at a much higher rate than the population at large. Mothers with asthma are at particularly high risk. Severe preterm births fewer than 28 weeks into pregnancy increased by 52% for mothers with asthma exposed to high levels of air pollution. Studies found that high temperatures were tied to an increased risk of premature birth ranging from 8% to 21%. Every temperature increase of 1°C in the week before delivery corresponds with a 6% greater likelihood of stillbirth. Another study of almost half a million births in Florida in 2004 and 2005 found that for every three miles closer a mother lives to a plant that uses garbage to produce energy, the risk of low birth weight increases by 3% (American Lung Association, 2020; Lakhani, 2020; Flavelle et al., 2020; Flavelle, 2020a: A24).

Teaching Documents

Thawing of Permafrost May Disturb Historic Cattle Burial Grounds in East Siberia

By Boris Revich and Marina Podolnaya, *Global Health Action*, 4(1), 2011

Questions

1. What disease emerged with the melting of the Siberian permafrost?
2. According to this study, why does climate change bring an increased risk of zoonoses?

Climate warming in the Arctic may increase the risk of zoonoses (diseases transmitted to humans from animals) due to expansion of vector habitats, improved chances of vector survival during winter, and permafrost degradation. Monitoring of soil temperatures at Siberian cryology control stations (study of snow and ice) since 1970 showed correlations between air temperatures and the depth of permafrost layer that thawed during summer season. Between 1900s and 1980s, the temperature of surface layer of permafrost increased by 2° to 4°C, and a further increase of 3°C is expected. Frequent outbreaks of anthrax caused the deaths of 1.5 million deer in Russian North between 1897 and 1925. Anthrax among people or cattle has been reported in 29,000 settlements of the Russian North, including more than 200 Yakutia settlements (Yakutia, also known as Sakha, are a Siberian ethnic group), which are located near the burial grounds of cattle that died from anthrax. Statistically significant positive trends in annual average temperatures were established in 8 of 17 administrative districts of Yakutia (a Russian Republic or subdivision in Eastern Siberia) for which sufficient meteorological data were available. At present, it is not known whether further warming of the permafrost will lead to the release of viable anthrax organisms. Nevertheless, we suggest that it would be prudent to undertake careful monitoring of permafrost conditions in all areas where an anthrax outbreak had occurred in the past.

Additional Teaching documents at https://alansinger.net:
Abstracts from scientific journals underscore the medical dangers associated with climate change.
- Fossil Genes and Microbes in the Oldest Ice on Earth
- Thirty-thousand-year-old Distant Relative of Giant Icosahedral DNA Viruses With a Pandoravirus Morphology
- Discovery and Characterization of the 1918 Pandemic Influenza Virus in Historical Context
- *Carnobacterium Pleistocenium* Isolated From Permafrost of the Fox Tunnel in Alaska

12 Climate Change Deniers and Minimizers

The writer Upton Sinclair was the unsuccessful Democratic Party candidate for governor of California in 1934. In a self-published post-election chronicle, *I, Candidate for Governor: And How I Got Licked*, Sinclair famously wrote: "It is difficult to get a man to understand something, when his salary depends on his not understanding it" (Sinclair, 1935: 100). Sinclair could well have been writing about late 20th century and 21st century climate deniers and minimizers.

Mathematics is a closed system that generally corresponds to the real world but has its own internal logic, so mathematicians can have absolute proof. Scientists, social scientists, and historians weigh evidence, and sometimes there is a predominance of evidence or even an overwhelming predominance, but there is never absolute proof because there are always new things to be discovered. In a sense, all scientists, social scientists, and historians are existentialists; we make the best choices we can make based on the available evidence but recognize that new evidence might require new explanations. The evidence that human-caused climate change through the burning of fossil fuels threatens life on Earth as we know it is overwhelming. When climate deniers and climate minimizers challenge this, they are really challenging science itself and the historical process.

Since the 1970s, fossil fuel corporations have been adopting a strategy first deployed by the tobacco industry in the 1950s as evidence mounted of the connection between smoking and cancer. The tobacco and fossil fuel industries each used heavily funded public relations campaigns to undermine an emerging scientific consensus by suggesting there was uncertainty and conflict within the scientific community. Rather than attacking science, they posed as its defenders, demanding more research, not less, while promoting skepticism about existing evidence. They funded their own "science" to protect their industry from charges that they were motivated by self-interest However, the goal of these companies was to undercut public health efforts and minimize government regulations that might interfere with corporate profits (Brandt, 2012; Uscinski, Douglas, and Lewandowsky, 2017). Advertisements placed by the Tobacco Industry Research Committee (1954) repeatedly reminded the public "There is no conclusive scientific proof of a link between smoking and cancer;" "Medical research points to many possible causes of cancer;" and

DOI: 10.4324/9781003200864-12

"The millions of people who derive pleasure and satisfaction from smoking can be reassured that every scientific means will be used to get all the facts as soon as possible." However, internal documents released as part of a Tobacco Master Settlement Agreement in November 1998 revealed that the tobacco companies were privately aware of the cancer risks they were publicly denying (Public Health Law Center, 2019).

While there is a nearly unanimous scientific consensus that human-caused global warming is happening and presents a serious global problem in the immediate future, public opinion polls in the United States show the impact of corporate and political denials. According to a 2013 poll conducted by Public Policy Polling, 37% of respondents believed that "global warming is a hoax," and a 2016 poll conducted by Fairleigh Dickinson University found that 41% of respondents thought it was definitely or possibly true that "global warming is a myth concocted by scientists" (Uscinski, Douglas, and Lewandowsky, 2017; Wiltgen, 2013; Cassino, 2016).

Corporate-funded think tanks like the Heartland and Cato Institutes have taken the lead in promoting climate denial or misdirection. In 2012, a billboard campaign by the Heartland Institute compared "believers in global warming to 'murderers and madmen' such as the Unabomber, Charles Manson and Osama bin Laden." In 2017, after Donald Trump announced the withdrawal of the United States from the Paris Climate Agreement, Joseph Bast, CEO of Heartland, declared, "We are winning in the global warming war." Heartland finances its initiatives with millions of dollars in support from ExxonMobil and foundations and political action committees associated with Koch Industries, a major petroleum producer (Banerjee, 2017). The Cato Institute, which is largely funded by Koch Industries–affiliated groups, takes a different tack. On its website, it recognizes that human activity has contributed to global warming, but "global warming is also a very complicated and difficult issue that can provoke very unwise policy in response to political pressure." The Cato Institute charged that legislative proposals to reduce carbon dioxide emissions lacked the technology needed to achieve their goals. However, addressing climate change did not require emergency measures, at least according to the Cato Institute. "[C]ontrary to much of the rhetoric surrounding climate change, there is ample time to develop such technologies, which will require substantial capital investment by individuals" (Cato Institute).

The Cato Institute website highlights "uncertainty" claims made by Robert Pindyck, an MIT economist (Van Doren, 2020; Pindyck, 2020). According to Pindyck, who is primarily interested in the cost-benefit of climate policies and is not a climatologist:

> There is a lot we know about climate change, but there is also a lot we don't know. Even if we knew exactly how much carbon dioxide (CO2) and other greenhouse gases (GHGs) the world will emit over the coming decades, we wouldn't be able to predict with any reasonable precision how much the global mean temperature will rise as a result. Nor would

we be able to predict other aspects of climate change, such as rises in sea levels, and increases in the frequency and intensity of storms, hurricanes and droughts. And even if we were able to predict the extent of climate change that will occur over the coming decades, we can say very little about its likely impact—which in the end is what matters. The fact is that we face considerable uncertainty over climate change, and as we'll see, that uncertainty has crucial implications for policy.

(2)

However, what Cato leaves out from Pindyck's analysis is his conclusion.

So what, exactly, is the value of 'climate insurance?' . . . The very uncertainties over climate change that create a value of insurance prevent us from determining exactly how large that value is . . . [T]he simple numerical examples we explored suggest that the insurance value is likely to be large. And what is most important, the very fact that there is an insurance value is a reason why *the correct policy response to uncertainty is not to sit back and wait to see what happens.*

(35) (italics added)

The Cato Institute also misrepresents arguments about climate uncertainty made by Myles Allen and David Frame, Oxford University physicists, in *Science* magazine (2007). Allen and Frame do not deny the threat of climate change; their work focuses on the "unpredictability" of how severe its impact will be. In an article titled "Call off the Quest" cited by the Cato Institute, they meant call off the quest for a formula that would permit precise predictions about the impact of climate change, not the quest to figure out necessary responses. Allen contributed to research on climate change for the United Nations Environment Programme and the Third Assessment Report of the Intergovernmental Panel on Climate Change. Frame, whose research focuses on the impact of methane on climate change, is director of the New Zealand Climate Change Research Institute (Van Doren and Brannon, 2020–2021: 61; Allen and Frame, 2007: 582).

According to a report by Joe Uscinski, Karen Douglas, and Stephan Lewandowsky on climate conspiracy theories for *Oxford Research Encyclopedia, Climate Science*, climate change deniers keep shifting their position as they argue their case. They claim there "exists no scientific consensus on climate change," and when that is refuted, they argue that "many voices of dissenting scientists are drowned out by vocal climate change ideologues" or that "evidence showing the consensus was faked or otherwise flawed" (2017). They maintain these claims, although it would be impossible to keep secret a conspiracy involving virtually every scientist across the global.

In another report, Lewandowsky and his co-authors argued that accusations by climate skeptics that climate change is a hoax, scam, cover-up or deception are frightening and effective. "In response to constant, and sometimes toxic, public challenges, scientists have over-emphasized scientific uncertainty, and have inadvertently allowed contrarian claims to affect how they themselves speak, and perhaps even think, about their own research" (Lewandowsky et al., 2013).

Climate denial has powerful support in U.S. state and federal governments. The American Legislative Exchange Council (ALEC), a major Koch Industry–financed lobbying group, has been influential in shaping state legislative initiatives that limit the regulation of the fossil fuel industry. ALEC maintains that since "global climate change is inevitable," policy goals should be based on "economic and political realism" because "international efforts to decrease emissions have proven politically infeasible and unenforceable." ALEC "discourages impractical visionary goals" and "supports free markets because markets are more effective than onerous regulation at achieving optimal economic and environmental outcomes" (American Legislative Exchange Council, 2017).

U.S. Senator James Inhofe (Rep.-Oklahoma), chair of the Senate Committee on Environment and Public Works, is the author of *The Greatest Hoax: How the Global Warming Conspiracy Threatens Your Future* (2012), which was published by the far-right fringe group World Net Daily (WND). Inhofe, whose campaigns are heavily supported by the fossil fuel industry, believes "global warming can be beneficial to mankind," compared the Environmental Protection Agency to the German Gestapo, and presented a snowball on the floor of the Senate to disprove climate change (Center for Responsive Politics, n.d.; Hamburger, 2014; Bump, 2015).

One of the more prominent academic climate minimizers and skeptics is Bjørn Lomborg, president of the Danish think tank Copenhagen Consensus Center and a visiting fellow at the Hoover Institution, Stanford University. Bjørn Lomborg is neither an economist nor a climate scientist; he bases his analysis on the cost of responding to climate change on the work of William Nordhaus, a Nobel Prize–winning economist at Yale University. Nordhaus claims that according to his calculations, the cost of addressing climate change would be too enormous, not justifying a massive social investment. Nordhaus advocates more minimal responses, including a carbon tax to reduce greenhouse gas emissions. Joseph Stiglitz, another Nobel Prize–winning economist and a lead author of the Intergovernmental Panel on Climate Change's Second Climate Assessment, responded to Nordhaus' work accusing him of underestimating the damage associated with climate change including the impact of increased acidification of the oceans, rising sea levels, more extreme weather events, intense hurricanes, and droughts and floods. According to Stiglitz, in 2017 alone, the United States lost 1.5% of its gross domestic product to climate-related events (Stiglitz, 2020: SBR 11).

Taking a position similar to that of the Cato Institute, Bjørn Lomborg agrees that climate change is happening but doesn't believe the impact will be as serious as projected. In his latest book, *False Alarm: How Climate Change Panic Costs Us Trillions, Hurts the Poor, and Fails to Fix the Planet* (2020a), Lomborg's main argument is "current policy won't solve climate change—not even close" and will "waste trillions of dollars along the way" (123). He accuses climate scientists of promoting "apocalyptic threats" to attract research dollars and blames the "hyperventilating media" for creating a crisis where one does not really exist (19; Lomborg, 2020b). Lomberg makes his living writing and speaking about climate change and working for the Copenhagen Consensus Center, a non-profit organization registered in the United States, that paid him $775,000 in 2012 and almost $500,000 in 2018 (Readfearn, 2014; non-profit tax records are available online).

Big fossil fuel companies also use advertising campaigns in which they masquerade as workers and small business owners to push their agenda that addressing climate change is too expensive and will wreck the economy. The Texans for Natural Gas website urged voters to "thank a roughneck" and support natural gas fracking. The Arctic Energy Center campaigned to end federal restrictions on drilling for oil in the protected Arctic wildlife refuge. The Main Street Investors Coalition warned that climate activism hurt small stock market investors. The three groups, which circulate pro-industry petitions and videos and place opinion pieces in local newspapers, are part of a network organized by FTI Consulting, which also created a phony Facebook page for a fictional middle-aged Texas woman so the company could help keep track of anti-fossil fuel protesters. FTI Consulting works for a number of large oil and gas companies, including ExxonMobil (Tabuchi, 2020: A1).

Joseph Stiglitz (2020: SBR:11) responds that Lomborg and Nordhaus and people who oppose taking forceful action to reverse climate change are putting the cost on future generations. "As the atmospheric concentration of carbon increases, we are entering uncharted territory." The Earth has not had the current carbon dioxide levels in the atmosphere for three million years when sea levels were 30 to 60 feet higher than today. Stiglitz calls their position "ethically indefensible and economically nonsensical."

In his January 17, 1961, farewell address to the nation, President Dwight Eisenhower warned, "In the councils of government, we must guard against the acquisition of unwarranted influence, whether sought or unsought, by the military-industrial complex. The potential for the disastrous rise of misplaced power exists and will persist. We must never let the weight of this combination endanger our liberties or democratic processes." If Eisenhower were speaking today, he could make the same warning about the "unwarranted influence" of the climate denier-industrial complex who put private profit ahead of human needs (Eisenhower, 1961).

Teaching Documents

Exxon: What Did They Know, and When Did They Know It?

In 2015, research revealed that Exxon knew about the dangers posed by climate change and the burning of fossil fuels at least since the 1970s. Exxon's response to the exposé was that the company is the victim of a "coordinated campaign perpetuated by activist groups with the aim of stigmatizing" it (E. Holden. 2020, January 8. "How the oil industry has spent billions to control the climate change conversation," *The Guardian*). Greenpeace and the Center for International Environmental Law put together a timetable documenting Exxon and oil industry sponsored studies on climate change and exposing their campaign of denial of the scientific findings they helped to produce. Examine evidence from the "timetable" to decide whether Exxon was unfairly stigmatized or is guilty as charged.

Exxon's Climate Denial History: A Timeline

Source:www.greenpeace.org/usa/global-warming/exxon-and-the-oil-industry-knew-about-climate-change/exxons-climate-denial-history-a-timeline/;

1. October 1957: Scientists working for a predecessor company that evolved into ExxonMobil, published a study in *EOS, Transactions American Geophysical Union*. Its title was "Radiocarbon Evidence on the Dilution of Atmospheric and Oceanic Carbon by Carbon from Fossil Fuels" (v. 38 n. 5: 643–650). "Of particular interest" to the scientific team was "the fate of the enormous quality of carbon dioxide which has been introduced into the atmosphere since the beginning of the industrial revolution in the 19th century, and the manner in which the added carbon dioxide has been distributed in the carbon cycle." By analyzing tree-rings and marine shells, they found evidence of an increased concentration of CO_2 in the atmosphere and the oceans during the industrial era. "They concluded "Although appreciable amounts of carbon dioxide have undoubtedly been added from soils by tilling of land, apparently a much greater amount has resulted from the combustion of fossil fuels" (www.smoke-andfumes.org/documents/7).

2. February 1968: A report prepared for the American Petroleum Institute by the Stanford Research Institute, "Sources, Abundance, and the fate of Gaseous Atmospheric Pollutants," disputed the fossil fuel industry's claim that there were other explanations for the CO_2 increase in the atmosphere. The paper warned that the "'green-house' effect" produced by a significant rise in CO_2 in the atmosphere would lead to "melting of the Antarctic ice cap, a rise in sea levels, warming of the oceans, and an increase on photo-synthesis. . . . Changes in ocean temperature would change the distribution of fish and cause a retreat in the polar sea ice. This has happened in recent time on a very limited scale. . . . Although there are other possible sources for the additional CO_2 now being observed in the atmosphere, none seems to fit the presently observed situation as well as the fossil fuel emanation theory. . . . It is clear that we are unsure as to what our long-lived pollutants are doing to our environment; however, there seems to be no doubt that the potential damage to our environment

could be severe . . . the abundant pollutants which we generally ignore because they have little local effect, CO_2 and submicron particles, may be the cause of serious world-wide environmental changes" (www.smoke-andfumes.org/documents/16).

3. 1972–2004: ExxonMobil placed advertisements in *The New York Times* every Thursday at a cost of over $30,000 each promoting the company's positions on a number of issues, including efforts to raise doubts about climate science (I. Johnson. 2017, August 23. "ExxonMobil: Oil and gas giant 'misled' the public about climate change, say Harvard experts," *Independent*; G. Supran and N. Oreskes. 2017, August 22. "What Exxon Mobil Didn't Say About Climate Change," The *New York Times*).

4. July 1977: James Black, a scientist working with Exxon's Products Research Division, presented a slideshow to top Exxon executives in which he detailed the "general scientific agreement that the most likely manner in which mankind is influencing the global climate is through carbon dioxide release from the burning of fossil fuels. . . . [C]arbon dioxide from the burning of fossil fuels was warming the planet and could eventually endanger humanity." In a 1978 talk, Black warned, "Some countries would benefit but others would have their agricultural output reduced or destroyed. . . . Present thinking holds that man has a time window of five to ten years before the need for hard decisions regarding changes in energy strategies might become critical." Initially, Exxon committed to increased research on the impact of the burning of fossil fuels on CO_2 concentrations in the atmosphere and climate change, but it later curtailed funding for carbon dioxide research and adopted a strategy of climate change denial (N. Banerjee, L. Song, and D. Hasemeyer, 2015, September 16. "Exxon's Own Research Confirmed Fossil Fuels' Role in Global Warming Decades Ago," *Inside Climate News*).

5. 1979–1982: An American Petroleum Institute Major task force met regularly to discuss the science and implications of climate change. Task force members included representatives from Exxon, Mobil, Amoco, Phillips, Texaco, Shell, Sunoco, Standard Oil, and Gulf. The goal of the task force was developing "ground rules for energy release of fuels and the cleanup of fuels as they relate to CO_2 creation" (N. Banerjee. 2015, December 22. "Exxon's Oil Industry Peers Knew About Climate Dangers in the 1970s, Too," *Inside Climate News*).

6. November 1982: The Environmental Affairs Programs manager for Exxon distributed a primer on the "CO2 'Greenhouse' Effect" to Exxon management with a warning that "it should be restricted to Exxon personnel and not distributed externally." The primer described "potentially catastrophic events" if fossil fuel use was not reduced. In 2018, the documents were included as evidence in a lawsuit filed by the City of New York in federal court against fossil fuel companies. The lawsuit asserted "a corporation that makes a product causing severe harm when used exactly as intended should shoulder the costs of abating that harm" (N. Banerjee,

L. Song, and D. Hasemeyer, 2015, September 16. "Top executives were warned of possible catastrophe from greenhouse effect, then led efforts to block solutions," *Inside Climate News*; B. Van Voris. 2018, January 11. "New York City sues oil companies over climate change costs," *Bloomberg News*).

7. October 1982: Exxon Research and Engineering Co. President Edward David told a global warming conference "Few people doubt that the world has entered an energy transition away from dependence upon fossil fuels and toward some mix of renewable resources that will not pose problems of CO2 accumulation." David, however, was "generally upbeat about the chances of coming through this most adventurous of all human experiments with the ecosystem" (N. Banerjee, L. Song, and D. Hasemeyer, 2015, September 16. "Exxon's Own Research Confirmed Fossil Fuels' Role in Global Warming Decades Ago," *Inside Climate News*).

8. 1989: Companies and trade organizations tied to fossil fuel industries, including Exxon and the American Petroleum Institute, established the Global Climate Coalition. Until it was disbanded in 2002, the oil-, coal-, and auto industry–funded coalition aggressively lobbied government agencies and launched public relations campaigns disputing the emerging scientific consensus that the burning of fossil fuels produced heat-trapping gases and global warming. In its publications, the coalition claimed, "The role of greenhouse gases in climate change is not well understood." It continued to publicly argue this position even though a 1995 internal industry memo, *Predicting Future Climate Change: A Primer*, acknowledged "The scientific basis for the Greenhouse Effect and the potential impact of human emissions of greenhouse gases such as CO2 on climate is well established and cannot be denied." Coalition documents became public in 2007 as the result of lawsuits filed by the automobile industry against Vermont and California. Auto manufacturers attempted to prevent these states from placing restrictions on vehicular emission of carbon dioxide (A. Revkin, 2009, April 24. "Industry Ignored Its Scientists on Climate," *New York Times*, A1; *New York Times*, "Advisors to Industry Group Weigh In on Warming."). Exxon was also a member of the American Legislative Exchange Council, supporting its lobbying efforts against regulation of the fossil fuel industry with $2 million between 1998 and 2014 (S. Higgins. 2014, September 30. "Exxon Mobil refutes report it has quit ALEC," *Washington Examiner*).

9. April 1998: *The New York Times* reported on efforts by the American Petroleum Institute, supported by Exxon and other fossil fuel companies, to recruit scientists to present a "sound scientific alternative" to the Intergovernmental Panel on Climate Change and challenge the Clinton administration's support for the Kyoto Protocol on climate change. The companies pledged $5 million to the campaign (J. Cushman, 1998, April 26. "Industrial Group Plans to Battle Climate Treaty," *New York Times*, A1).

10. August 2015: The Independent Petroleum Association of America and the Alaska Oil and Gas Association started the Arctic Energy Center to "advance greater public understanding of energy development in the American Arctic" (www.ipaa.org/ipaa-aoga-launch-new-digital-arctic-energy-center). The group claimed it was representing the interests of Alaskans, including indigenous groups. According to EnergyFactor, an ExxonMobil website, Exxon was a major supporter of the Arctic Energy Center and opening up the Alaskan wilderness preserves for oil exploration and exploitation (https://energyfactor.exxonmobil.com/perspectives/door-open-arctic-energy). Exxon was also a major supporter of other groups that claimed to be grassroots pro-oil organizations, including the Main Street Investors Coalition and Texans for Natural Gas (H. Tabuchi. 2020, November 12. "Global Firm Casts Big Oil's Messages as Grass-Roots Campaigns," New York Times, A1).

Additional Teaching Documents at https://alansinger.net:
- A Frank Statement to Cigarette Smokers
- ExxonMobil's *New York Times* Advertising Campaign
- Masquerading as "Ordinary People"

13 A Short Cold Snap of About 500 Years

Jump up and down. Look left and right. Check out the sky above and the floor below. From our perspective as individual living beings, it seems as if we live on a large, flat table – Mesa Earth – with two miniature orbiting bodies that travel through the sky on a daily basis, kind of like described in ancient Greek myths. But scientific observation over thousands of years has established that the Earth is spherical; is billions of years; orbits an immensely larger sun, 330,000 times more massive than the Earth, in a solar system that is infinitesimally small when compared with the Milky Way galaxy where it resides in a seemingly unending and every expanding universe. Mind boggling.

The world we experience on a daily basis and what is are not the same thing. Humans also survive in a very small window of time and a very small range of temperature. If you are lucky, you may get to live to 100. Civilizations have been around for about 12,000 years, the human species for between 100,000 and 150,000 years. But the Earth is an estimated 4.5 billion years old, the sun is at least 100 million years older, and the universe may be almost 14 billion years old – that is 14 followed by nine zeroes. While 500 years is a long time in human history, it is a very, very short time in the history of the Earth and even shorter in the history of the universe.

Our temperature zone is similarly a tiny segment of the temperature range. On Earth, at sea level, water boils at 100°C (212°F) and freezes at 0°C (32°F). But the temperature in the Sun's core reaches 15 million degrees C (27 million degrees F) and in deep space plunges to absolute zero, –273°C (–460°F), where there is no longer observable sub-atomic activity.

Humanity also exists in a world of repeating cycles. In the Broadway musical *Fiddler on the Roof*, at their daughter Tzeitel's wedding, Tevye and Golde sing about sunrise and sunset and season following season. There is a well-known passage from the Judeo-Christian Bible, Ecclesiastes 3:1–8, "to every thing there is a season," that was turned into a popular song "Turn! Turn! Turn!" in the 1950s by folk artist Pete Seeger. Pacific currents generated by oceanic heat fluctuation like El Niño and La Niña that repeat every two to seven years have an impact on climate.

But some natural phenomena, time spans, and cycles are so broad that it is difficult for the human imagination to comprehend, at least for most of us,

DOI: 10.4324/9781003200864-13

and they are definitely difficult to explain. One of those phenomena is natu-rally occurring climate cycles, known as Milankovich cycles that are driven by variations in the Earth's orbit. Milutin Milanković was a Serbian mathemati-cian, astronomer, and climatologist, in the first half of the 20th century who explored the climate implications of long-term changes in Earth's relation-ship to the Sun, including periodic ice ages (Buis, 2020a). According to Milanković, climate on the Earth is influenced by the elliptical shape of its orbit around the sun (eccentricity), the angle that Earth's axis is tilted (obliquity), and the "wobble" as the Earth spins on its axis (precession) and these change at set rates. Eccentricity, obliquity, and precision affect the amount of sunlight and energy the Earth absorbs from the Sun. They can cause up to 25% variabil-ity in the amount of solar radiation that reaches the Earth's temperate middle latitudes, the region where most humans live (Buis, 2020b).

Writing for NASA's Jet Propulsion Laboratory, Alan Buis explains the intricacies and eccentricities of the Earth's orbit Milankovich cycles and their impact on climate. We don't feel it, but the gravitational pull of Jupiter and Saturn affects the Earth and changes the shape of its orbit around the Sun from circular to an oval or ellipse. As a result of orbital eccentricity, at different times during the year, the Earth is closer to or farther from the Sun. In practical "cli-mate" terms, this means that currently, summers in the Northern Hemisphere are 4.5 days longer than winters, and spring is longer than autumn. No com-plaint so far unless you are a big skiing fan or really like to shovel snow. But the shape of the Earth's orbit is not constant; it changes back and forth from more elliptical to more circular approximately every 100,000 years. If you manage to stick around long enough, winters will get longer.

The main reason for seasons is the tilt of the Earth's axis, obliquity, which varies between 22.1 and 24.5 degrees in a cycle that takes 41,000 years. The greater the tilt, the more extreme are seasonal differences because the pole pointing at the Sun has a hotter summer while the pole pointing away has a colder winter. Milanković calculated that periods of greater tilt angles tend toward deglaciation (the melting and retreat of ice caps). The Earth is now at is mid-obliquity cycle. The last ice age ended about 20,000 years ago, and it would start another one in about 10,000 years, except for the affect of the eccentricity cycle. Between one and three million years ago, ice ages did occur every 41,000 years. But in the past 800,000 years, the eccentricity cycle has lengthened the time frame for an ice age to repeat to about every 100,000 years, which is definitely good news.

There is also another cycle affecting climate on Earth as well, the "wobble," or precession. The Earth spins like an off-kilter top because the gravitational pull of the Sun and Moon create a bulge along the Equator. This cycle repeats every 25,771.5 years, so about 13,000 years from now, we can expect the Northern Hemisphere to experience more extreme solar radiation while sea-sons in the Southern Hemisphere grow more moderate (Buis, 2020a).

Scientists believe that Milankovich cycles are probably the cause of the Earth's relative cooling and warming and periodic ice ages. Variations in the amount of sunlight and radiant heat during Northern Hemisphere summers trigger "feedback loops" that intensify the impact of warming or cooling. During an interglacial period, as sea ice and snow retreat, there is reduced sunlight reflected back into space, increased atmospheric water vapor traps even more heat, the thawing of permafrost release methane and carbon dioxide, and warming oceans discharge dissolved carbon dioxide. During glacial periods, these processes are essentially reversed, ice cover increases, more sunlight is reflected into space, there is less water vapor in the atmosphere, and permafrost and the oceans retain onto greenhouse gases (Herring and Lindsey, 2020). As the result of Milankovich cycles and feedback loops, since the end of the last ice age about 20,000 years ago, average global temperature has risen between 3°C and 8°C (5° F to 14°F) (Climate Change Committee, n.d.).

Milankovich cycles have their greatest impact on the Earth's climate when all three variables – orbit, rotation, and wobble – line up. Think about Hurricane Sandy, which struck the East Coast of the United States in 2012. The wind and the rate of rainfall from Hurricane Sandy were moderate for a hurricane, but flooding was extensive because a number of factors lined up – the size of the storm, that it was traveling from east to west and slow moving, and that it made landfall during a full moon at high tide when high tides are at their highest (Stein and Hamilton, 2012).

And these are just the Earth's orbital cycles; the Sun, which provides energy for life on Earth, also goes through cycles, 11-year cycles when levels of solar ultra-violet radiation, magnetism, and sunspot activity rise and fall. One solar cycle began in January 2008 and ended in late 2020, producing the lowest level of sunspot activity recorded since 1750. According to the United Nations' Intergovernmental Panel on Climate Change (IPCC), variations in solar activity generally play only a minor role in the Earth's climate. IPCC scientists estimate that since 1750, the impact of greenhouse gases on global warming has been 50 times greater than warming caused by solar cycles. However, periodically, a solar "grand minimum" can have a greater impact. A "Little Ice Age" from roughly the start of the 14th century until the middle of the 19th coincided with a "grand minimum." Scientists studying the solar "grand minimum" phenomenon suggest that if one started now, it could slow down but not reverse global warming and that the cooling effect would be quickly reversed by fossil fuel emissions. Shorter periods of reduced sunspot activity, known as a "Maunder Minimum," also might impact on climate, but their impact would be temporary (NASA, 2019, 2021).

During the past four decades, climatologists have pieced together an accurate account of climate conditions over the past 2,000 years including climate cycles. There were relative cooling periods of varying lengths between 1000 BC and 400 BC, 100 and 200 AD, and 600 and 800 AD, and between approximately 1300 AD and 1850 AD, there was a 50-year-long cooling, or cold snap, which we now know as the Little Ice Age. British archaeologist Brian Fagan, in his book *The Little Ice Age: How Climate Made History, 1300–1850* (2000), shows how increasing cold destroyed the Viking North Atlantic trade network and left Iceland as the most genetically isolated and homogenous community in the world; lowered sea temperatures and changed the location of ocean fisheries; contributed to social unrest in France, culminating in revolutionary upheaval; and led to agricultural advances in Great Britain and the Industrial Revolution. To document climate change, Fagan drew on a range of unusual sources such as tithing records that show the dates of wine harvests and cloud types depicted in portraits and landscapes. He also explored human adaptation such as the way the Dutch built sea walls as protection against rising sea levels and increased their farmland by a third between the late 16th and early 19th centuries. The Dutch experience demonstrates that humans can respond before catastrophe strikes if they have the will.

Brian Fagan opens his examination of the impact of climate change on European civilizations discussing what he describes as the "heyday" of the Norse between 800 AD and 1200 AD when a North Atlantic warm period facilitated their exploration, raids, conquest, and settlement in the area stretching from present-day Norway to Iceland, Greenland, and Labrador in Canada and including parts of Scotland, Ireland, and England (7).

Climate in this region is deeply affected by three ocean currents, the Labrador and East Greenland currents sweeping south from the Arctic Ocean and the warmer Irminger Current, a branch of the tropical Gulf Stream. When the currents meet, colder water forces warmer water to release the salt, changing the weight of the water, temperatures, and current direction. This interaction is called the High North Atlantic Oscillation Index or NAO (24–28). Where the currents meet and how they interact determine which areas in the far northern North Atlantic are frozen and which areas are ice free and conducive to agriculture. In bad ice years on Iceland, Fagan cites the 1180s, 1287, and 1350 to 1380, the local population starved as crops failed, villages were invaded by polar bears, and sea trade connecting them to the outside world was interrupted (10).

During the Medieval Warming Period that coincided with the era of Norse exploration and colonization in the North Atlantic, agriculture flourished in European feudal societies and population increased despite disease and war as average temperature was even warmer than in the 20th century, between 0.7°C (1°F) and 1.0°C (2°F) in coastal western Europe and as much as 1.4°C (3°F) higher in the center of the continent (17). At the end of the 11th century, the estimated population of England was less than 1.5 million people. By 1300, it was 5 million. The population of the area included in present-day France rose from tripled to almost 18 million (33). Grapes flourished across Europe, and grain production expanded farther north. Villages became towns, and towns became cities. In urban areas, burghers and clerics built gothic cathedrals like Notre Dame in Paris, Chartres outside of the city, and Canterbury in England. An unanticipated problem was the spread of agriculture into marginal lands with sandy soil or more vulnerable to floods and frost.

In the 13th century, Iceland and Greenland experienced increasing cold temperatures. Sea ice spread, growing seasons shortened, frost interrupted planting and harvest, and crops began to fail in north central Europe, including breadbaskets like Poland and Russia. But these patterns were erratic. Warmer years like 1315 brought their own problems, including excess rain and flooding. A cold August and heavy rains in August 1315 destroyed crops before they could be harvested. By Christmas 1315, many parts of Europe, which had much larger populations than in previous centuries, faced famine (28–29).

Fagan discusses the impact of climate change on Wharram Percy, a well-documented and now abandoned British village that is preserved as a national historic site. Fagan argues that its cycle of growth and decline is representative of what happened to other villages during the period as climate shifted. Wharram Percy, about 20 miles northeast of present-day York, was continuously occupied for about 600 years from the 9th century to the early 16th century when it was deserted. Today it is a British historical site. It flourished between the 12th and early 14th centuries, a period of relatively mild climate before the Little Ice Age (34–36).

Between 850 and 950, the village sprung up in the agricultural region with a wooden church on its central green. William the Conqueror later confiscated Wharram, and by 1086 control over the village and surrounding lands had been transferred to William de Percy, a Norman baron. During the late Middle Ages following crop failure in 1315 and 1316, with the rising price for wool, feudal landowners in the region switched from farming to sheep raising. The shift meant eviction for peasant families that were already impoverished, and there was a sharp decrease in the village's population by the middle of the 15th century (Oswald, 2013). Fagan speculates that the shift from farming to sheep husbandry and the decline of the village were attributable to the changing climate, not just economic decisions made by feudal landlords. As the countryside was transformed by climate variability and famine, people turned to grave robbing to survive or fled to larger towns and cities where they became beggars. Fagan notes this was also a period of religious revivalism as desperate people searched for answers to the inexplicable (41).

Fagan opened the second section of *The Little Ice Age* with a passage from *The Second Shepherds' Play*, a medieval style English play dating from c. 1450 about the hoped-for return of Christ to Earth to redeem the world from its sins (45). While the shepherds were punished by the weather, humanity's sins are clearly blamed on landlords who have "oppressed" their countrymen to the "point of misery." The harsher weather of the Little Ice Age is also evident in paintings by Peter Breughel the Elder, *Hunters in the Snow*, painted in 1565, and a 1567 painting of the three Biblical kings paying homage to the baby Jesus, not in the hot and dry Middle East but in a cold and snowy landscape (48).

We rarely consider how dependent human civilization is on climate moderation and predictability. Fagan notes it is 15,000 years since the last Ice Age. For the past 6,000 years of the Holocene, the geological age of humankind, the Earth's climate has been especially moderate and predictable; however, this does not mean climate has not varied, either in localities or globally (47). Think of climate as a narrow sine curve in the moderate range above and below the y-axis with the y-axis representing the climate zone where human civilization can prosper.

Brian Fagan dates the start of the Little Ice Age at about 1300 AD with the expansion of the Greenland ice sheet. This would be just before the harsh weather that led to famine in winter 1315–1316. He argues it definitely ends by 1850. However, some scientists narrow the time period, arguing cold periods on both ends were not part of a prolonged climate shift but were normal fluctuations. Volcanic eruptions like Tambora in Indonesia in 1815 definitely impacted the broader trends. Again, as with today, we are looking at average annual temperature for the entire Earth, not in just one region. The coldest periods on one continent or even within a continent were not necessarily the coldest in another. However, from 1590 to 1610, it seems that everywhere on Earth was colder (49–50).

Hundred Years' War: 1337–1453

After the 11th century Norman invasion and conquest of England, descendants of the Duke of Normandy, now the Plantagenet kings of England, continued to claim land in France and the French throne. It remains unclear how much the Hundred Years' War, fought during the first century and a half of the Little Ice Age in Europe, and the result of dynastic infighting were influenced by climate change and decline in agricultural production on feudal lands. Based on Fagan's account of the Little Ice Age, I do not believe it is just coincidence. An otherwise long-forgotten war remains immortalized in two iconic national remembrances. A surprising English victory at the Battle of Agincourt in 1415 is central to William Shakespeare's play *Henry V* (c. 1599). Henry's speech to his vastly outnumbered troops before the battle was used to inspire British forces during World War II. In France, the national heroine, Jeanne d' Arc, led the French to victory at the Siege of Orleans in 1429 and then was executed as a witch in 1431 for claiming that she was directed by God through angelic visions to lead French troops into battle.

Teaching Documents

Seeking the Cause of Ice Ages

The American Museum of Natural History in New York City has an online "Earth Inside and Out" curriculum collection edited by Edmond A. Mathez, Director of the Earth and Planetary Sciences Department. It includes material for teaching about the formation of mountains, forecasting earthquakes, using tree rings to map climate change, continental drift, and the cause of the ice ages. www.amnh.org/learn-teach/curriculum-collections/earth-inside-and-out

Milutin Milankovitch: Seeking the Cause of the Ice Ages

> **Source:**www.amnh.org/learn-teach/curriculum-collections/earth-inside-and-out/milutin-milankovitch-seeking-the-cause-of-the-ice-ages

Questions

1. What contribution did Milutin Milankovitch make to understanding the Earth's climate?
2. What did Milankovitch's calculations demonstrate?
3. Why were findings that were dismissed later accepted?

    1. "In 1911 a young Serbian mathematician, Milutin Milankovitch, decided to chart the ice ages of the Pleistocene. (The Pleistocene is the epoch that began 1.8 million years ago and ended about 11,500 years ago. It was characterized by lengthy ice ages, when glaciers covered large regions of the continents, interrupted by short interglacial periods, when the climate was temperate.) All Milankovitch's calculations were done by hand, and he worked at them obsessively for the next thirty years. He incorporated new information about small variations in the tilt of the Earth's axis, and factored in small orbital changes caused by the gravitational tug of other planets. Each of these orbital variations has its own time scale, and consequently they interact in different ways over time, but each one is regular. Going back 600,000 years in his computations, he carefully calculated the effect of these factors on incoming solar radiation across the Northern Hemisphere. The charts and tabulations Milankovitch created are still used today. He also measured summer solar radiation curves in high northern latitudes, where the ice age glaciers originated, linking certain low points with four previous European Pleistocene ice ages. Ultimately, the mathematician arrived at a complete astronomical theory of glaciation."
    2. On the basis of his analysis, Milankovitch concluded that Earth's orbit changes in three cycles of different lengths. The shape of Earth's orbit around the Sun changes from less to more and back to less elliptical in about 96,000 years. The Earth is tilted on its axis of rotation relative to the solar plane, currently at an angle of 23.5 degrees. This tilt changes, however, from 21.5 to 24.5 degrees and back again in about 41,000 years. Finally, the Earth's axis of spin wobbles with a period of 23,000 years. The challenges for Milankovitch were to understand when the three cycles were coincident with each other

and how they worked together to influence insolation (the amount of solar radiation received by the Earth). Based on his computations, Milankovitch theorized variations of more than 20% in the amount of sunshine reaching the northern latitudes. In his 1941 account, *Canon of Insolation and the Ice Age Problem*, he suggested that this caused the waxing and waning of the great continental ice sheets.

3. Like that of several predecessors, Milankovitch's work was greeted with considerable excitement but was then largely dismissed. Ice ages are difficult to date, partly because each erases much of the traces of its predecessor. However, the tables were turned by the late 1960s. Technical advances made it possible for geologists to study deep-sea sediment cores that contain a climate record going back millions of years. This climate record shows remarkably regular variations, which correlate with the mathematician's figures and which are now known as Milankovitch cycles. However, it is also clear that astronomical factors alone cannot cause the large changes that the Earth experienced. Other factors must also influence climate, but scientists still do not know how.

Additional Teaching Documents at https://alansinger.net: The Second Shepherds' Play

14 Power of Ice

Anyone who drives a car on wintery roads knows the power of ice to disrupt; people keep getting taken by surprise by weather and climate, something humanity can no longer afford. In February 2021, Texans learned first-hand the power of ice and the implications of climate change. In the midst of winter storms and record-breaking low temperatures, the power grid collapsed as demand for electricity to operate electric heaters soared while pipelines carrying natural gas to the state's power plants froze, and without heating units, many of Texas' wind turbines stopped working. An estimated four million people were left without electricity, heat, and water. Electrical systems can be engineered to operate during the more extreme weather that is accompanying climate change, but Texas was not prepared. Alice Hill, who assessed climate risks for the U.S. National Security Council during the Obama Administration, commented, "We base all our choices about risk management on what's occurred in the past, and that is no longer a safe guide" (Plumer, 2021: A1; Flavelle, Plumer, and Tabuchi, 2021: A1). The same storm created a different infrastructure disaster in Jackson, Mississippi, where the freezing weather almost destroyed an antiquated water delivery system. A month later, people were still forced to boil tap water before using it (Fentress and Fausset, 2021: A21).

Long Island, New York, where I teach at Hofstra University, stretches about 120 miles from east to west and was formed by ice. Glaciers from the last North American Ice Age ended on what is now the rocky northern shore of Long Island depositing boulders and soil swept south from the mainland. The table-like area south of the glacial moraine is an outwash plain, or "sandur," formed by sediment from melt water as the glacier receded. Sandurs like the Long Island central and southern plain are common on the Icelandic coast because geothermal activity there melts the ice, and water, stone, sand, and soil stream together downhill toward the ocean (Cohen, 2014; Hine, Boothroyd, and Nummedal, 2013).

During the same Ice Age that formed Long Island, the indigenous settlers of the Americas migrated across the Bering land bridge connecting Asia and North America, a bridge that submerged when the ice cap melted and ocean waters rose. Ten thousand years ago, the southern area of the North Sea

DOI: 10.4324/9781003200864-14

between England and France was a marshy plain inhabited by Stone Age hunter and gatherer bands. About 6,000 years ago, rising seas flooded the plain, creating the modern coastline. Sea levels rose again about 1000 AD, flooding the European Atlantic lowland countries, and storms killed hundreds of thousands of people in current-day Denmark, Belgium, and the Netherlands. The sea gradually retreated, but in the 17th century, the Dutch, to extend habitable land, started to dig channels and build massive dykes. Money for this construction came from profits from the trans-Atlantic slave trade. Much of the coastal destruction caused by an angry Atlantic was the result of lower temperatures that are recorded in the ice sheets of Greenland (Fagan, 2000: 63).

To examine the impact of climate change on a more micro-level, Brian Fagan in *The Little Ice Age* takes a close look at the depopulation of Norse Greenland in the 14th century. Norse agricultural settlements on the Greenland coast were always vulnerable to harsh weather conditions. A village could probably store enough hay to feed its cows and enough seafood to feed the human population to survive a bad year, but it was unlikely villagers could survive two years, let alone the two decades that stretched from 1343 to 1362 when ice-core analysis shows summers were much colder than when the colony was established (67).

Nipaatsoq was a Viking farm site that lay buried under glacial sands for six centuries. The edge of Greenland's ice cap is now six miles from the site, and in the mid-14th century, it was probably closer.

The farm was part of the Norse Western Settlements established around 1000 AD. Its population eventually reached about 1,500 people and then was abandoned around 1350. Debris from the final devastating winter remained on the floor of a large multi-family house, left behind when the remaining population abandoned the settlement and moved farther south. Glacial sand covered Nipaatsoq in the early 1400s, and it remained covered until 1990, when hunters spotted pieces of ancient wood jutting out from the eroded bank of a stream (Brooke, 2001: F5).

Norse artifacts, buried under the glacial sand and in permafrost, included broken items, stools made from whale vertebra, and a wooden weaver's loom too large to easily move. Skeletal remains buried at what was once a church-yard indicate that the diet of the Norse settlers increasingly depended on marine life, seals and fish, as it became more difficult to raise cattle and sheep as the climate cooled. The remaining cattle were butchered during the final winter, and their hooves were uncovered when the site was rediscovered. There is also evidence that starving families ate their hunting dogs (Fagan, 67–68).

Increasing cold also had some positive impacts as people adjusted to climate change. Fagan documents changes in agriculture starting in Flanders and the Netherlands as farmers developed new techniques, including the use of wind-mills for drainage and irrigation and cold-resistant crops (107). Salted cod and herring were major food sources, especially in Roman Catholic lands where red meat was banned on Fridays and during Lent (69). Shifting ocean currents and cooler water temperatures changed fish breeding grounds and moved fisheries. To access fishing grounds in dangerous waters, the Dutch developed much larger fishing boats that combined fishing with gutting and salting. European boat builders also shifted from creating the outside shell first and the internal structure after to building the internal skeleton first and then adding the outside shell. This made possible construction of larger and stronger boats capable of surviving intense ocean storms and crossing the Atlantic, making possible the Columbian Exchange (74). However, the new construction techniques did not benefit everybody as the Columbian Exchange meant the decimation of the indigenous peoples of the Americas and the trans-Atlantic slave trade. Agricultural innovation also had a negative impact. Land holdings were consolidated, and marginal lands were pressed into use for commercial agriculture that led to the displacement of peasant farmers without legal claim to plots farmed by their families for generations (106).

Potatoes were another blessing that proved to be a curse. The Spanish found potatoes in the Peruvian Andes when they conquered and destroyed the Inca Empire. Potatoes gradually took hold in Europe, especially Ireland and Central Europe, as a crop to feed the peasantry when grain was expropriated by landlords. The potato was a hardy crop that survived on marginal and rocky soils and in different weather conditions, but single-crop agriculture left the population exceedingly vulnerable to crop failure, which happened repeatedly and most devastatingly in Ireland from 1845 to 1852 (110–112).

Fagan also points at climate changes as a cause of the Bubonic or Black Plague that struck Europe in the middle of the 14th century. "Bubonic" refers to infected glands that emitted a black pus, hence the two names for the plague. The plague bacteria were brought to Europe by Mongol merchants and armies from the Gobi Desert in Asia. One hypothesis is that drier conditions on the Asian steppes or plains forced Mongolian herders to seek new pasture farther and farther west. Fleas carrying the plague bacteria followed the herds. Europeans may have been especially vulnerable to the plague because cooler and wetter climate conditions meant people were forced to huddle indoors in dirty clothing and blankets accompanied by rats that were infected by the fleas. Fleas were the bridge that carried the bacteria from the rats to the people (81–82).

As kingdoms and incipient nation-states emerged in Europe during the 14th century, government records, basically tax records, as noble, church, and royal masters enriched themselves by extracting wealth from the 90% of the population that were agricultural peasants, add to our understanding of climate. Competition in the form of war between kingdoms, especially France, England, and Spain, sometimes in the name of religion and sometimes for empire, may also have been stimulated by the harsher climate of the Little Ice Age. From 1337 to 1453, French and English rulers fought a Hundred Years' War over who would control the western coast of present-day France (83–84). Note they were not any better at math in those days; the war went on for 116 years. Between 1455 and 1485, English noble houses fought the

War of the Roses to determine which family would control the monarchy. The Eighty Years war between 1568 and 1648 over control of the Low Countries along the west coast of the North Sea, which was also a Thirty Years Religious War between 1618 and 1648 involving much of Central Europe. During these wars, the Spanish Armada was sunk in violent Atlantic storms off the coast of Ireland. This list does not include periodic peasant rebellions and continuous war on Europe's eastern front as the Ottoman Turkish and Russian empires expanded.

Brian Fagan argues what historians must do is use the past to illuminate the present and the present to illuminate the past. In Chapter 6 of *The Little Ice Age*, Fagan described a visit he made to subsistence farmers in Africa when "The specter of hunger was always in the air, never forgotten" (101). During the visit, he "received a firsthand lesson in the harsh realities of subsistence farming, the brutal ties between climate shifts and survival" in a world where agriculturalists have "virtually no cushion against hunger" (102). It was this trip that helped him understand the impact of the Little Ice Age on the peasant populations of Europe.

Teaching Documents

Storms Exposing a Nation Primed for Catastrophe

> By Christopher Flavelle, Brad Plumer, and Hiroko Tabuchi. *The New York Times*, February 21, 201: A1
> www.nytimes.com/2021/02/20/climate/united-states-infrastructure-storms.html

Questions

1. Why does Alice Hill argue "We are colliding with a future of extremes"?
2. How is climate change impacting on infrastructure in unanticipated ways?
3. Why do the authors believe the United States is a nation primed for catastrophe?
4. Do you share the authors' concerns? Explain.

> 1. "We are colliding with a future of extremes," said Alice Hill, who oversaw planning for climate risks on the National Security Council during the Obama Administration. "We base all our choices about risk management on what's occurred in the past, and that is no longer a safe guide." While it's not always possible to say precisely how global warming influenced any one particular storm, scientists said, an overall rise in extreme weather creates sweeping new risks. Sewer systems are overflowing more often as powerful rainstorms exceed their design capacity. Coastal homes and highways are collapsing as intensified runoff erodes cliffs. Coal ash, the toxic residue produced by coal-burning plants, is spilling into rivers as floods overwhelm

barriers meant to hold it back. Homes once beyond the reach of wildfires are burning in blazes they were never designed to withstand.

2. In September, when a sudden storm dumped a record of more than two inches of water on Washington in less than 75 minutes, the result wasn't just widespread flooding but also raw sewage rushing into hundreds of homes. Washington, like many other cities in the Northeast and Midwest, relies on what's called a combined sewer overflow system: If a downpour overwhelms storm drains along the street, they are built to overflow into the pipes that carry raw sewage. But if there's too much pressure, sewage can be pushed backward, into people's homes – where the forces can send it erupting from toilets and shower drains. This is what happened in Washington. The city's system was built in the late 1800s. Now, climate change is straining an already outdated design.

3. Higher storm surges can knock out coastal power infrastructure. Deeper droughts can reduce water supplies for hydroelectric dams. Severe heat waves can reduce the efficiency of fossil-fuel generators, transmission lines, and even solar panels at precisely the moment that demand soars because everyone cranks up their air conditioners. Sometimes even small changes can trigger catastrophic failures. Engineers modeling the collapse of bridges over Escambia Bay in Florida during Hurricane Ivan in 2004 found that the extra three inches of sea-level rise since the bridge was built in 1968 very likely contributed to the collapse because of the added height of the storm surge and force of the waves. . . . Crucial rail networks are at risk, too. In 2017, Amtrak consultants found that along parts of the Northeast corridor, which runs from Boston to Washington and carries 12 million people a year, flooding and storm surge could erode the track bed, disable the signals, and eventually put the tracks underwater.

Additional Teaching Documents at https://alansinger.net:
- Frigid Onslaught Stretches Limits Of Electric Grids
- Officials Falsely Hold Windmills at Fault

15 Climate Repercussions

Cold waves have many repercussions. Even today, hypothermia kills the elderly and the very young when indoor room temperature falls below 8°C (46°F) for a prolonged period of time. When someone becomes deeply chilled, their blood pressure rises, their pulse rate accelerates, and they shiver uncontrollably. All this places stress on the heart. Eventually, the shivering stops when body temperature falls below 35°C (95°F). Then blood pressure drops, and the heart rate slows until it stops and the person dies of cardiac arrest. Hypothermia is the cause of at least 1,500 deaths a year in the United States. Males tend to have a higher metabolic rate than females and are more susceptible to hypothermia. It may because female bodies contain a higher percentage of body fat, which enables them to support fetuses during pregnancy (Healthwise, 2020; Brown et al., 2012).

I have had frostbite twice but avoided serious medical complications because of general good health and quick action. As the United States was preparing to invade Iraq, I marched in an anti-war demonstration in Manhattan holding a giant puppet of President George Bush with what Donald Trump would call a "nasty" slogan. The police had us penned in for hours, and eventually, my hands started to hurt, and I couldn't even open them to put down the puppet. When I was finally able to put down the puppet and take off my gloves, I saw that my hands were purple. I was a hiker and had been a camp counselor, so I knew what to do. You can either hold your hands under your armpits until circulation resumes or stick them in your pants between your legs. Once you have had frostbite, you are more likely to get it again. The second time was because I was biking to a school in Brooklyn for a student teaching observation when the wind chill factor was below 10°F, which was pretty stupid on my part.

In 1816, the writer Mary Godwin, the poet Percy Bysshe Shelley, and their son joined a group that included the poet Lord Byron, with plans to spend the summer in a villa near Geneva, Switzerland. It was a year without a summer because of the Tambora eruption in Indonesia. Huddling at night around the fireplace, they shared ghost stories they were working on during days spent indoors. One night, while the group was debating the nature of the life, Godwin questioned whether it was possible for a human corpse to be re-animated.

DOI: 10.4324/9781003200864-15

That question became the basis for Mary Shelley's novel *Frankenstein or the Modern Prometheus*, published two years later (Wood, 2015).

All cold weather stories are not so benign. Hunger, starvation, disease, riots, mass hysteria, victimization, and revolution were all products of climate cooling. In 1739, the high-pressure region near the North Pole expanded south over England. Easterly winds from the Russian Arctic brought extended periods of sub-zero temperatures to London. January and February 1740 set record low temperatures. Spring came late with repeated frosts. The summer was cool and dry. The next year was the same, and winter 1741–1742 was even worse. The annual mean temperature in England during the early 1740s was less than 7°C (45°F), the lowest average temperature between 1659 and 1973 (Fagan, 2000: 138).

France suffered as well. Bitterly cold winters in the 17th century caused food shortages, grain price inflation, and bread riots. During the winter of 1693–1694, an estimated 10% of the population died from hunger and because weakened conditions left people susceptible to disease. During the winter of 1739–1740, Paris was caught in a cold wave that produced 75 consecutive days of frost. After 1770, climate fluctuation became even more extreme. As a result, in some years, there was no food; in other years, markets were glutted. Spring 1788 was dry, and during the summer, much of the country struggled with drought. Paris was hit with a hailstorm in July so severe that some hailstones measured 16 inches in diameter. The next winter was bitterly cold again. Heavy snow crippled the transport of goods, and when the snow melted in the spring, it flooded fields, preventing planting. Bread riots broke out in villages and towns and then spread to Paris. On July 14, 1789, Parisian women stormed the Bastille, sparking the French Revolution (Fagan, 2000: 154–166).

The winter of 1740–1741 was a miserable period for the poor in New York City. There were threats of war with Spain and its allies, and an economic depression was aggravated by record low temperatures and snowfall. Many people were threatened with starvation or freezing to death. People burned whatever they could to stay warm. New York was a wooden city, and the proliferation of warming fires caused a proliferation of building fires. New York was also a slave city, and white New Yorkers blamed enslaved Africans, about 15% of the population, for starting the fires as part of a rebellious plot. The fear of an uprising by enslaved Africans in the city led to the arrest of 152 enslaved Africans and 20 white co-conspirators. Eighty-one of the Africans confessed to participation in the conspiracy to save their own lives or the lives of loved ones. Seventy had their lives spared and were transported to the sugar islands of the Caribbean. Thirty-four Blacks and four whites were executed. Thirteen of the Blacks were burned alive (Lepore, 2006).

During the 19th century, cold in New York was even worse. In 1821, the Hudson River froze solid. Thousands of people crossed the ice from New York to New Jersey, and shelters were set up mid-river so people could get warm. Because it is smaller and shallower than the Hudson, the East River froze at least seven times. During the 1850s alone, the East River froze four times. However, the most famous freeze was in 1866–1867. In January, ice choked the river and halted ferry service, and people had to walk across the frozen river to get to work (Spilman, 2018).

In April 1815, the Earth cooled again, this time not from a long-term climate shift but from dust blanketing the Earth after the eruption of Mount Tambora. So much dirt and ash was thrown into the atmosphere and spread across the planet over the next two years by the Jet Stream that after the eruption, the summit of Mount Tambora was over 4,000 feet closer to sea level. Global sunlight was probably reduced by more than 20% during the next few years. 1816 was the year without summer. As Godwin, Shelley, and Byron huddled in their Swiss cabin, cold temperatures, violent thunderstorms, and hail destroyed crops in the Northern Hemisphere. In England, the yield of wheat was at its lowest point in 40 years. In Germany, there was famine. Pillaging, riots, criminal violence, and religious millennialism erupted across Europe. There were outbreaks of typhus and Bubonic Plague. Farmers in Ireland abandoned failed plots. French peasants and workers blocked shipments of grain marked for export. Tens of thousands of people migrated to the new North America nation the United States. But North America was not much better. It snowed in the Catskill Mountains of New York State during the summer. In New England, sheep froze, and crops withered. Three-fourth of the northern corn crop was unfit for human consumption (Wood, 2015; Fagan: 170–177).

In *The Little Ice Age* (2000), Brian Fagan began his exploration of the climate impact of prolonged periods of cold with discussion of the European famine of 1315. He ended it with one of the greatest catastrophes in European history, the Great Irish Famine, An Ghorta Mór, from 1845 to 1852. The immediate cause of the famine was failure of the potato crop because of a fungus and the failure of the British government (Ireland was a colony or Great Britain) to act decisively and provide aid. An underlying cause was the chill, damp, weather of the mid-19th century and prevailing winds that dispersed the fungal spores.

Because of the Gulf Stream, Ireland has a damp, moderate climate with mild winters. While its climate was usually supportive of an agricultural society, periodic climate shifts or just plain bad weather at the wrong time of year meant hunger and hardship. The potato, a tuber brought to Europe from the Peruvian Andes by the Spanish, was the primary food source for Irish tenant peasants. Grains belonged to the landlord. About 65,000 people died in Ireland when the potato crop failed in 1816. At least a million people died from famine and disease, and another 1.5 million people were forced to migrate between 1845 and 1852 (Gray, 1982; Fagan: 188–194).

Human-caused climate change is now seriously impacting the survival of other species, and some of that will blow back on humans. Species always went extinct in the past, but now they are going extinct at an alarming and accelerating rate. Scientists are aware of over 500 species that disappeared during the past 100 years, something that would have taken 10,000 years before the human population explosion and capitalist industrialization changed their environments. Scientists warn the Earth is in the midst of a vast extinction with major repercussions for the loss of biodiversity, water resources, food supplies, plants that clean the air, and organisms that control pests and diseases. Bats eat insects. Honeybees pollinate plants. If the current rate of climate change and human expansion into formerly uninhabited habitats continues unabated, an estimated 500 terrestrial vertebrate species will become extinct within the next two decades because they already have fewer than 1,000 members. Males and females are too far apart to meet at appropriate times, which means breeding in the wild may soon become impossible. Imagine if the only way you could date a prospective mate was via email or Zoom (Nuwer, 2020: A13).

Depleted Lakes

Global factors cause climate change, but consequences are often regional and local. Best-case scenarios for the reduction of carbon dioxide emissions into the atmosphere may come too late to prevent severe regional and local consequences. Climate-driven drying in many regions of the world will cause substantial lake level decline in Asian, African, and American basins. These changes in lake levels do not draw sufficient global attention because they can be masked by other factors affecting freshwater lakes, including irrigation for farmland, dams, and diversion of water to supply urban areas. The depletion of large inland lakes will definitely feed economic competition between nations bordering the lakes and can also result in military conflict.

Additional Teaching Documents at https://alansinger.net
- The Other Side of Sea Level Change
- Looking for Sharks
- Sandy Coastlines Under Threat of Erosion
- Destruction of the Amazon
- The Mediterranean Is Heating Up

16 Water Scarcity, Water's Vengeance

In his poem "The Rime of the Ancient Mariner" (1798), which is about a sailor aboard a ship that is stranded in the Pacific Ocean, Samuel Taylor Coleridge wrote: "Water, water, every where, Nor any drop to drink." In the end, the entire crew dies except for the poem's narrator. Water can be destructive, but it is the biological basis for life itself and crucial for modern technology.

Water Scarcity

During the second half of the 19th century, in the 1850s, 1870s, and 1890s, three severe droughts struck the North American Great Plains. They contributed to the near extinction of the American bison and the destruction of Native American cultures that depended on the buffalo for survival. The 1870s drought, which was related to a La Niña event in the Pacific, was accompanied by a plague of locusts, while the 1890s drought caused a reduction in agricultural production along with a decline in American settlement on the Great Plains (Seager and Herweijer, 2010).

As a historian, coincidences always make me suspect and search for a causal relationship. The 1850s drought was also the time of "Bloody Kansas." Passage of the 1854 Kansas-Nebraska Act established the principle of popular sovereignty, which meant white men living in a territory would decide if it would be a free or slave state. Between 1854 and 1859, northern Free-Staters and southern slaveholders battled for control over Kansas as it prepared to enter the union. In the midst of a drought that must have severely exacerbated conditions, Free-Staters and the slaveholders fought a mini-civil war, approved different constitutions, and established different capitals and governments. Kansas was finally admitted to the Union as a free state in January 1861, after Southern states had begun to secede and just before the start of the American Civil War.

It turns out that locusts love droughts. Dry conditions seem to awaken locusts, speed maturation, and stimulate their hunger for plant life, while weakening the natural defenses of vegetation and reducing fungal disease that limit the size of locust swarms. In 1875, a swarm of over three trillion locusts blanketed much of the Great Plains. Locust swarms are now threatening agriculture in East Africa as the climate warms and dries.

DOI: 10.4324/9781003200864-16

The 1870s drought meant devastation for the American bison population and the native people of the Great Plains that depended on the buffalo for survival. While other factors played a role in the U.S. conquest of the plains, military and weapon superiority, the telegraph, the railroad, and the employment of hunters to wipe out buffalo herds, the drought and the locust infestation definitely weakened the ability of both bison and the indigenous population to survive. During droughts, bison and the Plains Indians moved to river valleys, where they could take advantage of remaining water and grassland, but these were the same areas that the locusts targeted; congregation in more confined space left both populations vulnerable to attack by the U.S. military and railroad company henchmen.

During the 1890s drought, farmers on the Great Plains rose up to challenge corrupt state governments controlled by railroad companies and organized the Populist or People's Party. *The Wonderful Wizard of Oz* (1900) is actually an allegorical tale written by a Populist leader. Dorothy represents the common people of Kansas caught up in a tornado and dust storm. The Scarecrow represents farmers, the Tin Man workers, the Lion is Populist spokesperson William Jennings Bryan, the fake wizard is President William McKinley, and the witches and their evil hoard are the railroads, monopolies, and their minions. I do not think it is an accident that the farmers' rebellion coincided with harsher conditions on the Great Plains.

In the 1930s, drought struck the Great Plains again, this time creating an enormous "Dust Bowl" as dry storms swept across the plains, wiping out agriculture and forcing three million people to abandon their farms and a mass migration to other areas of the United States. Between 1895 and 2013, 1934 was the driest year on the Great Plains, and 1936 was the second driest. Drought struck again in 1939 (NOAA, 2021b). The droughts caused topsoil to dry out, turn powdery, and blow away in enormous clouds of dust. The novel *Grapes of Wrath* (1939) by John Steinbeck tells the story of the Joads, a family from Oklahoma that flees to California, where they work as migrant laborers. In the world they left behind, at night "stars could not pierce the dust to get down, and the window lights could not even spread beyond their own yards. Now the dust was evenly mixed with the air. . . . Houses were shut tight, and cloths wedged around doors and windows. . . . In the morning the dust hung like fog, and the sun was as red as ripe new blood" (3). People suffered from "dust pneumonia" as their lungs filled with dust (Cook, Miller, and Seager, 2008). These droughts may have been caused, or they were at least exacerbated, by La Niña–like conditions in the Pacific (Seager et al., 2004).

More recently, northern China suffered enormous dust storms that forced the cancelation of airplane flights and school closings. The dust combined with human-made pollutants to form a life threatening "airpocalypse" that turned the air yellow-orange as the sun rose in the morning and "soupy gray" during the afternoon. The dust migrated south and east from arid areas in Mongolia and along the Chinese-Mongolian border that have increasingly desertified because of climate change (Myers, 2021: A10).

Human beings cannot survive without potable water. For adequate daily hydration, the National Academies of Sciences, Engineering, and Medicine recommends 3.7 liters (15.5 cups or about 4 quarts) of fluid from water, other beverages, and food for men and 2.7 liters (11.5 cups or about 3 quarts) for women. If an individual participates in activities that make them sweat profusely on hot days (workouts or physical labor), they need extra fluid to remain hydrated. Very active people exposed to hot weather can require at least six liters of fluid (25 cups or 6 quarts) to remain hydrated (NASEM, 2004).

But will there be enough water? At the beginning of the Neolithic era, approximately 12,000 years ago, the Earth's population was probably about 5 million people, though, of course, there was no census then, so this is a pretty rough estimate. Between 2,000 and 3,000 years ago, the time of the Roman Empire in the Mediterranean and Confucius in China, when the Aksum Empire ruled modern-day Ethiopia and the Olmec dominated Central America, there were probably between 200 and 300 million human inhabitants of the Earth. It took another 1800 years until the Earth's human population reached 1 billion. With the start of the Industrial Revolution and the development of modern medicine, the rate of human population growth increased astronomically. It took 130 years for the Earth's human population to double to 2 billion, and it doubled again to four billion in only 45 years. In 2013, the Earth's human population was about 6.5 billion. Seven years later, in 2020, it was an estimated 7.8 billion. If the current growth rate continues, it will be 10 billion by 2060 (Emmott, 2013; Kaneda and Haub, 2020).

As the human population increases, so does the demand for water, food, land, minerals, transport, and energy, but water, as climate changes, may be humanity's undoing. Ice melts and redirects ocean currents, water floods low-lying areas, ocean water salinates farmland and fresh water sources, rainwater fails to fall from the sky, and subterranean water dries up and is no longer available for irrigation. In the United States, most tap water is potable; however, there have been serious problems in Flint, Michigan, and Newark, New Jersey, but not because of climate change. Except during emergencies, water is usually readily available in plastic containers at local stores and supermarkets. Unfortunately, that is not the case in many parts of the world, and the situation is growing more drastic because of climate change (Denchak, 2018; Nathanson, 2020).

Humans use an enormous amount of water. The average American uses almost 100 gallons a day to cook, bathe, wash clothing, and clean up after meals. It takes about 660 gallons of water to produce a 1/3-pound hamburger – only one. Americans eat 50 billion burgers a year. I think I eat about 50 of them. At 660 gallons of water per burger, that is 33 trillion gallons of water a year. It takes 11 gallons of water to produce a single slice of bread, from watering the grain through kneading the dough, and 240 gallons to manufacture an entire loaf (Hallock, 2014).

It takes around 1,500 gallons of water to produce a three-pound chicken and over 50 gallons to produce a single egg. Americans eat an estimated

8 billion chickens ranging in weight from three to six pounds each a year, which means those chickens are the equivalent of at least 20 trillion gallons of water. It takes 450 gallons of water to make one 3.5-ounce (100-gram) chocolate bar and 37 gallons to produce the coffee beans needed for a single cup of coffee. This doesn't include water used in the brewing process or cleaning up. If every person in the world drank a single cup of coffee each day, it would require 32 trillion gallons of water a year. Americans drink 150 billion cups a year. I am more guilty than most here. I drink about six cups of coffee a day, over 2,000 a year, which comes out to about 75,000 gallons of water a year, give or take a few gallons (United States Geological Survey, n.d.; Postel, 2015; Hallock, 2014).

Enormous amounts of water are used in standard manufacturing processes, creating the electronic devices that operate our cell phones, computers, and cars and are essential for modern life. A modern car requires more than 3,000 computer chips to operate. The manufacture of a miniature electronic circuit can require the use of 2,200 gallons of water because components must be repeatedly bathed. A large factory producing semiconductors, a building block of the electronics industry, uses 4.8 million gallons of water a day. The semiconductor industry is also highly energy intensive; a typical factory has a carbon footprint equivalent to a small city (Ewing and Boudette, 2021: A1; Zafar, 2019; China Water Risk, 2013).

While demand for water increases, supply is becoming more erratic as a result of climate change. Data gathered by NASA satellites that track water cycles and measure fresh water supplies show climate change creating greater extremes in the frequency and magnitude of floods and droughts and impacting on food production and human survival. In the United States, from 1958 to 2016, there was an increase of 55% in "heavy rainfall events" in the northeastern states, by 42% in the Midwest, and by 27% in the Southeast, overwhelming the ability of local watersheds to absorb excessive water. In the near future, parts of Asia is expected to become wetter, while the southwestern United States, Central America, the Sahel region of East Africa, Australia, and Europe will become drier. NASA scientists predict that the U.S. Southwest could experience "megadroughts" that linger for decades (Gray and Merzdorf, 2019). Droughts in these regions will affect food availability, prevent the shipment of essential goods along rivers as water levels drop, make forests more susceptible to fire, and interfere with electrical power from plants that rely on water for cooling systems (Pugh, 2021).

The impact of shifting rain patterns and warming temperatures is already being felt in the Eastern Mediterranean and the U.S. Pacific coast. The Syrian Civil War, which started in 2011 and at this writing had lasted a decade, was preceded by a drought between 2006 to 2010. By some measures, it was the worst experienced in the region in the previous 900 years. The United Nations estimated that the drought caused almost three-quarters of Syrian farms to fail and a mass migration from the Syrian countryside to urban areas (Kelley et al., 2015; Stokes, 2016; Cook et al., 2016). Intense wildfires in the western United States are the result of a combination of declining rainfall and higher water evaporation rates from soil as the average temperature rises (Cook, 2018).

Ancient Civilizations

Drought was probably responsible for both the growth and collapse of a number of ancient civilizations. Around 5,500 years ago, shifts in monsoon rains led to increased desiccation in the Egyptian Sahara, population concentrating along the Nile River, and the formation of the earliest pharaonic dynasties. Tomb paintings and inscriptions in Egyptian tombs suggest that that the environment in the Sahara and along the Nile River became even more arid about 2200 BC and caused the end of the Old Kingdom. This is confirmed by studies of mud sediment cores from the Nile basin (Carey, 2006; Lawler, 2015). At the same time, in Mesopotamia, Akkadian civilization died when precipitation decreased by 30%, crops withered in the fields, and winds blew away the dried topsoil (Linden, 2006: 53).

Mayan civilization on the Yucatan Peninsula and Central America, which flourished between roughly 250 AD and the middle of the 9th century, collapsed when water started to run out. Mayan agriculture relied on subterranean water that they mistakenly believed was a constantly refilled renewal resource. Each of their sites is near a cenote, a surface entry to limestone caverns. As their population grew and the water level dropped and was more difficult to access, the Mayan city-states were unable to sustain agricultural production at a high enough level, which led to warfare between neighboring communities and the collapse of their civilization by 950 AD. The fate of the Maya is telling for the world today. China, Iran, and Mexico are all depleting their aquifers. Major freshwater lakes like Titicaca in South American and the Aral Sea in Asia are receding. Egypt, the Sudan, and Ethiopia are fighting for control over the Nile headwaters. One cause of the civil war in Syria and outside intervention is that Syria, Iraq, Turkey, and the Kurds are battling for Tigris River water that they all depend on for survival. The need for fresh water may trigger wars as climate change brings new and more prolonged droughts to a number of regions (Linden, 2006: 68–74; Collins, 2017; Hackley, 2018: 4).

Water's Vengeance

Throughout the book, I have discussed the destructive power of water – water's vengeance – but it is worth revisiting. Global warming means rising sea levels and more intense storms, both producing destructive floods. Rising sea levels are eating away at Shinnecock Indian lands on the narrow south fork of Long Island, about 100 miles from New York City. While this endangers the long-term survival of the Shinnecock people, other consequences of sea-level rise are even more threatening (Sengupta and Lawal, 2020: A20).

According to a survey by the World Nuclear Association, in 2020 there were over 440 commercial nuclear reactors in operation worldwide, including 94 in the United States. Because the reactors need massive amounts of water for their cooling systems, about 25% are located along coastlines. Nine U.S. nuclear plants are located less than two miles from the coast at an average of about 20 feet above sea level with minimal sea wall protection, and at least four of them are considered vulnerable to storm surges. In 2012, when Superstorm Sandy struck the east coast of the United States, three nuclear power plants were shut down because of risks from a storm surge, while another was put on alert. The March 2011 tsunami storm-surge following an earthquake off Japan's eastern Pacific coast flooded the Fukushima Daiichi nuclear power plant. It released radiation into the atmosphere and contaminated water leaked into the ocean, forcing the evacuation of over 150,000 people living within 12 miles of the plant. The surge was 45 feet above sea level (WNA, 2021; Vidal, 2018; Lipscy, Kushida, and Incerti, 2012; Associated Press, 2012).

According to the National Oceanic and Atmospheric Administration (NOAA), in 2019 there were record levels of high-tide flooding (HTF), water rising more than 20 inches above the normal daily high-tide mark, in coastal regions of the United States. The frequency of HTF increased because sea levels are about 13 inches higher than they were a century ago. Corpus Christi and Galveston, Texas; Annapolis, Maryland; and Charleston, South Carolina, all set or tied records for the number of days of HFT. With 64, Eagle Point, Texas, in Galveston Bay, had the most HTF days in the country. NOAA projects that by 2030, the number of days with HTF in U.S. coastal regions could double or triple, and it could be as much as 15 times greater by 2050. In 2020, 14.6 million properties in the United States were at risk from flooding with the number continually climbing. (Flavelle, 2020b: A18; Ivanova and Layne, 2020).

Sea-level rise and increased storm intensity are responsible for severe infrastructure damage. Even when rising water levels do not cause obvious flooding and surface damage, they still can affect subsurface infrastructure like storm-water infiltration, sewer lines, tunnels, and subways. Many of the more than 90,000 dams in the United States are at risk of failing because they were not designed for new weather conditions with increasing severe storms. In May 2020, a dam on the Tittabawassee River in Central Michigan was overwhelmed by water after five inches of rain fell in the area over the course of two days. The Tittabawassee River Dam collapse forced the evacuation of about 40,000 people and threatened a chemical complex and toxic waste cleanup site (Fountain, 2020: A20).

In 2012, Superstorm Sandy inflicted over $50 billion in damage, making it the second-costliest hurricane in the United States up until that time. At its peak, it was a Category 3 hurricane; however, when it made landfall in New York City on October 29, 2012, wind speed had dropped, and it was a tropical storm, hence the name Superstorm Sandy. Its storm surge flooded streets, tunnels, and subway lines and cut power in the city and the surrounding area. Approximately 100,000 homes on Long Island were destroyed or severely damaged, including 2,000 that were declared uninhabitable. At the time, Sandy was described as a once in a century event; by the middle of the 21st century, similar destructive flooding in the region may become a once in a decade event (CNN, 2013; Critchton, 2012; Marsooli and Lin, 2020).

Even small climate changes can trigger catastrophic infrastructure failures. Bridges that collapsed in 2004 in Escambia Bay, Florida, during Hurricane Ivan were built in 1968. Engineers investigating the collapse concluded that a three-inch sea level rise with higher storm surges probably was responsible. Amtrak's Northeast corridor train service between Boston and Washington, DC, is threatened by flooding and storm surges that can erode the underlying track bed, disable vital electrical signals, and leave stretches of tracks underwater (Flavelle, Plumer, and Tabuchi, 2021: A1).

In the 1955 folk song "Where Have All the Flowers Gone?" Pete Seeger asks, "When will they ever learn? Oh, when will they ever learn?" Seeger may well have been singing about the impact of hurricanes intensified by climate change. Climate change has made hurricanes wetter and slower.

In May 2020, Cyclone Amphan struck India and Bangladesh, forcing the evacuation of over two million people. It was the worst cyclone in the Bay of Bengal at least since 1999. In Bangladesh, rice paddies were flooded and destroyed by salt water from the storm surge. In the West Bengal, India, city of Kolkata, where its population of 14 million already faced food shortages because of the COVID-19 pandemic, electricity and phone service were cut off, leaving people who were quarantined in total isolation (Berlinger, Regan, and Rahim, 2020; BBC News, 2020).

In August 2020, heavy rains in China's Sichuan Province flooded the Yangtze River and threatened the Three Gorges Dam, where water levels were at their highest since it opened in 2003. It was the fifth time the river had flooded in one year with the last flood setting a high water record. Over 60 million people were affected, more than 50,000 homes were destroyed, and damage was at least $30 billion (Myers, 2020: A10).

Before the 1990s, hurricane-like cyclones, known as Medicanes, rarely happen in the Mediterranean Sea because the climate is generally dry; now they are a more regular occurrence and are expected to increase in frequency along with climate change. In September 2020, the western Ionian islands of Greece were battered by Cyclone Ianos that flooded streets, destroyed crops just prior to harvest, tore down buildings, and caused millions of dollars in damage (Specia, 2020: A12; Romero and Emanuel, 2017).

Following devastating wildfires in 2020, in March 2021 massive storms, a once in a 100-year event that is projected to be much more frequent, produced record-breaking floods in Eastern Australia. Schools were closed, homes were destroyed, and sections of a 500-mile stretch of highway were impassable. Climate researchers believe the fires, storms, and flooding are interconnected events caused by climate change. Warming leads to drought and causes remaining moisture in the soil to evaporate, making forests more susceptible to fire. Increased moisture in the atmosphere, coupled with new wind patterns, generates torrential rains and floods (Cave, 2021: A10).

Hurricane Sally stalled over the warm waters of the Gulf of Mexico in September 2020, absorbing power and water and then flooded coastal communities in Florida, Alabama, and Mississippi. In recent decades, the average speed of Atlantic hurricanes has slowed by more than 15%. Summer to fall 2020 was a record season for Atlantic named storms. The 30 named storms included 13 hurricanes with winds over 74 mph and caused over $50 billion worth of damage. The year 2020 also had the second most hurricanes in one season, surpassed only by 15 hurricanes in 2005. According to James P. Kossin, a climate scientist with NOAA, warmer ocean temperatures are "absolutely responsible for the hyperactive season," and "It's very likely that human-caused climate change contributed to that anomalously warm ocean" (Fausset, Rojas, and Fountain, 2020: A1; Penney, 2020: A19).

More powerful hurricanes with higher wind velocities are striking closer to home, at least in the New York metropolitan area where I live. In 2012, I was trapped in my Brooklyn apartment for days when elevator service was turned off because of the impact of Superstorm Sandy. According to Dr. Kerry Emanuel, a professor of atmospheric science at the Massachusetts Institute of Technology, "If Sandy's storm surge had occurred in 1912 rather than 2012, it probably wouldn't have flooded Lower Manhattan." In 2012, it also flooded large parts of Brooklyn (Penney, 2020: A19). In 2020, I was staying in a summer vacation house in Connecticut, where twice within two weeks storm winds took down trees that fell on power lines and interrupted electrical service. Food spoiled in the refrigerator, the stove wouldn't light, the toilet wouldn't flush, the air conditioners were dead, and television and Internet service were cut. We were lucky we could drive home until power was restored, but other people were not so lucky.

Water – we can't live with it, and we can't live without it. It is the incarnation of the Hindu God Shiva, the god of creation and also the god of destruction.

Teaching Documents

Things We Know About Climate Change and Hurricanes

Sources: www.nytimes.com/2020/11/10/climate/climate-change-hurricanes.html; www.nytimes.com/2020/11/11/climate/hurricanes-climate-change-patterns.html

Question: Why are hurricanes placing communities at greater risk?

1. Higher winds: Hurricanes are becoming more powerful. One of the key factors that determine how strong a storm becomes is ocean surface temperature. Warmer water provides more of the energy that fuels storms. Stronger winds mean downed power lines, damaged roofs and, when paired with rising sea levels, worse coastal flooding.

2. More rain: Warming increases the amount of water vapor that the atmosphere can hold. Every degree Celsius (1.8°F) of warming allows the air to hold about 7% more water, so we can expect future storms to unleash higher amounts of rainfall.

3. Slower storms: Hurricanes over the United States have slowed 17% since 1947. Combined with the increase in rain rates, storms are causing a 25% increase in local rainfall. Slower, wetter storms worsen flooding.

4. Slower decay: Fifty years ago, as a typical storm traveled over land, it lost more than three-quarters of its intensity in the first 24 hours. Today the storm would lose only half of its strength in the same time period.

5. Wider-ranging storms: Because warmer water helps fuel hurricanes, climate change is enlarging the zone where hurricanes can form. Storms are moving out of the tropics into middle latitudes, threatening the United States and Japan.

6. More volatility: Expect storms to intensify more rapidly. If a Category 1 hurricane develops into a Category 4 hurricane overnight, there is no time to evacuate people.

Additional Teaching Documents at https://alansinger.net:
- Emergency from Climate Change on Two Coasts
- Droughts, Floods and Food

17 Technology Debate

Advocates for technological solutions to halt or even reverse climate change argue that technological solutions, also known as geoengineering, can be the "silver bullet" that reduces the need for a shift away from fossil fuels and avoids potentially major economic dislocation. Paul Crutzen, a Dutch atmospheric chemist and Nobel Prize winner for his work on the hole in the ozone layer that surrounds the Earth, proposes injecting sulfate aerosols into the stratosphere, roughly 12 miles up, to block sunlight and cool the Earth. Crutzen argues that technological solutions offer the world a contingency plan because so far, attempts to limit fossil fuel emissions have been grossly unsuccessful. According to Crutzen, "If sizeable reductions in greenhouse gas emissions will not happen and temperatures rise rapidly, then climatic engineering . . . is the only option available to rapidly reduce temperature rises and counteract other climatic effects. Such a modification could also be stopped on short notice, if undesirable and unforeseen side-effects become apparent, which would allow the atmosphere to return to its prior state within a few years" (Crutzen, 2006: 212, 216; Connor, 2006).

If geoengineering works, humanity can have its cake (a carbon-based economy) and eat it, too (neutralize the impact of greenhouses gases), although Crutzen, believes "the very best would be if emissions of the greenhouse gases could be reduced so much that the stratospheric sulfur release experiment would not need to take place" (217). Critics of the "contingency plan" fear the search for a technological solution will be seen as a panacea and delay placing limits on the burning of fossil fuels past the point where the environmental damage caused by climate change cannot be healed.

Prominent research institutions and governmental agencies in the United States and other countries are investing in research seeking a way to artificially cool the Earth. Greenhouse gases trap heat in the atmosphere, raising the average temperature on the Earth's surface and producing a range of changes in climate. Solar geoengineering proposals are designed to reduce global temperature by reflecting some sunlight back into space before it enters the atmosphere. It would have the same cooling effect as volcanic ash thrown into the atmosphere by eruptions but, in theory, could be repeated and adjusted to provide a consistent lower average temperature. The United States National

DOI: 10.4324/9781003200864-17

Oceanic and Atmospheric Administration is conducting research into new technologies as is the government of Australia, which is committed to saving the Great Barrier Reef. Michael Gerrard, director of the Sabin Center for Climate Change Law at the Columbia Law School is a geoengineering advocate. "We're facing an existential threat, and we need to look at all the options. I liken geoengineering to chemotherapy for the planet: If all else is failing, you try it" (Flavelle, 2020c: B3).

SilverLining is a private initiative with roots in the tech investment world. It is committed to finding and funding "options to address near-term climate risk" (www.silverlining.ngo). According to its webpage "Historic weather extremes, natural disasters, and changes such as the weakening of Antarctic glaciers pose unprecedented risks to the safety of communities and the stability of natural systems in the next 10–30 years. Reducing and removing the greenhouse gases that cause climate change are imperative, but may act too slowly to prevent abrupt changes in natural systems and catastrophic impacts on people." Funding from its Safe Climate Research Initiative goes to major universities and research centers looking for technological quick fixes such as injecting aerosol particles into clouds to make them brighter and more reflective of sunlight.

There are a number of questions about solar geoengineering, even among its supporters. Where should the aerosol be targeted, in what amounts, at what precise elevation, and how frequently? What will be the impact on the strength of hurricanes, agriculture yields, and forest fires? Will some regions of the Earth benefit at the expense of others? Will a temporary reprieve buy time for humanity to wean off fossil fuels, or will it provide false hope that change is unnecessary?

The Australian government is exploring a different approach to cloud seeding, making clouds more reflective of sunlight by spraying saltwater into the air. In theory, salt particles will stimulate the formation of small water droplets, increasing the brightness of the clouds, without potential side effects that would accompany aerosol. However, unlike the proposals for aerosol, spraying saltwater into the atmosphere would be a very localized solution. Scientists estimate it would take between 500 and 1,000 spraying platforms to cover the 1,400-mile length of the Great Barrier Reef.

Barbara Unmüssig, President of the Heinrich Böll Foundation in Germany, is one of the leading critics of geoengineering as a solution, even as a temporary one, to climate change. The foundation is part of the German Green Party environmental movement. Unmüssig argues that proponents of geoengineering "feed the illusion that there is a way to engineer an exit from the climate crisis, meet the goals of the 2015 Paris climate agreement, and maintain a consumption-heavy lifestyle. . . . Betting on climate engineering – either as a planetary insurance policy or as a last-ditch measure to combat rising temperatures – is not only risky; it also directs attention away from the only solution we know will work: reducing carbon emissions" (Unmüssig, 2017).

Solar geoengineering proposals include potential environmental risks that its proponents either ignore or minimize. The only way to test the impact of spraying aerosol or saltwater into the atmosphere is to actually do it. Computer models, however, suggest that this could alter global precipitation patterns and damage the ozone layer, threatening the lives and livelihoods of millions of people. Unmüssig and the Heinrich Böll Foundation are also concerned that the new technology "could spawn powerful weapons, giving states, corporations, or individuals the ability to manipulate climate for strategic gain."

Other proposed technological solutions carry their own ecological risks. One suggestion is to remove CO_2 from the atmosphere. Occidental Petroleum and United Airlines are partnering in what they call a "direct air capture" facility located in Texas. It will be equipped with fans and use chemical agents including calcium carbonate to remove CO_2 from the atmosphere and then inject it underground, where it will be stored. Even if the plan is economically and technologically feasible, if the stored CO_2 were somehow released back into the atmosphere, there would be catastrophic consequences. Planting CO_2 capturing plants on a large enough scale necessary to have any impact on CO_2 concentrations in the atmosphere would require utilizing one-third of the world's arable land. Fertilizing oceans with "carbon-sequestering plankton" was banned in 2008 because of potential damage to marine life. It is also unclear how any of these proposals could amass sufficient support to ensure international cooperation. The United Nations–affiliated Intergovernmental Panel on Climate Change estimates that to be effective, CO_2 removal plans will have to capture and remove between 100 billion and 1 trillion tons of CO_2 from the atmosphere this century (Plumer and Flavelle, 2021: B5; Krauss, 2019: B1).

As of 2021, worldwide, there were approximately two dozen different "carbon capture" projects, some supported by the fossil fuel industry. The construction and operation costs were high, making them economically unfeasible largely because of the amount of energy required by the different processes. There was also corporate concern about legal liability if local environments were polluted or if the stored carbon dioxide escaped into the atmosphere. In the United States, government funded research has focused on cutting the cost of carbon capture with technologies that utilize more efficient carbon solvents. Mike Childs of Great Britain's Friends of the Earth, where a massive project was underway with participation by British Petroleum, charged "Carbon capture is being used as a Trojan horse by the fossil fuels industry to keep demand for fossil fuels alive." He recommended investing in processes that did not "create pollution in the first place" (Reed, 2021: B12; Frimpong et al., 2021; Jiang et al., 2021).

In an article in the Bulletin of the Atomic Scientists, Alan Robock, a climatologist at Rutgers University, listed 20 reasons that he considers geoengineering a very bad idea (2008: 14–18). Proponents of solar geoengineering models often refer to the cooling effect of volcanic eruptions as evidence that their proposals are replicating a natural phenomenon. Robock points out that the climate impact of these eruptions varies from region to region across the globe and in some areas have negatively affected food supply. An eruption in Iceland in the late 18th century contributed to famine in parts of Africa and in India and Japan. It is also not clear if aerosol sprayed at one elevation or in one region of the world could be prevented from dispersing or whether scientists could reverse the impact of geoengineering if the intervention proved to be excessive and the impact of climate cooling was too extreme.

According to Robock, there are just too many poorly understood consequences to risk pumping aerosols into the atmosphere. The continued acidification of the oceans through the absorption of CO_2 would still threaten the global food chain, spraying aerosols into the atmosphere could damage the ozone layer, and blocking sunlight would interfere with the use of solar power as an alternative to fossil fuels. Robock worries about potential military use of climate technology, private, for-profit, corporate control over climate technology and who decides where to set the thermostat, assuming it can be set.

There is another underside to technology as a solution to the climate crisis. Sometimes proposed solutions are misleading in their promises or may be harmful to the environment. While all-electric cars emit far fewer greenhouse gases than either gas-fueled or hybrid cars, they still leave a carbon footprint. Because they draw from the local power grid, if that electricity is generated by coal-fueled plants, they could even have a greater carbon foot print than a hybrid car (Tabuchi and Plumer, 2021: B5). Bitcoin is the cryptocurrency that hopes to pioneer a cashless and possibly greener financial future. The problem is that the greenhouse gas emitted while generating the electricity needed to power Bitcoin computers is greater than the amount produced by New Zealand or Argentina. A Bitcoin transaction has a carbon footprint equivalent to over 700,000 credit card purchases (Sorkin, 2021: B1).

There is another problem with electric cars that is rarely discussed – their lithium batteries. The mining process for lithium requires that billions of gallons of ground water be used to flush the lithium up from deep below the Earth's surface. The water, which could have been used for agricultural production, is now toxic waste (Penn and Lipton, 2021: A1).

Alan Robock didn't cite the science fiction movie *Total Recall* (1990) starring Arnold Schwarzenegger in his article questioning geoengineering, but he could have. In the movie, a private company controls Earth's Mars colony by rationing air as it exploits Mars' resources.

Teaching Documents

Can Technology Save the Planet?

Instructions: The excerpts from "As Climate Disasters Pile Up, a Radical Proposal Gains Traction" and "20 reasons why geoengineering may be a bad idea" offer different perspectives about the possibility for and safety of technological solutions to climate change. Examine the two excerpts. (1) What evidence do they present to support their position? (2) On balance, do you think geoengineering is a realistic and safe solution to the problems caused by climate change? Explain.

1. Radical Proposals

> **Source:** C. Flavelle, "As Climate Disasters Pile Up, a Radical Proposal Gains Traction," *The New York Times*, October 29, 2020. www.nytimes.com/2020/10/28/climate/climate-change-geoengineering.html

1. "As the effects of climate change become more devastating, prominent research institutions and government agencies are focusing new money and attention on an idea once dismissed as science fiction: Artificially cooling the planet, in the hopes of buying humanity more time to cut greenhouse gas emissions. That strategy, called solar climate intervention or solar geoengineering, entails reflecting more of the sun's energy back into space – abruptly reducing global temperatures in a way that mimics the effects of ash clouds spewed by volcanic eruptions. The idea has been derided as a dangerous and illusory fix, one that would encourage people to keep burning fossil fuels while exposing the planet to unexpected and potentially menacing side effects. But as global warming continues, producing more destructive hurricanes, wildfires, floods and other disasters, some researchers and policy experts say that concerns about geoengineering should be outweighed by the imperative to better understand it, in case the consequences of climate change become so dire that the world can't wait for better solutions."

2. "One way to cool the earth is by injecting aerosols into the upper layer of the atmosphere, where those particles reflect sunlight away from the earth. That process works, according to Douglas MacMartin, a researcher in mechanical and aerospace engineering at Cornell University. . . . 'We know with 100 percent certainty that we can cool the planet,' Dr. MacMartin said in an interview. What's still unclear, he added, is what happens next. Temperature, Dr. MacMartin said, is a proxy for a lot of climate effects. 'What does it do to the strength of hurricanes? What does it do to agriculture yields? What does it do to the risk of forest fires?' To help answer those questions, Dr. MacMartin will model the specific weather effects of injecting aerosols into the atmosphere above different parts of the globe, and also at different altitudes."

3. "Injecting aerosol into the stratosphere isn't the only way to bounce more of the sun's rays back into space. The Australian government is funding research into what's called 'marine cloud brightening,' which is meant to make clouds more reflective by spraying saltwater into the air. The goal is to get salt particles to act as nuclei in those clouds, encouraging the formation of many small water droplets, which will increase the brightness

of the clouds. Australian researchers say they hope the technique can save the Great Barrier Reef. Rising water temperatures during so-called marine heat waves are accelerating the die-off of the reef, and making marine clouds more reflective may be able to cool water temperatures enough to slow or stop that decline.

2. Is Geoengineering a Bad Idea?

Source: Robock. A. 2008, May/June. "20 reasons why geoengineering may be a bad idea," *Bulletin of the Atomic Scientists,* http://climate. envsci.rutgers.edu/pdf/20Reasons.pdf

1. "Since scientists became aware of rising concentrations of atmospheric carbon dioxide, . . . some have proposed artificially altering climate and weather patterns to reverse or mask the effects of global warming. Some geoengineering schemes aim to remove carbon dioxide from the atmosphere, through natural or mechanical means. Ocean fertilization, where iron dust is dumped into the open ocean to trigger algal blooms; genetic modification of crops to increase biotic carbon uptake; carbon capture and storage techniques such as those proposed to outfit coal plants; and planting forests are such examples. Other schemes involve blocking or reflecting incoming solar radiation, for example by spraying seawater hundreds of meters into the air to seed the formation of stratocumulus clouds over the subtropical ocean. Two strategies to reduce incoming solar radiation – stratospheric aerosol injection . . . and space-based sun shields (i.e., mirrors or shades placed in orbit between the sun and Earth)—are among the most widely discussed geoengineering schemes in scientific circles."

2. "Geoengineering proponents often suggest that volcanic eruptions are an innocuous natural analog for stratospheric injection of sulfate aerosols. The 1991 eruption of Mount Pinatubo on the Philippine island of Luzon, which injected 20 megatons of sulfur dioxide gas into the stratosphere, produced a sulfate aerosol cloud that is said to have caused global cooling for a couple of years without adverse effects. . . . The Pinatubo eruption caused large hydrological responses, including reduced precipitation, soil moisture, and river flow in many regions. . . . Scientists have also seen volcanic eruptions in the tropics produce changes in atmospheric circulation, causing winter warming over continents in the Northern Hemisphere, as well as eruptions at high latitudes weaken the Asian and African monsoons, causing reduced precipitation . . . The eight-monthlong eruption of the Laki fissure in Iceland in 1783–1784 contributed to famine in Africa, India, and Japan."

3. "Scientists may never have enough confidence that their theories will predict how well geoengineering systems can work. With so much at stake, there is reason to worry about what we don't know. The reasons why geoengineering may be a bad idea are manifold, though a moderate

investment in theoretical geoengineering research might help scientists to determine whether or not it is a bad idea. . . . The crux of addressing global warming is political. The U.S. government gives multibillion-dollar subsidies to the coal, oil, gas, and nuclear industries, and gives little support to alternative energy sources like solar and wind power that could contribute to a solution. Similarly, the federal government is squashing attempts by states to mandate emissions reductions. If global warming is a political problem more than it is a technical problem, it follows that we don't need geoengineering to solve it."

Additional Teaching Documents at https://alansinger.net:
- G.M. Phasing Out Cars and Trucks Using Gas by 2035
- G.M. Decision To Go Electric Rocks Industry
- All Roads Lead to China In G.M.'s Electric Car Push
- No Tailpipe Doesn't Mean No Emissions

18 Saving the Amazon Rainforest

The Amazon River is almost 4,000 miles long and runs roughly along the Equator eastward from the Andes Mountains to the Atlantic Ocean. Its immense tropical rainforest, containing about half of the Earth's remaining rainforests, is 2.6 million square miles in size with 1.4 billion acres of dense forest and covers approximately 40% of the land area of South America. The rainforest extends into seven countries, Brazil, Bolivia, Peru, Ecuador, Colombia, Venezuela, Guyana, Suriname, and one European colony, French Guiana, although most of its acreage is in Brazil. Brazil is the fifth-largest country in the world, it is the seventh most populous, and it has the eighth-largest economy. Sixty-two percent of the country is forested, and less than 10% is considered arable. Brazil's carbon footprint ranks the country 13th in the world for contributing CO_2 to the atmosphere; China, the United States, and India rank 1, 2, and 3 (Rice, 2019; WWF; CIA). Economic expansion by Brazil continually puts it at loggerheads with global environmental concerns because it would come at the expense of the rainforest, which has been described as the "lungs of the planet" (De Bolle, 2019).

Because of its size and location, the Amazon Rainforest is home to about 25% of the Earth's biodiversity and plays important roles in several of the planet's natural cycles that influence climate. Its plants and trees annually absorb two billion tons of carbon dioxide, approximately 5% of CO_2 emissions. Nearly 100 billion tons of carbon is stored in the Amazon's trees, which equates to almost 400 billion tons of carbon dioxide that is kept out of the atmosphere. As water evaporates from the tropical rainforest, it also acts as a giant cooling system (Rice, 2019).

Amazonas, located in the northwestern portion of the country along Brazil's borders with Venezuela, Columbia, and Peru, is the largest of Brazil's 26 states. It is named after the Amazon River and encompasses a major portion of the Amazon's watershed. The sparsely populated region was initially claimed by Spain in the 17th and 18th centuries, but nominal sovereignty was transferred to Portugal with the Treaty of Madrid in 1750. Today the population of Amazonas is estimated at fewer than four million people with over half living in the state capital of Manaus. The indigenous population of Amazonas is probably less than 200,000 people. Because of the region's size and rainforest

DOI: 10.4324/9781003200864-18

habitat, population density is fewer than seven people per square mile and much less if you do not include Manaus (World Data Atlas, n.d.).

Starting in the mid-19th century, Europe and capitalism started the rape of the Amazon and the exploitation of its indigenous population. The Industrial Revolution in Europe created demand for rubber, produced from latex sap of the Amazonian pará rubber tree. Between 1850 and 1880, the demand for rubber increased fivefold and then accelerated with its use in bicycle, wagon, and car tires. There was a major rubber boom between 1880 and the start of the first World War. Eventually, the value of Brazilian rubber declined as trees were planted in other regions of the world and after World War II when rubber was increasingly replaced by synthetic fibers (Davis, 1996).

The 19th century expansion of rubber production led to the enslavement of the Amazon's indigenous Amerindians, who were forced to work on the rubber plantations as *seringueiros* (rubber tappers); many died from disease and overwork. Rubber producers recruited slave catchers, known as *muchachos*, in the British Caribbean to control the enslaved workforce. British diplomat Roger Casement, who visited the region in 1910 and 1911, documented the treatment of the Amazonian people. In his report, he wrote, "The crimes charged against many men now in the employ of the Peruvian Amazon Company are of the most atrocious kind, including murder, violation, and constant flogging" (Collis, 2012; Hardenburg, 1912: 264).

The Amazon rainforest may be humanity's most important bulwark against catastrophic climate change. Despite this, global warming, coupled with the burning of forest for agriculture and pastures, is transforming the Amazon from carbon absorber to carbon emitter. For decades, the Brazilian government has encouraged deforestation through road construction and other infrastructure projects while promoting mining, logging operations, soybean production, and cattle ranching. Continued deforestation will damage the Amazon's ability to recycle moisture with major repercussions for the entire Southern Hemisphere. Water evaporating from the rainforest generates a significant amount of the Earth's cloud cover and rain. It forms clouds that slide south along the eastern side of the Andes Mountains and then turn east, bring water to dryer areas of southern Brazil and across the Atlantic Ocean, to South Africa. São Paulo, the largest city in South America and Capetown in South Africa, will face increasingly severe water shortages as the Amazon shrinks in size (Hess, 2020; Kaiser, 2019; Watts, 2017).

During the 2020 presidential campaign, Joseph Biden proposed that the United States organize an international fund of $20 billion to prevent the destruction of the Amazon Rainforest. The plan included economic consequences for countries and companies responsible for deforestation. Unfortunately, the proposal drew the immediate ire of Brazil's President Jair Bolsonaro (Friedman, 2021a: A10).

On Twitter, Bolsonaro responded to Biden's proposed international environmental fund (in Portuguese, https://twitter.com/jairbolsonaro/status/1311325732866588678?s=20):

O candidato à presidência dos EUA, Joe Biden, disse ontem que poderia nos pagar U$ 20 bilhões para pararmos de 'destruir" a Amazônia ou nos imporia sérias restrições econômicas.

[US presidential candidate Joe Biden said yesterday that he could pay us $ 20 billion to stop "destroying" the Amazon or impose serious economic restrictions on us.]

O que alguns ainda não entenderam é que o Brasil mudou. Hoje, seu Presidente, diferentemente da esquerda, não mais aceita subornos, criminosas demarcações ou infundadas ameaças. NOSSA SOBERANIA É INEGOCIÁVEL.

[What some have not yet understood is that Brazil has changed. Today, its president, unlike the left, no longer accepts bribes, criminal demarcations, or unfounded threats. OUR SOVEREIGNTY IS NON-NEGOTIABLE.]

After Bolsonaro assumed the Brazilian presidency in January 2019, the Brazilian Amazon was subjected to an expanded wave of environmental exploitation. Between 2018 and July 2019, more than 3,700 square miles of the Amazon was destroyed either legally or illegally, and the "legal" operations were also often questionable. Destruction of forest acreage was 30% higher than in the previous 12-month period and represented the worst attack on the Amazon region in a decade. Carlos Nobre, a climate scientist with the University of São Paulo's Institute for Advanced Studies, described what was happening in the Amazon as "completely lawless" with environmental criminals feeling "more and more empowered" (Sandy, 2019: A12). Bolsonaro opposed plans for the conservation of the Amazon as a break on Brazil's economic progress and as foreign interference with Brazil's sovereignty. His administration cut funding for government agencies that were supposed to enforce environmental regulations, including the prevention of illegal logging and mining and the expansion of cattle ranches (Londoño and Casado, 2019: A4).

According to Nobre, by 2019, intentionally set fires have already destroyed between 15% and 20% of the Amazon rainforest. He feared "if you exceed 40 percent total deforested area in the Amazon, then you have a tipping point. About 60 to 70 percent of the Amazon forest would turn into a dry savanna, especially in the southern and northern Amazon, areas that now border savannas. Only the western Amazon near the Andes, which is very rainy, the forest will still be there." In addition to the burnings, "if the temperature in the Amazon increases up to 4 degrees Celsius (7 degrees Fahrenheit), this will mean a hydrological cycle change with less rain and a longer dry season." Nobre warned, "at the current rates of deforestation, we are 20 to 30 years off from reaching this tipping point" (Montaigne, 2019).

In the lead up to the April 2021 Leaders Climate Summit sponsored by the United States, the Biden Administration renewed the offer to provide a massive international fund to protect the Amazon rainforest, and Bolsonaro responded with a promise to eliminate illegal deforestation by 2030. Bolsonaro's promise was met with skepticism in Brazil. João Doria, governor of São Paulo, Brazil's most populous state, charged, "Bolsonaro has demonstrated a total disregard for the environmental agenda and he hasn't done anything to suggest he has any intention of changing his behavior" (Nugent, 2021). Marcio Astrini, head of Brazil's Climate Observatory, warned the international community, "This is not a trustworthy government: not on democracy, not on the coronavirus and far less so on the Amazon" (Andreoni and Londoño, 2021: A9).

Influential former United States cabinet officials and climate negotiators who were involved in the 1992 Rio Earth Summit and in drafting the 1997 Kyoto Protocol and the 2015 Paris Climate Agreement are promoting a set of climate principles that include an Amazon Protection Plan. They advocate a coordinated private and public approach, international cooperation, and forest-friendly trade agreements, and call on the United States to leverage its foreign assistance programs to ensure forest conservation, agree to finance 25% of international climate initiatives, and "prohibit the importation of agricultural commodities grown on illegally deforested land" (Climate Principals, 2021: 3). In testimony before a sub-committee of the United States House of Representatives Committee on Foreign Affairs, Dr. Monica de Bolle, Johns Hopkins University, described preservation of the Amazon Rainforest as a shared global "moral imperative" (De Bolle, 2019). Sadly, it is not certain these collaborative efforts will happen.

Visiting the Amazon

In August 1969, after my sophomore year in college, I traveled on the Ucayali River, one of the major Amazon tributaries, by river from Pucallpa to Iquitos, Peru, just north of where the Ucayali enters the Amazon. My friends and I then flew by seaplane to Leticia, Colombia, near where Peru, Brazil, and Columbia meet. In the late 19th century, Iquitos and Leticia were major river ports and centers for the global rubber trade. The 330-mile trip from Pucallpa to Iquitos took eight days as the slowly traveling boat delivered supplies to riverside villages and picked up and dropped off passengers. The entire trip was through dense tropical rainforest and at night there was no light except on the boat. Most or our fellow travelers slept on deck, but as Americanos with a little more money, we slept on cots in small cabins. We were permitted to dive off of the boat to swim but regularly had to climb back onboard because of "alerts." Much of the food we ate was caught from the river, and we all ended up pretty sick for a good part of the voyage. There are a number of good movies about the Amazon. *The Emerald Forest* (1985) is about indigenous people in Brazil whose area of the forest and way of life are threatened by construction of a dam. *The Motorcycle Diaries* (2004) is based on journals kept by Ernesto "*Che*" Guevara, who in his early twenties traveled across the lower half of South America. In the final sections of the movie Guevara is at a leper colony on the Amazon. *When 2 Worlds Collide* (2016) is a documentary about late 2000s resistance by indigenous leaders to oil and gas exploration that was suppressed by the Peruvian government. *The Burning Season – The Chico Mendes Story (1994)* is about the struggle of environmental activist Mendes, who was murdered in 1988 by ranchers who wanted to burn the forest for cattle raising.

Teaching Documents

Documenting the Exploitation of the Amazon Rainforest and Its People

Questions

1. Why is Nobre concerned about the deforestation of the Amazon?
2. According to Nobre, how does climate change exacerbate the deterioration of the rainforest?
3. What does de Bolle see as the solution to prevent further deforestation?
4. De Bolle calls preserving the Amazon rainforest a moral imperative. Do you agree? Explain.

   "Will deforestation and warming push the Amazon to a tipping point?"— Interview with Carlos Nobre, University of São Paulo's Institute for Advanced Studies by Fen Montaigne (Yale Environment 360)
   Source: https://e360.yale.edu/features/will-deforestation-and-warming-push-the-amazon-to-a-tipping-point

1. "There have been many, many studies about what climate change, deforestation, and increased vulnerability to forest fires might do to the Amazon system as a whole . . . The post-deforestation climate will no longer be a very wet climate like the Amazon. It will become drier, it will have a much longer dry season, like the long dry seasons in the savannas in the tropics in Africa, South America, and Asia. What we know today is that if we would have only deforestation – [with] zero climate change – that if you exceed 40 percent total deforested area in the Amazon, then you have a tipping point. About 60 to 70 percent of the Amazon forest would turn into a dry savanna, especially in the southern and northern Amazon, areas that now border savannas. Only the western Amazon near the Andes, which is very rainy, the forest will still be there. So that's one tipping point – 40 percent deforested area. Then we look at what climate change might do. We concluded that if the temperature in the Amazon increases up to 4 degrees Celsius (7 degrees Fahrenheit), this will mean a hydrological cycle change with less rain and a longer dry season. It's the same

mechanism – savannization. So if you put all the perspectives together – deforestation, global warming, increased vulnerability to forest fires – we conclude that with the current rate of global warming, if we exceed 20 to 25 percent deforestation, then we reach the tipping point and 50 to 60 percent of the Amazon forest would become a savanna. That's why we are making this warning – today we already have 15 to 17 percent total deforestation in the Amazon. So at the current rates of deforestation, we are 20 to 30 years off from reaching this tipping point."

2. "Rains will be more concentrated in the rainy season, a typical savanna climate level: six months of rain, six months of drought, and much hotter temperatures. In Central and South American savannas, maximum temperatures may easily reach 40 degrees centigrade (104 degrees F). But maximum temperatures in a forest like the Amazon are 34 degrees centigrade (93 degrees F). Forests have this cooling effect. And our calculations and many other studies show that the rainfall in and over these forests will decline between 20 and 25 percent. This will have a tremendous impact on all river hydrology, aquatic ecology. There will be less stream flow. And we have studied what might be the remote impacts in South America. We found that a lot of that moisture travels south of the Amazon, parallel to the Andes. And that flow of moisture feeds a lot of the rain in southern Brazil, Paraguay, Uruguay, and parts of Argentina. And in many of these calculations and simulations, there will be a reduction of about 15 to 20 percent in the rainfall over that area I mentioned."

3. "Many studies have looked at how strong the Amazon is as a carbon sink. The rates of removal of carbon dioxide from the atmosphere in the Amazon vary between 1 billion and 2 billion tons a year. Two billion tons is 5 percent of all carbon dioxide from human activities. On the other hand, because of deforestation and fires, the Amazon is a source of 500 million to 700 million tons of carbon a year. So if the deforestation continues, all that area is not acting as a carbon sink anymore. So in the next 20 to 30 years, the Amazon will become only a source of carbon.

"It can be reversed, but we really have to put a lot of hope in the global agribusiness markets and also the global mining companies, because there is a lot of illegal mining. "About 10 percent of deforestation comes from that infrastructure and mining. But the critical thing is beef and soy. Beef is No. 1, soy is No. 2, and illegal timber is No. 3."

Additional Teaching Documents at https://alansinger.net:
- The Putumayo, the Devil's Paradise
- Sir Roger Casement's Report
- Preserving the Amazon: A Shared Moral Imperative

19 Capitalism vs. the Climate

In 1947, the *Bulletin of the Atomic Scientists* created a Doomsday Clock to symbolize how close humanity was to apocalyptic self-destruction. The Doomsday Clock was originally set at seven minutes to midnight and was advanced five minutes closer in 1953 when the United States and the U.S.S.R. began testing hydrogen bombs. In 2020, the Doomsday Clock was set at 100 seconds to midnight because of a triple threat to civilization, nuclear weapons, the COVID-19 pandemic, and the failure to address climate change.

The January 2021 *Bulletin of the Atomic Scientists* explained climate changes role in the 100-second warning:

> Governments have also failed to sufficiently address climate change. A pandemic-related economic slowdown temporarily reduced the carbon dioxide emissions that cause global warming. But over the coming decade fossil fuel use needs to decline precipitously if the worst effects of climate change are to be avoided. Instead, fossil fuel development and production are projected to increase. Atmospheric greenhouse gas concentrations hit a record high in 2020, one of the two warmest years on record. The massive wildfires and catastrophic cyclones of 2020 are illustrations of the major devastation that will only increase if governments do not significantly and quickly amplify their efforts to bring greenhouse gas emissions essentially to zero.
>
> (Mecklin, 2021: 2–3)

International cooperation is definitely required to address the climate crisis. Initial efforts were made with the Kyoto Protocol (1997) and the Paris Climate Agreement (2015) and with monitoring reports from the United Nations Intergovernmental Panel on Climate Change. But despite these efforts, as noted in *Bulletin of the Atomic Scientists*, "atmospheric greenhouse gas concentrations" continue to increase, and this is despite a global economic slowdown caused by the COVID-19 pandemic. While more effective international cooperation is necessary to combat the worse impacts of climate change, it may not be sufficient. The problem may require changing the globalized economic system itself – capitalism.

DOI: 10.4324/9781003200864-19

In *This Changes Everything: Capitalism vs. the Climate* (2014), Naomi Klein's principal argument is that that the impending climate catastrophe cannot be resolved in a global economy dominated by neoliberal or laissez-faire free market economic theory because capitalism is fundamentally hostile to the regulation and cooperation necessary to address climate change. She quotes Venezuelan political scientist Edgardo Lander: "The total failure of climate negotiation serves to highlight the extent to which we now live in a postdemocratic society. The interests of financial capital and the oil industry are much more important than the democratic will of people around the world. In the global neoliberal society profit is more important than life" (363).

Naomi Klein, a Canadian author, filmmaker, and climate change activist, is on the Board of Directors of the environmental group 350.org. Following the election of Donald Trump in 2016, she called for international economic sanctions on the United States if the Trump Administration refused to abide by the terms of the Paris Climate Agreement. She was also critical of what she considered inadequate climate measures by the Obama Administration. Klein argues the global economy is "born of the central fiction . . . that nature is limitless, that we will always be able to find more of what we need" (Klein, 2009, 2011, 2017).

350.org demands that the world "accelerate the transition to a new, just clean energy economy"; "Stop and ban all oil, coal and gas projects"; and "Cut off the social license and financing for fossil fuel companies." They call this policy "divest, desponsor and defund" (350.org).

Capitalism is an economic system based on private ownership of a society's means of production and distribution, its land, buildings, factories, marketplaces, and banks, even intangible ideas. Commercial capitalism has its roots in the European early modern period with the expansion of trade through networks like the Hanseatic League in the Baltic Sea and financial centers like the Medici in Florence and the Dutch city-states. Trade vastly expanded with the Columbian Exchange in the 16th century, the trans-Atlantic slave trade, the production and sale of slave-produced commodities, and colonial empires. Management of the trans-Atlantic slave trade and control over slave-produced commodities led to the development of stock markets, insurance instruments, and limited liability corporations. Capital accumulation, wealth, invested in infrastructure, and technologies led to capitalist industrialization, the Industrial Revolution, in the mid-18th century, which led to a drive for control over resources and markets and fueled European Imperialism. Since World War II, finance capitalism has dominated world economies and promoted globalization using investment and debt to control corporations and countries. In all three stages of capitalism, commercial, industrial and financial, private enterprise either worked with political power or controlled political power to maximize the power and wealth of dominant social classes. Klein argues that the system of production and distribution under the control of private individuals and corporations whose goal is maximization of profits and domination over markets, something she calls extractivism, is antithetical to environmental protection and the reversal of climate change (185).

"Laissez-faire" is a 19th century French term that basically means "leave it alone." In classical economics, it means government should not intervene in the economy through regulation, laws that favor particular industries or groups, or excess taxation on wealth. These ideas were revived in the second half of the 20th century when they became known as neoliberalism. Neoliberal economic theory promotes a high-consumption, carbon-hungry system and encourages mega-corporate mergers, trade agreements hostile to environmental and labor regulations, global financial hypermobility, and obscene levels of profit and economic inequality. The outsized power of major corporations manipulates and undermines the democratic process so fossil fuel companies are able to demand public subsidies and treat the air, land, and water as a "waste dump" (Klein, 2014: 70).

According to Klein, the villain in global warming is not greenhouse gasses but industrial and finance capitalism. Klein believes the path to correcting the ecological balance requires a transformation of a failed economic system and building something radically better. During the 2020 presidential campaign, Bernie Sanders and Congressional Representative Alexandria Ocasio-Cortez were leading advocates for a Green New Deal, rebuilding the American economy with climate-friendly policies, although neither discussed abandoning capitalism. Klein endorses the idea of a Green New Deal and believes it is compatible with a new form of capitalism. Rather than toss out capitalism, it needs to "shift to a dramatically more humane economic model" (Klein, 2019: 33). The current model benefits the wealthy, is indifferent to life, exploits workers, and decimates the planet, placing the entire planet at risk.

Fossil fuel companies were not big donors to Donald Trump's 2016 presidential campaign, but they made massive donations to his inaugural festivities to make up for their late support. Chevron, Exxon, BP, and Citgo Petroleum each donated at least $500,000. Other larger donors to the Trump inauguration were private equity firms with major investments in oil, gas, and coal. This continued in 2020 when fossil fuel companies became major contributors to Trump's reelection campaign. Robert Murray, a coal magnate with ties to Donald Trump's 2016 campaign that pledged to revive the coal industry, hosted a fundraising dinner for the 2020 campaign that raised an estimated $2.5 million. Another big Trump fundraiser is Texas lobbyist Jeff Miller. Miller raised about $1 million for the Trump Victory Committee in the second quarter of 2020 (Lavelle, 2017; Stone, 2020; Mandel, 2019).

Capitalists and defenders of the current system, including former President Trump and most of the Republican Party, believe that the kind of regulation demanded by the Green New Deal would hobble economies and argue that unregulated or minimally regulated capitalism will spur technological innovation that will solve the climate problem. Many are climate deniers who claim that the situation is not as dire as portrayed by scientists. Others deny capitalism is the problem and point to state-managed economies like China that continue to pollute and third world non-industrial countries like India and Indonesia that are increasingly contributing to pollution (Gardner, 2019).

Klein responds that the addiction of modern capitalism to maximized profit and growth is digging the Earth deeper into irreversible climate catastrophe. She claims the only way to rein in climate change is to rein in corporate power over the economy and politics, which also means rebuilding local economies and reclaiming democracy in the United States. She fears that in democracies where government policy is virtually dictated by corporate lobbyists and major donors, giant polluters win while the people and the planet die. According to Klein, "Any attempt to rise to the climate challenge will be fruitless unless it is understood as part of a much broader battle of worldviews. Our economic system and our planetary system are now at war" (Klein, 2014: 21).

This Changes Everything: Capitalism vs. The Climate is divided into three sections. The first section details how the environmental movement has been derailed by corporate promotion of climate denial. Exxon has known since the 1970s about the causes of climate change and the dangers climate disruption poses. In 1978, an internal memo by Exxon's Products Research Division warned that human-caused emissions could raise global temperatures and result in serious consequences. Between 1979 and 1983, representatives of ten major fossil fuel companies, including Exxon, met regularly as part of a task force to discuss the science and implications of climate change. Exxon's response was to cut funding for climate research, and in 1989 Exxon and other fossil fuel companies organized a Global Climate Coalition to oppose mandatory reductions in carbon emissions, claiming "The role of greenhouse gases in climate change is not well understood." In 1992, Exxon became a member of the Koch Industries American Legislative Exchange Council (ALEC), which actively undermines action on climate change at the federal and state levels (Curry, n.d.; Hall, 2015).

ALEC is the political arm of Koch Industries. Koch Industries is involved in the extraction, refining, and distribution of petroleum through its network of pipelines. It is the largest non-Canadian producer of oil from Canadian tar sands and is the second largest privately held company in the United States. Koch opposes limits on greenhouse gasses, low carbon fuel standards, efforts to turn tar sands into fossil fuels, and government regulation of industry.

In July 2019, the Competitive Enterprise Institute (CEI), a free-market research organization that disputes climate change, organized a fund-raising gala in Washington, DC. According to the CEI, "The claim that 97% of climate scientists believe humans are the primary cause of global warming is simply false." CEI supports work disputing the science of climate change and the think tank has played an outsized role influencing the Trump Administration (Root, Freidman, and Tabuchi, 2019; O'Neil, 2019).

It is no surprise that the gala's sponsors included the Charles Koch Institute and the American Fuel and Petrochemical Manufacturers. What was surprising is that the list of included major corporations like Google, Microsoft, and Amazon; these companies are pledged to support the Paris Climate

Agreement. A spokesperson for Amazon told *The New York Times* that Amazon "may not agree with all of the positions of each organization" but believed that its $15,000 contribution to the event "will help advance policy objectives aligned with our interests." In a statement defending its participation in the gala published in the journal *Mother Jones*, Microsoft responded, "Our commitment to sustainability is not altered or affected by our membership or sponsorship of an organization" (Mencimer, 2019).

The second section of the book discusses what Naomi Klein calls the "magical thinking" of those who propose technical fixes for climate change. She argues that technological fixes like dimming the rays of the sun with sulphate-spraying helium balloons bring many risks because scientists do not know enough about the Earth system to be able to re-engineer it safely. Klein expects madcap schemes will be attempted when abrupt climate change gets seriously under way (Klein, 2014: 187, 268).

In the third section, Klein discusses social movements that are springing up to address climate change and also challenge capitalist neoliberal control over politics and the economy. Klein believes the divestment movement against Big Carbon, such as the one promoted by 350.org, is gathering force. She doesn't think it will bankrupt the mega-corporations, but it can reveal unethical practices and triggered debate about the values that should underlie a healthy economy and political system and prohibit some of their more extreme practices. Klein emphasizes that she is against extreme or disaster capitalism, extractivism, not capitalism itself, and believes that the current economic system can be fixed in ways that will protect the environment.

Critics charge that Klein ignores environmental devastation by non-capitalist economic systems such as China and the easiest way to eliminate the burden on the Earth's finite resources, which is to address overpopulation. While population growth is slowing in economically advanced societies, it continues unabated in developing countries. If population growth is the problem, not capitalism, climate change will not be reversed until population declines, no matter the economic system (Gray, 2014). However, waiting for population growth to abate is not a viable proposal since the world's population is not expected to peak until the start of the 21st century (United Nations, 2019). To say that China is as bad or not worse than the United State at fossil fuel emissions also doesn't address the immediate problem. From the left, Klein has been accused of failing to provide a systemic critique of capitalism as a system and of advocating for small-scale and localized alternatives that model possibility but are unlikely to bring about broader social change. It is a strategy to refocus capitalism rather than topple it (Smith and Foster, 2017; Kahle, 2015).

I agree with Klein that climate devastation and the impending catastrophe are not just related to carbon-based industrialization but are a direct result of classical, unregulated, or loosely regulated capitalism and that governments are too closely tied to the worst pollution offenders. In the United States, Republican administrations since Reagan in the 1980s have systematically eviscerated regulation and directly and indirectly subsidized the fossil fuel industry in the name of productivity and prosperity. However, industry has fled the United States and income inequality has increased at the same time that Republican beneficiaries have made record profits. This system of corporate influence over politics was officially sanctioned when the Supreme Court, dominated by Republican Party appointees, in Citizens United ruled that corporate donations to political campaigns could not be restricted because it violated their first amendment freedom of speech, which is funny, because I have never heard a company speak (Lau, 2019).

My problem with Klein's arguments is that I am not convinced that capitalism can be reformed, for two reasons. First, the enormous political power that money buys. Major corporations like the tech giants pour money into the coffers of both major parties to maintain influence no matter who wins, so both parties remain committed to their agenda, though to different degrees (Dorsch, 2020). The Democratic Party at least accepts that climate threats are real and regulation to protect air, land, and water is necessary. My second disagreement is related to the nature of capitalism itself. Because its driving engine is competition for resources, markets, and short-term profits, companies have little reason to protect the environment, in fact protecting the environment is viewed as an unnecessary expenditure. Corporations, competing for market shares, are also driven to overproduce, which means they are continually trying to spur consumption, which increases demand, production, and environmental destruction in an ever-expanding spiral.

Paul Krugman, Nobel Prize winner economist and *New York Times* columnist, who believes the "very scale and complexity of the situation requires a market-based solution" acknowledges that "There is no reason to assume that free markets will deliver an outcome that we consider fair or just." Krugman advocates for more vigorous government intervention in the economy including taxes on fossil fuel emissions but also acknowledges that the legislative "prospects for climate action do not look promising" given the enormous political influence of the fossil fuel industry (Krugman, 2010: 34).

In January 2021, *The New York Times* reported that a number of major corporations were presenting themselves to the public as environmental champions, including the investment house BlackRock, agricultural giant Cargill, Levi Strauss, Costco, Netflix, Google, and Microsoft. Yet while they had all proclaimed climate emission goals, some for 30 years down the line, details were not made public about how they would achieve their targets. According to Alberto Carrillo Pineda, a founder of Science Based Targets, "You can look at a company's website and see their sustainability report and it will look great, but then when you look at what is behind it, you'll see there is not a lot of substance behind those commitments or the commitments are not comprehensive enough" (Eavis and Krauss, 2021: B1).

The argument that skyrocketing population feeds environmental devastation has merit. The answer to that is social planning and higher standards of living, which brought down population growth in Western societies, but social planning and higher standards of living are not the goals of capitalism.

Market Solutions

According to the World Bank, at the start of 2021, 64 countries or national sub-divisions had instituted or planned to institute some form of carbon pricing as a capitalist market-based solution to climate change. The two most common programs were taxes on excess fossil fuel emissions or cap-and-trade programs that permit heavy offenders to purchase credits from non-polluters, keeping the overall balance of CO_2 entering the atmosphere under control or capped. At the time, Canada, Mexico, and most of western Europe had committed to carbon pricing but not the United States. However, some states, including California, Oregon, Washington, Pennsylvania, Massachusetts, and Virginia, either had a policy in place or one was scheduled for implementation.—World Bank Carbon Pricing Dashboard

Teaching Documents

(A) Climate Talk Versus Climate Walk

What's Really Behind Corporate Promises on Climate Change?
By Peter Eavis and Clifford Krauss, *The New York Times*, Feb. 23, 2021, B1
Source:www.nytimes.com/2021/02/22/business/energy-environment/corporations-climate-change.html

Questions

1. Why are major corporations presenting themselves as climate champions?
2. Alberto Carrillo Pineda skeptical about their commit to addressing climate change?
3. What is your car's carbon footprint? Check it out at www.carboncounter.com/#!/explore.

For the past several years, BlackRock, the giant investment firm, has cast itself as a champion of the transition to clean energy. Last month [January 2021], Laurence D. Fink, BlackRock's chief executive, wrote that the coronavirus pandemic had 'driven us to confront the global threat of climate change more forcefully,' and the company said it wants businesses it invests in to remove as much carbon dioxide from the environment as they emit by 2050 at the latest.

But crucial details were missing from that widely read pledge, including what proportion of the companies BlackRock invests in will be zero-emission businesses in 2050. Setting such a goal and earlier targets would demonstrate the seriousness of the company's commitment and could force all sorts of industries to step up their efforts. On Saturday, in response to questions from The New York Times, a BlackRock spokesman said for the first time that the company's 'ambition' was to have 'net zero emissions across our entire assets under management by 2050.' As the biggest companies strive to trumpet their environmental activism, the need to match words with deeds is becoming increasingly important. Household names like Costco and Netflix have not provided emissions reduction targets despite saying they want to reduce their impact on climate change. Others, like the agricultural giant Cargill and the clothing company Levi Strauss, have made commitments but have struggled to cut emissions. Technology companies like Google and Microsoft, which run power-hungry data centers, have slashed emissions, but even they are finding that the technology often doesn't yet exist to carry out their 'moonshot' objectives. 'You can look at a company's website and see their sustainability report and it will look great,' said Alberto Carrillo Pineda, a founder of Science Based Targets, a global initiative to assess corporate plans to reduce emissions. 'But then when you look at what is behind it, you'll see there is not a lot of substance behind those commitments or the commitments are not comprehensive enough.'

(B) Economists Debate Approaches to Environmentalism and Climate Change

Richard Stroup is president of the Political Economy Research Institute and a visiting professor of economics at North Carolina State University. Stroup argues for market-based solutions to environmental issues. Paul Krugman is a *New York Times* columnist and winner of the 2008 Nobel Memorial Prize in Economic Science. Krugman believes in a mixed market and governmental response. Jeff Sparrow, a columnist for the British newspaper *The Guardian*, advocates for a socialist approach as part of broader societal reorganization.

Questions

1. What proposal does each economist offer to combat the impact of climate change?
2. Which position do you find most convincing? Why?

Richard Stroup on Free-Market Environmentalism

Source: www.econlib.org/library/Enc/FreeMarketEnvironmentalism.html

1. "Free-market environmentalism emphasizes markets as a solution to environmental problems. Proponents argue that free markets can be more successful than government – and have been more successful historically

– in solving many environmental problems. . . . Growing evidence indicates that governments often fail to control pollution or to provide public goods at reasonable cost. Furthermore, the private sector is often more responsive than government to environmental demands."

2. "For markets to work in the environmental field, as in any other, rights to each important resource must be clearly defined, easily defended against invasion, and divestible (transferable) by owners on terms agreeable to buyer and seller. . . . When rights to resources are defined and easily defended against invasion, all individuals or corporations, whether potential polluters or potential victims, have an incentive to avoid pollution problems. When air or water pollution damages a privately owned asset, the owner whose wealth is threatened will gain by seeing – in court if necessary – that the threat is abated."

3. "Liability for pollution is a powerful motivator when a factory or other potentially polluting asset is privately owned. The case of the Love Canal, a notorious waste dump, illustrates this point. As long as Hooker Chemical Company owned the Love Canal waste site, it was designed, maintained, and operated (in the late 1940s and 1950s) in a way that met even the Environmental Protection Agency standards of 1980. The corporation wanted to avoid any damaging leaks, for which it would have to pay. Only when the waste site was taken over by local government . . . was the site mistreated in ways that led to chemical leakage."

4. "Because the owner's wealth depends on good stewardship, even a short-sighted owner has the incentive to act as if he or she cares about the future usefulness of the resource. This is true even if an asset is owned by a corporation. Corporate officers may be concerned mainly about the short term, but . . . even they have to care about the future. If current actions are known to cause future problems, or if a current investment promises future benefits, the stock price rises or falls to reflect the change. . . . This ability and incentive to engage in farsighted behavior is lacking in the political sector."

5. "Property rights tend to evolve as technology, preferences, and prices provide added incentives and new technical options. Early in American history, property rights in cattle seemed impossible to establish and enforce on the Great Plains. But the growing value of such rights led to the use of mounted cowboys to protect herds and, eventually, barbed wire to fence the range. . . . Advances in technology may yet allow the establishment of enforceable rights to schools of whales in the oceans, migratory birds in the air, and . . . even the presence of an atmosphere that clearly does not promote damaging climate change. Such is the hope of free-market environmentalism."

Paul Krugman presents a practical Keynesian approach to addressing climate change

Source:www.nytimes.com/2010/04/11/magazine/11Economy-t.
html

1. "There is no reason to assume that free markets will deliver an outcome that we consider fair or just. . . . But the logic of basic economics says that we should try to achieve social goals through "aftermarket" interventions. That is, we should let markets do their job, making efficient use of the nation's resources, then utilize taxes and transfers to help those whom the market passes by."

2. "One way to deal with negative externalities is to make rules that prohibit or at least limit behavior that imposes especially high costs on others. That's what we did in the first major wave of environmental legislation in the early 1970s: cars were required to meet emission standards for the chemicals that cause smog, factories were required to limit the volume of effluent they dumped into waterways. . . . But while the direct regulation of activities that cause pollution makes sense in some cases, it is seriously defective in others, because it does not offer any scope for flexibility and creativity. Consider the biggest environmental issue of the 1980s – acid rain. Emissions of sulfur dioxide from power plants, it turned out, tend to combine with water downwind and produce flora- and wildlife-destroying sulfuric acid. . . . Imposing a tough standard on all plants was problematic, because retrofitting some older plants would have been extremely expensive. By regulating only new plants, however, the government passed up the opportunity to achieve fairly cheap pollution control at plants that were, in fact, easy to retrofit."

3. "What has caught on instead is . . . a system of tradable emissions permits, a/k/a cap and trade. In this model, a limited number of licenses to emit a specified pollutant, like sulfur dioxide, are issued. A business that wants to create more pollution than it is licensed for can go out and buy additional licenses from other parties; a firm that has more licenses than it intends to use can sell its surplus. This gives everyone an incentive to reduce pollution, because buyers would not have to acquire as many licenses if they can cut back on their emissions, and sellers can unload more licenses if they do the same."

4. "The very scale and complexity of the situation requires a market-based solution, whether cap and trade or an emissions tax. After all, greenhouse gases are a direct or indirect byproduct of almost everything produced in a modern economy, from the houses we live in to the cars we drive. Reducing emissions of those gases will require getting people to change their behavior in many different ways, some of them impossible to identify until we have a much better grasp of green technology. . . . The only way to get people to change their behavior appropriately is to put a price on emissions so this cost in turn gets incorporated into everything else in a way that reflects ultimate environmental impacts."

Jeff Sparrow argues socialism is the answer to the climate catastrophe

Source:www.theguardian.com/commentisfree/2018/oct/24/is-socialism-the-answer-to-the-climate-catastrophe

1. "In a rational society, an imminent threat to planetary civilisation would constitute rather a big deal. In our society, not so much. . . . It's increasingly difficult to ignore the profound incompatibility between serious climate action and an economic system predicated upon the pursuit of profit in a ceaseless war of all against all. When our leaders privilege GDP over the environment, they do so because the economy must expand year after year, decade after decade – or else the world tips into crisis. We're locked into a frankly carcinogenic model, predicated on unplanned but relentless growth, conducted with complete indifference to long-term consequences."

2. "Marx defined capitalism as a regime of universal commodity production, in which goods were created not because they were useful but because they could be exchanged. It was, he said, a society in which things ruled people, rather than the other way around . . . From a human perspective, the argument 'if we don't mine the stuff someone else will' is obscene. Within the logic of capitalism it makes perfect sense, since amoral self-interest underpins the entire system. As a result, the measures for which the IPCC pleads – massive changes in transportation, industry, cities and land use as part of a thoroughgoing transition away from fossil energy – become almost impossible to implement."

3. "Many mainstream pundits can avoid acknowledging the profound failure of capitalism. . . . But for millennials, who can expect to see the IPCC's predictions unfold, what does liberal centrism – or indeed capitalism as a whole – offer? It's not just that the scientific consensus warns of the ruination of the planet. It's also that capitalist business-as-usual means the steady destruction of social welfare, a preposterously unaffordable housing sector, an increasingly sinister security state and a political culture dominated by race-baiting charlatans."

4. "There's every reason to expect various versions of socialism to play an increasingly important role in discussions about the climate catastrophe. After all, they all begin from the conviction that humans can and should collectively decide how they interact with the world. Let's remember that, for the overwhelming majority of recorded history, people created most objects to use, rather than exchange. In the age of nanotechnology and AIs and the Mars rover, do we truly think ourselves incapable of similar agency today? If we accept democratic control over politics, why shouldn't we exercise the same scrutiny over economics, so that production becomes subordinate to human need rather than global markets? Isn't that the obvious (perhaps only) solution to the environmental crisis – the conscious direction of resources away from fossil energy and towards planetary repair?"

5. "Marx and Engels . . . suggested that fundamental social divisions would culminate either in 'a revolutionary reconstitution of society at large' or in what they called 'the common ruin of the contending classes.' The IPCC's given us a terrifying image of what ruination could involve. It's well past time we started talking about the alternative."

Additional Teaching Documents at https://alansinger.net:
- Can Finance Capitalism Reverse Climate Change?
- Climate Change and Monetary Policy
- Managing Climate Risk in the U.S. Financial System
- International Monetary Fund Staff: Finding the Right Policy Mix to Safeguard our Climate

20 Climate Activism

In April 2021, there were two reasons to be excited about the possibility the world would finally vigorously respond to the climate emergency: 350.org and over 140 other national and international organizations and affiliates sponsored a virtual three-day Global Just Recovery Gathering. There were over 200 workshops offered by climate activists from around the world. Featured speakers included Dr. Vandana Shiva, India, Naomi Klein, Canada, Vanessa Nakate, Uganda, Greta Thunberg, Sweden, and Bill McKibben, United States (Singer, 2021). Two weeks later, the Biden Administration sponsored a virtual global Leaders Summit on Climate that was addressed by among others the Secretary-General of the United Nations; the presidents of China, France, and Russia; Pope Francis; the prime minister of India; the mayor of Paris; an indigenous leader from Brazil; and American business leaders (United States State Department, n.d.).

I participated in a workshop at the Global Just Recovery Gathering with three high school teachers who work with the Hofstra University teacher education program, Adeola Tella-Williams from Uniondale and Pablo Muriel and Dennis Morales from the Bronx, who discussed their thoughts on student activism and climate change, and a New York City high school student, Sadia Weiner from Brooklyn. Sadia read a climate change manifesto she wrote as a high school project that is included as a Teaching Document at the end of this chapter. Adeola, Dennis, and Pablo teach in minority communities, Dennis and Pablo in one of the poorest areas of New York City and Adeola in the suburbs. All three raised that their students had many issues in their lives that seem more pressing and immediate to them than climate change. As teachers, they try to help their students draw connections between issues like poverty, racism, unemployment, COVID-19, and the disproportionate climate vulnerability of minority communities that face greater risk of flooding and are often located in urban heat islands where rising temperatures negatively affect the health of residents.

The conference was organized in Europe so our session, scheduled for 9:15 AM was at 4:15 AM in New York City. We taped our presentation the night before, so I was the only one who had to appear "live" on Zoom. When I signed in, I was apprehensive that no one would show, but to my amazement,

DOI: 10.4324/9781003200864-20

99 people participated, and 95 stayed for the entire one hour and 45-minute workshop. Teachers and students from across the globe joined with a sense of urgency about addressing climate change. It was invigorating. A high school student from Australia wanted tips on how to organize classmates who were non-engaged despite fires raging in southwestern Australia and threats to the Great Barrier Reef; a student from Brazil had similar questions about defending the Amazon; and a group of students from the John Dewey School for Children in Manila, Philippines, presented a video that they made as a school project to mobilize support for climate action in their country (*Climate Change: An Inevitable Crisis*, www.youtube.com/watch?v=nbWRtNCOIb0). A young woman from Spain recounted that she was penalized by a teacher for missing class when she attended a climate change conference. In the chat, teachers from some Asian countries explained that they had less freedom to speak out or protest than in the United States and Europe. People were concerned that an impending climate catastrophe seemed to be ignored in the press and by the 24-hour cable news cycle, pushed off because of the overwhelming attention to the COVID-19 pandemic.

The Philippines students had a Climate and Nature Group at their school, and we discussed setting up student climate action clubs, web pages, and social media networks to educate students and mobilize them for action. One of activities of the Philippine Climate and Nature Group was visiting students in younger grades to teach them about the climate emergency. Adeola added that her own seven- and nine-year-old children formed a community cleanup action to emphasize the importance of caring about the environment. A teacher from Taiwan explained how her students were educating their parents and other adults to raise awareness about the threat of climate change.

In a follow-up email, a teacher-education student from Austria who plans to be a history and English teacher wrote that in her country teachers are expected to always be "neutral" and examine "both sides." I wrote back that as a high school teacher and university professor my commitment is not to false neutrality but to informed and respectful dialogue. One of my goals is to teach students how their ideas can be presented responsibly, supported by evidence, and held open to critical examination. Active citizenship in a democratic society requires critical thinking and the constant questioning of authority. If teachers are afraid to express their views in open discussion, how will students learn how to participate as active citizens in a democratic society? I agree it is important to introduce multiple perspectives and "sides" into discussion. But the question is not whether human-caused climate change is happening – it is – but how humanity should respond.

As a teacher, I constantly ask myself, "Does offering my opinion open up discussion or close it down?" If I find that my views are silencing students, I try to tone down my comments or keep them to myself. However, I find expressing my views usually leads to a broader exchange of ideas, and they are necessary to counter the propaganda students are often exposed to from the government and the media.

Prior to the conference, organizers distributed an open letter that laid out basic principles for revitalizing the climate change movement following a year-long virtual hibernation caused by the COVID-19 pandemic. The letter called for a global recovery effort focused on the needs of people and communities, not corporations and shareholders; the creation of millions of decent jobs that would both help in the recovery from the COVID-19 pandemic and in transitioning to a zero-carbon future; and recognition that the struggle to rebuild after the COVID-19 pandemic and to avert climate catastrophe required solidarity across borders and communities and a commitment to human rights, civil liberties, and democracy.

A reversal, a halt, or even just a slowing of climate change will depend on global civic action by masses of ordinary people to save local communities and human civilization from destructive forces unleashed by unfettered capitalist exploitation of the environment for the past 250 years. It is a difficult struggle, but there is no alternative. As one of the more popular signs on display at climate change rallies reads, "There is no Planet B."

Governments and international organizations have laid out goals, but as of this writing, they have not been effective. In February 2021, the United Nations Framework Convention on Climate Change released an updated report on global climate emissions. To anyone concerned with climate change, the report was frightening. António Guterres, Secretary General of the United Nations, declared the report a "red alert." Aubrey Webson, chair of the Alliance of Small Island States, countries most threatened by rising ocean levels, charged, "This report confirms the shocking lack of urgency, and genuine action" by the world's largest greenhouse gas polluters. "We are flirting dangerously with the 1.5° Celsius warming limit that the world agreed we need to stay within." Only 25% of the almost 200 parties to the 2015 Paris Climate Agreement submitted updated climate targets for 2030, and their combined plans would only reduce carbon dioxide emissions by about less than 1%, significantly less than promised in the Paris agreement. Among the world's larger emitters, Australia, Brazil and Russia, refused to update their fossil fuel projections, and Mexico actually lowered its climate commitment. The world's two biggest greenhouse gas emitters, China and the United States, had not submitted updated emission targets at all, although they promised to do so in the near future (Sengupta, 2021a: A9). A hopeful sign, however, was an agreement by China and the United States, following President Joseph Biden's call for a global leadership conference in conjunction with Earth Day 2021, to work together with "urgency" to achieve promised fossil fuel reduction targets (Colman, 2021).

At the April Leaders Summit on Climate, President Biden announced that the United States would reduce greenhouse gas emissions by between 50% and 52% below 2005 levels by 2030, but he did not offer a roadmap for achieving the goal. Japan, Canada, Great Britain, and the European Union made similar promises but also without offering any concrete plans. In his opening remarks at the Summit, President Xi Jinping pledged that China would "strictly limit increasing coal consumption" and cap its fossil fuel emissions by 2030, but that would mean an increase in CO_2 released into the atmosphere for almost a decade, probably enough to counter global reduction efforts. Russia, Mexico, Australia, India, and Indonesia, all major atmospheric polluters, made no new pledges to cut down on their use of coal, oil, or gas. I was also disappointed that none of the "leaders" involved in the Global Just Recovery Gathering were included in the program (Friedman, Sengupta, and Davenport, 2021: A1; Sengupta, 2021c: A1).

But there definitely were some hopeful signs to come out of the Summit. As a follow up to the meeting, the U.S. Environmental Protection Administration (EPA) announced it would sharply limit the use of hydrofluorocarbons in domestic and commercial air conditioners. Hydrofluorocarbons, which are created in chemical laboratories and are not found in nature, are thousands of times more powerful greenhouse gases than carbon dioxide. The EPA estimated that these new restrictions would eliminate the equivalent of about three years' worth of fossil fuel emissions by 2050 (Friedman, 2021b: A15). At the same time, in an effort to stop methane gas leakage, the United States reversed the Trump Administration's loosening of environmental protection regulations on oil and gas production. A study in the journal *Environmental Research Letters* estimated that cutting methane leakage from natural gas drilling sites could slow the rate of global warming by as much as 30% (Wire and Phillips, 2021; Ocko et al., 2021).

The United Nations climate report was highly technical and conciliatory rather accusing, noting that "Many Parties have strengthened their commitment to reducing or limiting GHG emissions by 2025 and/or 2030, demonstrating increased ambition to address climate change" (4). But it should have been accusatory. "Considering implementation of only the unconditional elements of the NDCs [nationally determined contribution], the estimates suggest the possibility of the Parties' emissions peaking before 2030" (5). "Peaking before 2030" means that rather than reducing their carbon footprint five years after signing the Paris Climate Agreement, the reporting countries were still increasing greenhouse gas emissions (United Nations, 2021).

There are at least four difficult problems preventing implementation of greenhouse gas limits proposed in the 1992 United Nations Framework, the 1997 Kyoto Protocol, the 2015 Paris Climate Agreement, and the 2021 Leaders Summit on Climate:

- Powerful transnational capitalist corporations, including the major fossil fuel companies, have enormous political clout within countries and the ability to shift their operations across national borders to avoid regulation.
- There are sharp disagreements between countries over limiting carbon dioxide emissions by economically developing nations that are trying to expand their industrial base and had small carbon footprints in the past.

- While climate change is a global phenomenon, we live in a world organized into sovereign nation-states, so all international agreements on
  carbon dioxide emission targets are non-binding.
- National debt and endemic poverty, exacerbated by the COVID-19 pandemic, prevent a number of countries from addressing climate change
  at all.

The United Nations Framework Convention on Climate Change was signed
by over 150 countries after a June 1992 Earth Summit in Rio de Janeiro; it was
a very hopeful sign for climate activism. At the Summit, a decision was made
by negotiators to establish three different categories or Annexes for participating countries. Thirty-eight economically developed countries were placed in
Annex 1. These countries were supposed to adopt national policies that would
limit national greenhouse gas emissions to 1990 emissions levels. A sub-group
of Annex I, countries with the most advanced economies, were labeled as
Annex II. They were expected to provide financial aid to developing poorer
countries, Annex III, so these countries could comply with fossil fuel emission
targets. In 1995, in an agreement known as the Berlin Mandate, countries
with less-developed economies, including China and India, both already major
atmospheric polluters, were exempted from setting carbon dioxide emission
limits. Because the Berlin Mandate was included as part of the 1997 Kyoto
Protocol, the United States Senate overwhelmingly rejected the agreement by
a vote of 95 to 0. By 2005, the United States had officially withdrew from the
Kyoto Protocol, an international agreement it had helped to write during the
previous presidential administration. Canada, which was developing new fossil
fuel resources in its northwest, followed in 2011 (Schiermeier, 2012).

Misgivings by the United States about the Berlin Mandate and Kyoto
Protocol proved to be justified. Although economically advanced nations,
especially countries that were part of the European Union, did lower their
greenhouse gas emissions, a shift in heavy industry to Asian nations where
factories and power plants were burning coal led to a disappointing overall
increase in carbon dioxide concentration in the atmosphere between 1990 and
2010. By 2010, India was producing 5.4% of global greenhouse gas emissions
and China 22% compared with 13% by the United States. India and China's
percentages of global greenhouse gas emissions continued increasing after
2010, reaching 7% (India) and 27% (China) in 2017 (UNEP, 2012: 1, 15–16;
FEU-US, 2019: i).

The United States has had a similar rocky relationship with the 2015 Paris
Climate Agreement. Although the agreement no longer exempted developing
economies from instituting greenhouse gas reduction plans, it permitted each
country to establish its own targets and had no legally binding authority. President Barack Obama described the newly negotiated pact as providing for "A
world that is safer and more secure, more prosperous, and more free" and used
the executive authority of the presidency to have the United States became a
party to the agreement. However, because the Paris Climate Agreement was

never submitted to the Senate as a formal treaty, Donald Trump, who campaigned for office as climate change skeptic, was able to summarily withdraw the United States from the agreement. After Joseph Biden was inaugurated as president in January 2021, one of his first actions was issuing an Executive Order to officially rejoin (UNCC, 2021; Denchack, 2021).

Unfortunately, a review of the Paris Climate Agreement by a team of international scientists affiliated with the Intergovernmental Panel on Climate Change found that "commitments to reduce emissions between 2020 and 2030 shows that almost 75 percent of the climate pledges are partially or totally insufficient to contribute to reducing GHG [green house gas] emissions by 50 percent by 2030, and some of the pledges are unlikely to be achieved." Seventy percent of the greenhouse gas reduction pledges by 128 countries were deemed insufficient. Even the pledges that were found to be acceptable were questionable because they were voluntary and "technicalities, loopholes and conditions continue to postpone decisive climate action." Both India and China were expected to increase carbon dioxide emissions as their economies continued to grow at least until 2030 (FEU-US, 2019).

While some countries continue to escalate their level of pollution, other countries lack the ability to respond to climate change. According to assessments by the World Bank and the International Monetary Fund, dozens of countries scattered around the globe have such enormous national debt problems that they are unable to take any effective climate change action. Creditor banks and countries are being pressured to provide debt relief but that may not come on acceptable terms. In the past, China, the world's largest creditor, has forced debt-ridden countries to sign over control of their natural resources and infrastructure. Some countries, like Belize and Guatemala in Central America and Zambia, Central African Republic, and Mozambique in Africa have few resources or infrastructure projects they can post as collateral (Sengupta, 2021b: B1; Servant, 2019).

The same week as the April 2021 Global Just Recovery Gathering, the U.S. National Oceanic and Atmospheric Administration announced that despite a worldwide economic slowdown caused by the COVID-19 pandemic, carbon dioxide levels in the atmosphere reached 412.5 parts per million, a higher level than at anytime in the previous 3.6 million years. About 3.6 million years ago, carbon dioxide concentrations in the atmosphere ranged between 380 to 450 parts per million. As a result, the average global temperature was 3.8°C (7°F) warmer than in the modern pre-industrial period, and sea level was about 80 feet higher than today. There has also been a significant increase in methane in the atmosphere. While methane is rarer than carbon dioxide, it is also a much more potent greenhouse gas. Increased levels of methane were attributed to an expansion of livestock ranching in areas that had once been rainforest and the decomposition of organic material, some of which had been trapped in melting permafrost (NOAA, 2021c).

A question for me and other teachers who are climate activists is "How do we best prepare a new generation to be active participants in preserving and transforming democratic societies, promoting international cooperation, and generating solutions that meet the needs of people across the globe?" Two thinkers that point the way are the American philosopher John Dewy and the Brazilian educator Paulo Freire. The key to Dewey's approach to education is recognizing that there is an "organic connection between education and experience" (Dewey, 1938/1963: 25). As an advocate for democracy, Dewey understood that students must experience democracy. By extension, active citizenship in a democratic society means that students must personally experience the power of activism to understand its implications to the fullest. Freire argued that progressive educational and social goals can only be achieved when students explicitly critique social injustice and actively organize to challenge oppression. The educational ideas of Dewey and Freire on experiential learning and critical analysis virtually mandate teacher support for student climate activism (Freire, 2004: 105, 144, 2000: 28; Muriel and Singer, 2020: 9).

Pairing civics education with student activism, including climate activism, is supported by the National Council for the Social Studies (NCSS) in its College, Career, and Civic Life (C3) Framework and social studies standards in a number of states. According to the NCSS, "students need the intellectual power to recognize societal problems; ask good questions and develop robust investigations into them; consider possible solutions and consequences; separate evidence-based claims from parochial opinions; and communicate and act upon what they learn," (6) and mastery of civic ideals is measured by their ability to "Apply a range of deliberative and democratic strategies and procedures to make decisions and take action in their classrooms, schools, and out-of-school civic contexts" (62). For students to "act upon what they learn" in "out-of-school civic contexts" is a call for informed student political action (Muriel and Singer, 2020: 47–48).

Student activism and its ability to contribute to the transformation of society is not a new phenomenon. Two of the most powerful examples are the role played by secondary school students in the campaign against apartheid in South Africa and in the African American Civil Rights movement in the United States. International student unrest in the 1960s and anti–Vietnam War and Black Power protests in the United States energized students who challenged conditions in their schools and communities.

The week before the September 20, 2019, global student strike for climate action, New York City Mayor Bill de Blasio tweeted: "New York City stands with our young people. They're our conscience. We support the 9/20 #ClimateStrike." The city's Department of Education (DOE) decided that students with parental permission to attend the September 20th climate action rally would receive an excused absence.

Then two days before the rally, de Blasio and the DOE backtracked. They announced that participation in the rally could not be part of a formal school trip and that teachers could not accompany their students. Unfortunately, the reversal came too soon before the rally to effectively challenge the decision. Tens of thousands of students ended up attending the New York City rally, a defining teachable moment, except their teachers were not with them to teach. De Blasio and the DOE were wrong. Civics education means teachers must be out there marching with their students modeling what it means to be active citizens promoting democracy and social justice and struggling to reverse the devastating climate change that threatens human civilization.

Where Do We Go From Here?

In sermons delivered at the Ebenezer Baptist Church in Atlanta, Georgia, on mental and spiritual slavery, the Reverend Dr. Martin Luther King Jr. questioned the desire to be "well-adjusted." King argued there are "some things in our world to which men of good will must be maladjusted. . . . Human salvation lies in the hands of the creatively maladjusted" (Carson et al., 2007: 327).

In many of the 2021 Global Just Recovery Gathering sessions, participants discussed strategies and tactics for expanding the environmentalist movement through education, action, and creative maladjustment. Strategies are incremental goals like stopping a particle fossil fuel company from expanding production or pushing for passage of specific legislation like the Green New Deal. Tactics are the on-the-ground activities climate activists pursue to achieve their goals.

Some of the "maladjusted" tactics discussed were very creative, while I think others such as provoking mass arrests could be counterproductive. Gatherings like the Global Just Recovery and mass marches build spirit and attract media attention. Community campaigns such as park cleanups and recycling initiatives connect the global with the local. Climate activists can lobby politicians with petition drives and at constituent meetings. People can put pressure on fossil fuel companies and the banks that loan them money by becoming stockholders and introducing climate change resolutions at stockholder meetings. Letters to the editor and Facebook posts draw attention to climate actions and expose polluters. Websites have been set up launching mock campaigns demanding justice for billionaires and food bailouts for the World Bank and circulating pretend corporate reports confessing to their environmental misdeeds. Activists can use social media for wide distribution of agit-prop climate change action videos. To promote concern for the environment, Australian activists ran an online election in which people voted for their favorite bird and learned about threats to their survival.

In one session, Greenpeace activist Kumi Naidoo described using a flotilla of boats to temporarily interrupt Arctic exploration. Employing a similar strategy, Pacific Climate Warriors used canoes and other small craft to block an Australian coal port. Eileen Flanagan of the Earth Climate Action Team described a pray-in at PNC stockholders meeting. When climate activists were told that protest signs would be illegal, they came wearing protest t-shirts.

One idea always put forward is provoking police or even military intervention. At Standing Rock oil pipeline protests in 2016 Lakota Sioux community activists and supporters put their bodies on the line to block construction, leading to arrests, convictions, and prison sentences. Flooding local jails was a successful tactic during the 1950s and 1960s African American civil rights movement in the segregated American South, but it required mobilizing large numbers of people who were willing to be arrested and stay in jail for pro-longed periods of time if necessary. I have been involved in social justice and antiwar movements since the 1960s, and I am not happy with symbolic arrest as a tactic. It drains the campaign of activists and resources, can alienate poten-tial allies, and shifts focus from the original goal to getting activists out of jail.

On the other hand, mobile protests that push up to the law enforcement line and then draw back can generate media attention. One tactic that was discussed and seems promising is pressuring fossil fuel companies to cut back exploration and production by "flooding" a company's gas stations. Teams of activists drive up to all the pumps, and instead of fueling, they park. They stay until ordered to move by police and then drive to another station and repeat the performance. Media should be advised of the protest schedule in advance so television reporters are on the scene and have time to set up.

Sadia Weiner, the high school junior who was part of our session on student activism, made an important point about failing to become a climate activist; it makes you complicit. Sadia told about skipping over a news article about annual flooding in the Florida Keys because

> Florida was so far away from New York, and flooding wasn't the worst thing that could happen if these people were used to it happening every year. Best not to think about it when it's miles away in the future. So, I went on with my daily life, going to school and my other activities not realizing that that is the problem. We are all deniers of climate change, even if we don't want to admit it.

Sadia's point is supported by what happened in metropolitan New York City after Hurricane Sandy in 2012. Immediately after disaster struck, there were calls to protect the city's infrastructure with massive storm surge barriers modeled on the Dutch "Maeslantkering." They have computer-controlled gates that close when the port of Rotterdam is threatened by flooding from the North Sea. While floodgates were eventually installed at entrances to tunnels in New York City, as memory faded, plans were dropped for a more extensive system to protect the harbor (Kimmelman, 2017; Pagano, 2017; Hickman, 2020). Meanwhile, vulnerable communities on Long Island and on the New Jersey coast ignored climate warnings and rebuilt (Cheng and Pavlovic, 2018).

A continuing theme at the Global Just Recovery Gathering was recogniz-ing that climate activism is a social justice movement that must build alliances with groups involved in pro-immigrant, anti-racist, pro-democracy, and eco-nomic reorganization campaigns. The climate crisis that confronts many of the poorest and least developed regions of the world is a product of capitalist industrialization that primarily benefited Europe and North America and a residue of centuries of Western colonialism and imperialism. It is made worse by a combination of neglect and continuing economic disadvantage. As with the COVID-19 pandemic, the people who are most endangered by climate change today and in the near future are the same people who have long been victimized by exploitation in the past.

On August 16, 1967, in Atlanta, Georgia, at the annual meeting of the Southern Christian Leadership Conference, The Reverend Martin Luther King, Jr. asked, "Where do we go from here?" It is a question people concerned with social justice are still asking today. Important civil rights legislation was passed in 1964 and 1965, but racism and inequality continued to shape conditions in the United States. King argued: "The movement must address itself to the question of restructuring the whole of American society" including the "capitalistic economy." For King, questioning the whole society" meant "ultimately coming to see that the problem of racism, the problem of exploitation, and the problem of war are all tied together. These are the triple evils that are interrelated" (King, 1967). Dr. King, of course, was speaking before there was widespread public awareness of the possibility of catastrophic climate change. If Dr. King were speaking today, I am sure he would refer to four evils, the "Four Horsemen of the Apocalypse," racism, capitalist exploitation, war, and the climate crisis.

As a historian, I study social movements and have written about the abolitionist campaign to end slavery in the United States (Singer, 2008, 2018). Social movements by their nature are broad umbrella coalitions that include people who disagree about other issues. The abolitionist movement was made up of whites and Blacks who opposed slavery but not necessarily for the same reasons. There were religious abolitionists who considered slavery fundamentally immoral but did not necessarily believe God created all people as equals, Free-Soilers who wanted to keep slavery out of the western territories but accepted racist stereotypes about Blacks, Northerners who did not like the disproportionate influence slavery gave the South in the national government, and free Blacks and a few whites who believed in racial equality with full citizenship rights for African Americans.

When slavery ended after the Civil War with passage of the 13th Amendment to the Constitution, the abolitionist coalition split. For most whites, its goal had been achieved. The split meant diminished political support for Black civil rights, the triumph of Jim Crow segregation and domestic terrorists in the American South, and the continuing legacy of institutional racism in the United States (Hannah-Jones, 2019). The break-up of the abolitionist coalition was repeated in the mid-1960s when many whites abandoned the African American civil rights movement once *de jure* segregation was no longer legal. In both cases, the first battle, the battle to change the law, was won, but the second battle, the battle to create a more just society and improve the condition of people's lives, was lost.

At this writing, the campaign to address climate change is similarly a broad, but internally segmented, coalition. More companies (including fossil fuel companies), financial institutions, politicians, and governments acknowledge that the science documenting climate change is uncontestable and cannot be ignored. But some coalition members are betting on technological solutions that will bail out current economic arrangements or are hoping to just slow the pace of climate change until societies can adapt and they can figure out opportunities to profit from new circumstances. Neither position views climate change as an impending global catastrophe that requires fundamental economic and political reorganization on a global scale.

The first battle for the climate change movement is to slow, halt, and possibly reverse carbon emissions to minimize the damage and displacement of climate change. Winning this battle requires both national and international mobilization and the cooperation of private industry. Getting companies, financial institutions, and governments to accept the imminent threat of climate change is a necessary first step but only a first step.

So far, proposals for a Green New Deal in the United States, proposals that have also been introduced in a number of European countries, remain general principles, not specific programs, and details will have to be negotiated. In the United States, legislation calls for "achieving net-zero greenhouse gas emissions; establishing millions of high-wage jobs and ensuring economic security for all; investing in infrastructure and industry; securing clean air and water, climate and community resiliency, healthy food, access to nature, and a sustainable environment for all; and promoting justice and equality" (Congressional Research Service, 2019). A proposed THRIVE Act (Transform, Heal, and Renew by Investing in a Vibrant Economy) includes many of the goals of the Green New Deal but also lacks specifics. It is not clear how these goals will be accomplished or whether a bill like this can pass a politically polarized U.S. Congress (www.congress.gov/bill/116th-congress/house-resolution/109; Friedman, 2019; Beitsch, 2020; Greenberg, 2021).

There are historic precedents for winning a battle like the one facing climate change activists. Before and during World War II, all of the parties involved transformed their economies and mobilized to promote the war effort. Women were brought into the factories to replace men who were called up as soldiers, and production shifted to military equipment and munitions. After the war, as tension increased between the United States and the Soviet Union, economies were kept on a war footing, and the United States, through the Marshall Plan, rebuilt the economies of Western Europe as part of a strategy to secure potential allies. Climate change activists, including Naomi Klein and Angelica Navarro Llanos, Bolivia's representative to a United Nations climate-change conference, are calling for a Marshall Plan for the Earth (Klein, 2014: 5).

The second climate change battle will even be more difficult to win and requires convincing billions of people, as well as at least some people currently in power, that the answer to the climate crisis will mean abandoning a global economic system of virtually unrestrained production for profit because that system not only produces tremendous inequality, but it is also responsible for the climate crisis that threatens human civilization. Adding to the difficulty of winning this second battle are the wealth and power of global capital and its supporters and because state-managed economies like China also have a very poor environmental record.

Capitalism is an enormously powerful historical force that remade human societies across the globe, producing enormous wealth, incredible technological achievements, and better living and working conditions for many but also devastating wars, imperialist exploitation, and environmental ruin. At least symbolically, it is the reincarnation of the Hindu God/Goddess Shiva, the God/Goddess of creation and destruction.

Capitalism is responsible for the growth of powerful nation-states and partnered with them to manage populations and protect private productive property from challenges by the dispossessed. Nation-states permitted capitalist industrialization to use the commons, public land, air and water, as their refuse dumps without consequence. However trans-national capitalism, now unleashed from national loyalties and regulatory restraints, supported by computerization and instantaneous communication, and utilizing mature financial and distribution networks, has a new dynamic with the potential to undermine the nation-state system that still organizes, governs, taxes, represents, and provides services for most of the people of the world. One possibility is that at least some major nation-states will reject destructive capitalism and embrace more fundamental political and economic change.

In the *Communist Manifesto* and other writings, Karl Marx predicted that capitalism, by mobilizing working-class opposition and organization, contained within itself the seeds of its own destruction, a prediction that has failed to materialize. It is possible that capitalism's exploitation of the environment, by producing cataclysmic climate change, and its rupture from the nation-state system may in the end succumb to a different dialectic. The question for me is whether climate mobilization will be able to prevent human society from going down with a sinking capitalist ship (Marx and Engels, 1848).

There is a message of hope in the study of earlier social movements. For over two decades, the abolitionist movement in the United States was stalled, internally divided, and on the margins of society. But as the United States expanded westward in the 1850s, the issue of slavery became a major dividing point in the nation, leading to civil war and the ultimate end of slavery. Similarly, the modern African American civil rights movement had gains and disappointments between the 1930s and the early 1960s when a national recounting led to the expansion of the movement and passage of major new laws.

The 2021 Global Just Recovery Gathering demonstrated that the infrastructure for a global climate change movement is in place. There have been advances and setbacks in campaigns to slow, halt, and reverse global warming and the burning of fossil fuels, but as climate threats increase, it is a movement that will, that has to, succeed. Our house is on fire. There is no Planet B.

Teaching Documents

A. Wake-Up Call on the Environment – A French Student Manifesto (English Version)

This is only the first section of the manifesto. The entire manifesto is included with the online teaching documents (https://manifeste.pour-un-reveil-ecologique.org/en).

Questions

1. According to the manifesto, why do "societies keep moving towards an environmental and human disaster"?
2. Why do the people who issued the manifesto believe "this bleak picture is not inevitable"?
3. Do you agree with the French student manifesto? Why or why not?

"We, students and recent graduates, make the following observation: despite the many calls from the scientific community, despite the irreversible changes already observed around the world, our societies keep moving towards an environmental and human disaster. Need we remind you? Each of the last three decades has been warmer than the previous one and all the other decades since 1850. In 2018, even the Scandinavian countries have been affected by forest fires of an unusual magnitude. 60% of species in Europe already reached an 'unfavorable' conservation status and one third of humanity is affected by desertification. As a result of an increase in the frequency of extreme weather events, of declining crop yields and rising disease levels, more than 100 million people are likely to fall below the poverty line by 2030. By 2050, 250 million people are expected to migrate due to extreme events related to climate change. The list is long so let's try to be concise. On a global scale we have crossed at least 4 of the 9 'planetary boundaries' beyond which the environmental degradation risks causing brutal changes of the Earth system, compromising further human activity. Do we have to wait until all boundaries are crossed? Of course, at COP21 in 2015, 195 countries, supported by groups of experts and NGOs, agreed on the need to contain global warming under 2°C to avoid climate change going beyond any control- but they agreed on that in a non-binding agreement. Given the gap between the promises made by the States and the emission reductions that are in fact required, we can only notice with frustration that the actions taken so far are fundamentally insufficient to face the challenges ahead of us.

"Insufficient because they do not address the root causes of the problem. The way our modern societies function, the fact that they are based on GDP growth goals without taking into account the issues linked to this indicator -that is the main reason why environmental and social challenges arise. Our economic systems have not yet comprehended the fact that resources are not infinite and that some of the damage caused to the environment is irreversible. They are unaware of their own fragility in the face of environmental disruption and widening inequalities. Our political systems are constrained by the expression of opposing interests, often very different from the public interest. As such they fail to offer a long term vision or to make ambitious decisions which would effectively renew our societies. Finally, our ideological systems value individualistic behaviors that pursue profit and unlimited consumption; behaviors that drive us to label as 'normal' ways of life that are yet far from being sustainable. We confine ourselves to ignorance at best, to denial at worst.

"We, the signatories of this manifesto, are nevertheless convinced that this bleak picture is not inevitable. Two options are open today. Either we stick to the destructive path our societies have chosen, being content with the commitment of only a minority of people, waiting to sift through its aftermath. Or we take our future into our own hands and collectively decide to anticipate and incorporate social and environmental ambitions into our daily lives and jobs; take action to change direction and avoid stalemate."

B. Sadia's Climate Manifesto

When she wrote this manifesto, Sadia Weiner was a 16-year old junior at Millennium Brooklyn High School in New York City. For one of her classes, she had to read a non-fiction book and present the main themes as a five-minute videoed speech. Sadia chose Naomi Klein's *This Changes Everything: Capitalism vs. The Climate* (2014). Sadia presented her climate manifesto at the 2021 Global Just Recovery Gathering.

Questions

1. Who does Sadia hold largely responsible for climate change?
2. Why does Sadia believe we are all complicit with climate denial?
3. Why does Sadia open and close with the quote from a speech by President John F. Kennedy?
4. Do you agree with Sadia? Why or why not?

"'Every inhabitant of this planet must contemplate the day when this planet may no longer be habitable.' This declaration was made by President John F. Kennedy in his 1961 speech in front of the United Nations. He, of course, was talking about nuclear war and the threat it could pose to humanity, however, his words can be associated with another, fast-approaching and categorical crisis.

"Climate Change, climate change, climate change.

"You've heard this phrase hundreds of times, but most don't understand the true gravity of the situation that humanity has gotten itself into. I have been a climate activist since middle school. I participate in demonstrations, and changed my diet and consumption patterns. The book, This Changes

Everything by Naomi Klein has strengthened my commitment to challenging abuses that threaten the planet. Government climate policies didn't start being passed until the 1990s, just a few decades ago. Former President Trump rolled back over 100 environmental guidelines, paving the way for capitalist corporations to think of new ways of plundering the earth and making life worse for communities that are already in need. According to the 2019 IPCC Special Report on Global Warming, many regions of the Earth, usually ones with higher amounts of disadvantaged groups of people, have warmed by over 1.5 degrees Celsius. If this number reaches 2 degrees Celsius, severe heat waves, droughts, and other natural disasters will frequent many areas of the world including cities with millions of people in them. A system that favors free-market capitalism and deregulation has allowed corporations to profit off of environmentally hostile trade agreements and an absence of labor restrictions. The climate denialism of capitalist corporations and government officials are to blame for the crisis. Their ads and commercials claim they are looking out for the environment and encourage middle class people to make sacrifices such as riding their bike to work or recycling, acts that will do little to change what is happening to the planet. Meanwhile corporations continue to extract resources and use fossil fuels. No need to practice what they preach when they are making money.

"Capitalist corporations need to be held accountable for their actions, and that's not going to happen overnight. They have been extracting and burning fossil fuels, releasing carbon dioxide into the atmosphere and they have been funding climate denial campaigns. People, especially the younger generations like us need to fully grasp what we are facing. Unless you want to leave a disaster-ravaged world for your children, it is up to us to solve the problems that our parents, grandparents, and great-grandparents created. We will be unable to change the minds of corporations, if we don't even truly believe what is already approaching. Our generation must pressure the federal and state governments to strongly regulate corporate practices to reduce greenhouse gas emissions.

"A few years ago, I came across an article about the Florida Keys. Every single year, this area is flooded by tides from rising sea levels due to the changing climate. I felt angry about what is happening to the environment and our world, and how so many people can choose to believe that it isn't. I closed out the article and continued scrolling through others on completely different topics. Florida was so far away from New York, and flooding wasn't the worst thing that could happen if these people were used to it happening every year. Best not to think about it when it's miles away in the future. So I went on with my daily life, going to school and my other activities not realizing that that is the problem. We are all deniers of climate change, even if we don't want to admit it.

"Assuming that eventually new technologies will magically find a fix to the problem, or that it's not up to us to try and make change, is just not going to cut it. Yes, buying food in paper packages rather than plastic containers may feel as if it is doing something, but in actuality, the real change needs to be made at the top. Corporations need to be held accountable for their actions. So how are we going to do this? Before you make a purchase, find out where the materials come from. Were exploitative practices of extraction used? If so, consider not buying from that company and research others that use similar practices. Next, if you have a social media platform or website, consider publicizing these corporations with problematic practices, and convince others to stop buying from them. In these media campaigns, refer to certain strategic decision makers such as politicians for people to contact. Lastly, encourage people to share your media campaigns so that word can spread about this issue, and how corporations are only making things worse by taking advantage of the environment and people in need just so that they can make a profit. As president Kennedy reminded us, "Every inhabitant of this planet must contemplate the day when this planet may no longer be habitable." Greta Thunberg argues our house is on fire. Our generation must put out that fire."

C. Will You Become a Climate Activist?

This is a modified version of a questionnaire developed at the University of Nevada (Las Vegas) to measure student willingness to become climate activists. Students were asked to respond to questions using scales ranging from "strongly disagree" to "strongly agree" and "not willing" to "willing enough to convince others."

Source: Sinatra, G.M., Kardash, C.M., Taasoobshirazi, G. & Lombardi, D. 2012. "Promoting attitude change and expressed willingness to take action toward climate change in college students. *Instructional Science 40*, 1–17 (2012).

1. Do you strongly disagree, disagree, are unsure, agree, or strongly agree with these statements?

---

1. Scientific evidence points to a warming trend in global climate.
2. The release of carbon dioxide from human activity plays a central role in raising the average surface temperature of the earth.
3. The Greenland ice cap is melting faster than had previously been thought.
4. Human activity is responsible for the continuing rise in average global temperature.
5. The likelihood that emissions are the main cause of the observed warming trend of the last 50 years is between 90 and 99%.
6. Claims about global climate change are mostly propaganda.
7. Natural phenomena such as solar variations combined with volcanic activity are the real cause of the warming effect.

8. Humans have very little effect on climate temperature.
9. An increase in carbon dioxide is directly related to an increase in global temperature.
10. It is arrogant to assume that humans can influence climate temperature.

2. Are you willing to take personal action?

1. Stop using plastic grocery bags and use recycled bags instead.
2. Stop buying bottled water because the manufacturing process for plastic water bottles is carbon intensive.
3. Trade in a SUV or small truck for a smaller car.
4. Pay more money to buy a hybrid car.
5. Use energy efficient fluorescent bulbs.
6. Pay a gas surcharge to support greenhouse gas reduction.
7. Raise the temperature on my home air conditioning system.
8. Require car manufacturers to raise the number of miles per gallon their cars get.
9. Reduce the numbers of hours a week using electronic devices (computer, cell phone, TV, etc.).
10. Support legislation reducing the legal speed limit to 55 miles per hour to reduce energy consumption.

3. Are you willing to take political action?

1. Petition local elected officials to adopt climate friendly laws.
2. Leaflet at school and in your community to promote pro-climate behavior.
3. Use social media to educate about climate change and alternatives.
4. Attend pro-climate rallies and marches.
5. Engage in civil disobedience to attract media attention, alert government officials, or interrupt destructive climate practices.

Additional Teaching Documents at https://alansinger.net:
- China's Teenage Climate Activist
- Federal Appeals Court Refuses to Act to Defend the Planet
- Excerpts from the Dissenting Opinion by Judge Josephine Staton

Appendix I
Annotated Bibliography

Books to Consider

Alley, Richard. 2000. *The Two-Mile Time Machine: Ice Cores, Abrupt Climate Change, and Our Future* (Princeton University Press). Alley is a geologist and Professor of Geosciences at Pennsylvania State University. This book explains how climatologists use Greenland ice cores to construct global climate history.

Berners-Lee, Mike. 2019. *There Is No Planet B: A Handbook for the Make or Break Years* (Cambridge University Press). Lee, an expert on the carbon footprint of ordinary things, is a professor at the Institute for Social Futures at Lancaster University in the United Kingdom.

Diamond, Jared. 2004. *Collapse: How Societies Choose to Fail or Succeed* (Viking). Diamond is a professor of geography at UCLA. In this book, he explains how environmental damage and climate change led to the demise of societies in the past and argues that in many cases, the situation was made worse by bad choices.

Fagan, Brian. 2000. *The Little Ice Age: How Climate Made History 1300–1850* (Basic Books). Fagan is Emeritus Professor of Anthropology at the University of California, Santa Barbara. In this book, he explores the impact of a 500-year-long cold snap that shaped world history and step the stage for the development of the modern world.

Gates, Bill. 2021. *How to Avoid a Climate Disaster: The Solutions We Have and the Breakthroughs We Need* (Random House). Gates, the cofounder of Microsoft, proposes a practical plan to achieve zero greenhouse gas emissions and avoid a climate catastrophe.

Gore, Al. 2006. *An Inconvenient Truth: The Planetary Emergency of Global Warming and What We Can Do About It* (Rodale). Gore is a former vice president of the United States. The book is based on a lecture tour by Gore and intended as a companion to the Academy Award–winning film. In 2009, Gore published a sequel, *Our Choice: A Plan to Solve the Climate Crisis* (Rodale).

Ghosh, Amitav. 2016. *The Great Derangement: Climate Change and the Unthinkable* (Penguin). Ghosh is a novelist and climate activist from

India. This non-fiction book points to the origins of the climate catastrophe in the history of European colonialism and imperialism.

Klein, Naomi. 2014. *This Changes Everything: Capitalism vs. the Climate* (Simon & Schuster). Klein is a Canadian journalist and climate activist. She argues that disaster capitalism has exacerbated the climate crises and must be, can be, reined in to reverse climate change. *On Fire: The (Burning) Case for a Green New Deal* (Simon & Schuster) is a 2019 collection of essays by Klein that calls for immediate action to defend the planet and oppose "climate barbarism."

Kolbert, Elizabeth. 2014. *The Sixth Extinction: An Unnatural History* (Henry Holt). Kolbert is an American science writer who reports on five mass extinction events in the Earth's history that were caused by natural phenomenon and a sixth extinction, now taking place, caused by human action. She is also the author of *Field Notes from a Catastrophe: Man, Nature, and Climate Change* (Bloomsbury, 2006) and *Under a White Sky: The Nature of the Future* (Crown, 2021), which explore proposed solutions to the climate crisis.

Krauss, Lawrence. 2021. *The Physics of Climate Change* (Post Hill Press). Krauss was a professor of physics at Case Western Reserve University. In this book, Krauss writes for a general audience about the science underlying our understanding of climate change.

Linden, Eugene. 2006. *Winds of Change: Climate, Weather, and the Destruction of Civilizations* (Simon & Schuster). Linden, a journalist who writes about environmental issues, explains devastating hurricanes such as Hurricane Katrina and their impact on communities by reviewing earlier climate history and the science behind climate change.

McKibben, Bill. 1989. *The End of Nature* (Anchor). McKidden is an American environmentalist and a leader of 350.org and a prolific author. This book is considered the first book on climate change written for a general audience.

Nakate, Vanessa. 2021. *A Bigger Picture: My Fight to Bring a New African Voice to the Climate Crisis* (Houghton Mifflin Harcourt). Nakate is a Fridays for the Future climate activist in Uganda and founded the Rise Up Climate Movement. Nakate discusses her experience as a young Ugandan woman whose community suffers the disproportionate consequences of the climate crisis.

Robinson, Mary. 2018. *Climate Justice: Hope, Resilience, and the Fight for a Sustainable Future* (Bloomsbury). Robinson is a former president of the Republic of Ireland. In this book, she highlights the role played by local women around the world in the struggle for a sustainable future.

Sobel, Adam. 2014. *Storm Surge: Hurricane Sandy, Our Changing Climate, and Extreme Weather of the Past and Future* (Harpers). Sobel is an atmospheric scientist at Columbia University's Lamont-Doherty Earth Observatory. In this book, he uses Hurricane Sandy, which devastated the East Coast of the United States in 2012, as a starting point to explain the forces emerging from global climate change.

Thunberg, Greta. 2019. *No One is Too Small to Make a Difference* (Penguin). As a teenager, Thunberg became the face of youth demands for climate action. This is a collection of speeches she delivered at different venues.

Weisman, Alan. 2007. *The World Without Us* (St. Martin's). Weisman, an American journalist, predicts what would happen as the Earth heals if humans disappeared.

Organizations (Some of the Larger International Groups)

350.org: A global network of climate activists founded in the United States. 350 refers to 350 parts per million, the safe concentration of carbon dioxide in the atmosphere. It supports grassroots campaigns opposing coal plants, mega-pipelines, and bank and government subsidies to the fossil fuel industry and lobbying for renewable energy solutions. It was active in campaigns against the Keystone XL and Dakota Access pipelines in the United States; pressuring insurance companies to stop insuring fossil fuel companies; against natural gas fracking in Brazil and Argentina; and for university, foundation, and church divestment from fossil fuel portfolios. The organization calls for a fast and just transition to 100% renewable energy for all.

Alliance for Climate Protection (The Climate Reality Project): Its focus is climate change education. It encourages government policies to limit greenhouse gas emissions and supports low-carbon power sources.

Climate Action Network (CAN): CAN has over 1,500 member organizations in 130 countries who are fighting the climate crisis. Member organizations have helped implement sustainable environmental solutions across the globe.

Environmental Defense Fund (EDF): EDF's leadership includes people prominent in a number of fields, including the financial sector. It supports researchers and activists.

Extinction Rebellion: Extinction Rebellion may be the most radical of climate change groups. Its members engage in dramatic non-violent direct action. Because governments and corporations have failed to address climate change, Extinction Rebellion proposes that they be replaced by independent Citizens' Assemblies that empower localities to achieve climate and ecological justice.

Fridays for the Future (FF): FFF started in August 2018 when Greta Thunberg and other Swedish youth sat in front their country's Parliament building for three weeks demanding climate action. FFF sponsors School Strike for Climate.

Friends of the Earth: Friends of the Earth International is a decentralized network of autonomous of environmental organizations. Climate justice is also economic justice and a defense of human rights.

Greenpeace: Greenpeace uses peaceful protest, creative communication, and interventions to expose global environmental problems. Greenpeace defends the natural world by investigating, exposing, and confronting environmental abuse.

Rainforest Action Network (RAN): RAN is committed to doing what is "necessary," as opposed to what is considered politically feasible, to protect rainforests as part of a broader campaign to protect the climate and human rights.

Sunrise Movement: The Sunrise Movement works through the political system in the United States to elect candidates who support of renewable energy and is a major advocate for a Green New Deal.

World Wildlife Fund (WWF): The WWF is a leading conservationist organization that works to protect the natural environment and endangered species.

Scientific and Governmental Groups that Focus on Climate Change

Bulletin of Atomic Scientists (https://thebulletin.org/climate-change/)
Center for Climate and Energy Solutions (C2ES) (www.c2es.org/about/)
Environmental Protection Administration (EPA) (www.epa.gov/climate-change)
IPCC (Intergovernmental Panel on Climate Change) (www.ipcc.ch/)
Lamont-Doherty Earth Observatory (www.ldeo.columbia.edu/)
NASA Global Climate Change (https://climate.nasa.gov/)
National Centers for Environmental Information (formerly NCDC) (www.ncdc.noaa.gov/)
NOAA (National Oceanic and Atmospheric Administration) (www.noaa.gov/categories/climate-change)
Science Moms (https://sciencemoms.com/)
Union of Concerned Scientists (www.ucsusa.org/climate)
United Nations Climate Change (https://unfccc.int/)
United Nations Environment Programme (www.unep.org/explore-topics/climate-change)
World Meteorological Organization (www.wmo.int/pages/index_en.html)

Appendix II
Resources for Teaching About Climate Change

In conjunction with Earth Day 2021 and the Biden Administration's Leaders Summit on Climate, *The New York Times* dedicated its Tuesday Science supplement to addressing questions about climate change. The supplement was written by Dr. Julia Rosen, a journalist with a PhD in geology who specializes in the study of Greenland and Antarctica ice cores. The supplement included a series of mini-articles with questions that can serve as lesson aims for an entire interdisciplinary high school unit.

The Science of Climate Change Explained: Facts, Evidence and Proof

Source: Rosen, J. 2021, April 20. "Explaining the science," *New York Times*: D2

1. How do we know climate change is really happening?
2. How much agreement is there among scientists about climate change?
3. Do we really only have 150 years of climate data? How is that enough to tell us about centuries of change?
4. How do we know climate change is caused by humans?
5. Since greenhouse gases occur naturally, how do we know they're causing Earth's temperature to rise?
6. Why should we be worried that the planet has warmed 2°F since the 1800s?
7. Is climate change a part of the planet's natural warming and cooling cycles?
8. How do we know global warming is not because of the sun or volcanoes?
9. How can winters and certain places be getting colder if the planet is warming?
10. Wildfires and bad weather have always happened. How do we know there's a connection to climate change?
11. How bad are the effects of climate change going to be?
12. What will it cost to do something about climate change, versus doing nothing?

Next Generation Science Standards

Sources: www.nextgenscience.org/; Gillis, J. 2013, April 10. "New Guidelines Call for Broad Changes in Science Education," *New York Times*, A15; Riddell, R. 2014, May 14. "Opposition to Next Generation Science Standards growing," *K-12 Dive*.

The Next Generation Science Standards (2013) were developed by a consortium of state Education Departments in conjunction with the National Science Teachers Association, the American Association for the Advancement of Science, the National Research Council and Achieve, an organization that collaborated on the development of national Mathematics and English Language standards. They are based on the "A Framework K – 12 Science Education" developed by the National Research Council. The standards introduce students on different grade levels to core ideas in different areas of study, science and engineering practices, and scientific concepts that cross discipline lines. There was some opposition to the standards because they include teaching about human-caused climate change and evolution.

According to the Next Generation Science Standards, by the end of fifth grade (or elementary school), students should understand that "If Earth's global mean temperature continues to rise, the lives of humans and other organisms will be affected in many different ways;" by the end of eighth grade (or middle school), students should understand that "Human activities, such as the release of greenhouse gases from burning fossil fuels, are major factors in the current rise in Earth's mean surface temperature (global warming). Reducing human vulnerability to whatever climate changes do occur depend on the understanding of climate science, engineering capabilities, and other kinds of knowledge, such as understanding of human behavior and on applying that knowledge wisely in decisions and activities;" and by the end of 12th grade (or high school), students should understand that "Global climate models are often used to understand the process of climate change because these changes are complex and can occur slowly over Earth's history. Though the magnitudes of humans' impacts are greater than they have ever been, so too are humans' abilities to model, predict, and manage current and future impacts. Through computer simulations and other studies, important discoveries are still being made about how the ocean, the atmosphere, and the biosphere interact and are modified in response to human activities, as well as to changes in human activities. Thus science and engineering will be essential both to understanding the possible impacts of global climate change and to informing decisions about how to slow its rate and consequences – for humanity as well as for the rest of the planet."

Social studies standards tend to be less specific about the impact of climate change. The National Council for the Social Studies College, Career, and Civic Life 3C Framework for Social Studies State Standards, a collaboration between major historical, social science, and educational organizations, makes recommendations for the teaching of social studies in elementary, middle, and high school and for the teaching of history, geography, civics, and economics. The study of climate change and its impact on human communities is part of its geography standard. Students should "evaluate the influence of long-term climate variability on human migration and settlement patterns, resource use, and land uses at local-to-global scales." Environmental concerns are also included in many state social studies standards as student examine of how people in traditional societies adapt to their environments and in final high school history units on contemporary issues.

Recommended Websites

Alliance for Climate Education (https://acespace.org/our-work/ #climate-education). This website focuses on youth activism.

Climate Change Live (https://climatechangelive.org/index.php?pid= 180). Lesson plans for Grades K-12 and links to other sites.

Morningside Center for Teaching Social Responsibility (www.morningside center.org/sites/default/files/2019-04/EarthDay2019Teachable MomentLessons.pdf). An online booklet developed in conjunction with Earth day 2019 has Teachable Moment lesson ideas across all grade levels.

National Center for Science Education (https://ncse.ngo/supporting-teachers/classroom-resources). Lesson plans on the scientific consensus, climate models, climate change in the past, local impacts, and climate solutions.

National Education Association (www.nea.org/professional-excellence/ student-engagement/tools-tips/climate-change-education-essential). Provides links to other websites.

National Public Radio (NPR; www.npr.org/2019/04/25/716359470/ eight-ways-to-teach-climate-change-in-almost-any-classroom). NPR has teaching recommendations and links to other sites.

NASA Global Climate Change (https://climate.nasa.gov/resources/ education). This website includes links to lesson plans prepared by the Jet Propulsion Lab that are aligned with the Next Generation Science Standards; NASA Wavelength, which provides instructional videos for different grade levels and subject areas; and for younger grades NASA has a Climate Kids page (https://climatekids.nasa.gov) with instructive videos.

National Oceanic and Atmospheric Administration (NOAA) Climate. gov (www.climate.gov/teaching). NOAA has a toolbox for teaching climate and energy with visuals, videos, and demonstrations.

PBS (https://ny.pbslearningmedia.org/collection/climlit/. PBS has lesson plans and videos promoting climate literacy that explore the greenhouse effect, global warming, and local climate impacts.

Stanford Earth (https://earth.stanford.edu/climate-change-ed/curriculum)

Teaching for Change (https://socialjusticebooks.org/booklists/environment). Booklists on environmental justice for elementary school, middle school, and high school students that include picture books for younger children.

Zinn Education Project (www.zinnedproject.org/campaigns/teach-climate-justice). "Teach Climate Justice" provides a number of lessons on its websites for different grade levels. They include Blockadia: Teaching How the Movement Against Fossil Fuels Is Changing the World; The Climate Crisis Trial: A Role Play on the Roots of Global Warming; Coal, Chocolate Chip Cookies, and Mountaintop Removal; Dirty Oil and Shovel-Ready Jobs: A Role Play on Tar Sands and the Keystone XL Pipeline; Meet Today's Climate Justice Activists: A Mixer on the People Saving the World; Mystery of the Three Scary Numbers: A Climate Change Teaching Activity; and From the New Deal to the Green New Deal: Stories of Crisis and Possibility.

References

350.org. "We are building a future that's just, prosperous, equitable and safe from the effects of the climate crisis," *350.org/about/*.

ACLED. 2021, January 15. *Armed conflict location & event data project.* https://acleddata.com/#/dashboard.

Ad Hoc Study Group on Carbon Dioxide and Climate. 1979, July 23–27. *Carbon dioxide and climate: A scientific assessment.* Washington, DC: National Academy of Sciences.

Ali, M. 2020, July 24. "Congressman John Lewis: A champion for civil rights and environmental justice," *The Hill.*

Allen, M. and Frame, D. 2007, October 26. "Call of the quest," *Science,* 318.

American Legislative Exchange Council, 2017. "ALEC energy principles."

American Lung Association. 2020. "State of the air: People at risk." www.stateoftheair.org/key-findings/people-at-risk.html.

Andreoni, M. and Londoño, E. 2021, April 22. "Antagonist of the Amazon wants billions to save it," *New York Times.*

Antonova, M. 2020, July 11. "Nearly 300 wildfires in Siberia amid record warm weather," *pays.org.*

Arango, T. and Baker, M. 2020, October 2. "What made this a record fire season? It started with lightning," *New York Times.*

Associated Press. 2012, October 30. "Superstorm Sandy puts NJ's Oyster Creek nuclear power plant on alert: NY's Indian point plant shut down." www.nj.com.

Ban, K. 2007, June 16. "A climate culprit in Darfur," *United Nations.*

Banerjee, N. 2017, December 22. "How big oil lost control of its climate misinformation machine," *Inside Climate News.*

Baum, F. 1900. *The wonderful wizard of Oz.* Chicago, IL: George M. Hill.

BBC. 2020, June 22. "Arctic circle sees 'highest-ever' recorded temperature," *BBC News.*

BBC News. 2020, May 21. "Amphan: Kolkata devastated as cyclone kills scores in India and Bangladesh," *BBC Asia.*

Beitsch, R. 2020, September 10. "Democrats push resolution to battle climate change, sluggish economy and racial injustice," *The Hill.*

Bell, A. and Streiber, W. 1999. *The coming global superstorm.* New York: Simon & Schuster.

Berlinger, J., Regan, H. and Rahim, Z. 2020. "May 20 Cyclone Amphan news," *CNN Asia.*

Berwyn, B. 2019, November 27. "Climate tipping points are closer than we think, Scientists warn," *Inside Climate News.*

Brandt, A. 2012, January. "Inventing conflicts of interest: A history of tobacco industry tactics," *American Journal of Public Health*, 102(1), 63–71.

Brodsky, R. 2020, September 14. "Conn. health officials warn of wound infections from LI Sound waters," *Newsday.*

Broecker, W. 1975, August 8. "Climatic change: Are we on the brink of a pronounced global warming?," *Science*, 189(4201), 460–463.

Broecker, W. 2010. *The great ocean conveyor.* Princeton, NJ: Princeton University Press.

Brooke, J. 2001, May 8. "Story of Viking colonies' icy 'Pompeii' unfolds from ancient Greenland farm," *New York Times.*

Brown, D., Brugger, H., Boyd, J. and Paal, P. 2012, November. "Accidental hypothermia," *The New England Journal of Medicine*, 367(20), 1930–1938.

Buis, A. 2020a, February 27. "Milankovitch (orbital) cycles and their role in Earth's climate," *NASA Global Climate Change.*

Buis, A. 2020b, February 27. "Why Milankovitch (orbital) cycles can't explain Earth's current warming," *NASA Global Climate Change.*

Bump, P. 2015, February 26. "Jim Inhofe's snowball has disproven climate change once and for all," *Washington Post.*

Burke, M. et al. 2009, November 23. "Warming increases the risk of civil war in Africa," *PNAS.*

Busby, M. 2018, August 3. "Europe's record temperature of 48C could be beaten this weekend," *The Guardian.*

Card, D., Mas, A. and Rothstein, J. 2008, February. "Tipping and the dynamics of segregation," The Quarterly Journal of Economics, 123(1), 177–218.

Carey, B. 2006, July 20. "Sahara Desert was once lush and populated," *LiveScience.*

Carlin, D. 2020, January 5. "A history of science change science and denialism," *History News Network.*

Carson, C., Carson, S., Englander, S., Jackson, T. and Smith, G., eds. 2007. *The papers of Martin Luther King, Jr. Volume VI: Advocate of the social gospel, September 1948–March 1963.* Berkeley, CA: University of California Press.

Cassino, D. 2016, May 4. "Fairleigh Dickinson University's public mind poll finds Trump supporters more conspiracy-minded than other republicans," Fairleigh Dickinson University.

Cato Institute. "Global warming." www.cato.org/research/global-warming.

Cave, D. 2021, March 23. "In Australia, devastating floods are part of the new normal," *New York Times.*

CDC. 2020a, March 11. "Mosquitoes," *Centers for Disease Control and Prevention.*
CDC. 2020b, June 3. "West Nile Virus," *Centers for Disease Control and Prevention.*
CDC. 2020c, November 20. "Anthrax," *Centers for Disease Control and Prevention.*
Center for Responsive Politics. n.d. "James M. Inhofe," *OpenSecrets.org.*

Cheng, P. and Pavlovic, K. 2018, June 13. "After rebuilding, Sandy homeowners now told by Long Island town to elevate," *NBC News 4.*

China Water Risk. 2013, July 11. "8 things you should know about water & semiconductors," *CWR.*

CIA. "Brazil," *The World Factbook.* www.cia.gov/the-world-factbook/countries/brazil/.

Climate Change Committee. n.d. "A natural climate cycle," *U.K. Climate Change Committee.*

Climate Principals. 2021. "Amazon protection plan." https://climateprincipals.org/amazon-plan/.

CNN. 2013, July 13. "Hurricane Sandy fast facts," *CNN Editorial Research.*

Cohen, P. 2014, March 15. "Geological history of Long Island," *Geohistories.*

Collins, G. 2017. "Iran's looming water bankruptcy," Center for Energy Studies, Rice University.

Collins, L. 2020, July 26. "Imagine Central Park as a rainforest," *New York Times.*

Collis, M. 2012. "The enslavement of Amazon natives during the rubber boom," *Iquitos Times.* http://www.iquitostimes.com/enslavement.htm.

Colman, Z. 2021, April 18. "U.S., China pledge to tackle climate change with 'urgency'," *Politico.*

Colpitts, T. et al. 2012, October. "West Nile Virus: Biology, transmission, and human infection," *Clinical Microbiology Reviews*, 25(4), 635–648.

Congressional Research Service. 2019, February 13. "S. J. Res. 8 (116th): A joint resolution recognizing the duty of the Federal Government to create a Green New Deal," Govtrack.us.

Connor, S. 2006, July 31. "Scientist publishes 'escape route' from global warming," *The Independent.*

Cook, B. et al. 2016, February 4. "Spatiotemporal drought variability in the Mediterranean over the last 900-years," *JGR Atmospheres*, 121(5), 2060–2074.

Cook, B. 2018, May 14. "Guest post: Climate change is already making droughts worse," *Carbon Brief.*

Cook, B., Miller, R. and Seager, R. 2008, May 4. "Did dust storms make the Dust Bowl drought worse?," Lamont-Doherty Earth Institute at Columbia University.

Cornwall, W. 2020, December 7. "'Godzilla' dust storm traced to shaky northern jet stream," *Science.*

Critchton, S. 2012, December 10. "Officials: Sandy destroys more than 2,000 LI homes," *Newsday.*

Crutzen, P.J. 2006. "Albedo enhancement by stratospheric sulfur injections: A contribution to resolve a policy dilemma?," *Climatic Change*, 77, 211.

Curry, R. n.d. "Exxon's climate denial history: A timeline," *Greenpeace.*

Cuvier, G. 1796/1998. "Memoir on the species of elephants, both living and fossil," in Rudwick, M., ed., *Georges Cuvier, Fossil Bones, and geological catastrophes.* Chicago, IL: University of Chicago Press, 18–24.

Daley, J. 2019, September 3. "Earth's orbital shifts may have triggered ancient global warming," *Scientific American.*

Davis, W. 1996. *One river: Explorations and discoveries in the Amazon rain forest.* New York: Simon & Schuster.

Davies, B. 2020, June 22. "Ice core basics," *AntarcticGlaciers.org.*

De Bolle, M. 2019, October. "The Amazon is a carbon bomb: How can Brazil and the world work together to avoid setting it off?" Peterson Institute for International Economics.

De Leon, C. and Schwartz, J. 2020, August 17. "Death Valley just recorded the hottest temperature on Earth," *New York Times.*

deMenocal, P. 2004, March. "African climate change and faunal evolution during the Pliocene-Pleistocene," *Earth and Planetary Science Letters*, 220(1–2), 3–24.

Denchack, M. 2021, February 19. "Paris climate agreement: Everything you need to know," NRDC.

Denchak, M. 2018, November 8. "Flint water crisis: Everything you need to know," NRDC.

Dennis, B., Mooney, C. and Kaplan, S. 2020, December 19. "The world's rich need to cut their carbon footprint by a factor of 30 to slow climate change, U.N. warns," *Washington Post*.

DeRoberts, N. 2019, June 24. "Columbia researchers provide new evidence on the reliability of climate modeling," Columbia University.

Dewar, H. and Sullivan, K. 1997, December 11. "Senate republicans call Kyoto Pact dead," *Washington Post*.

Dewey, J. 1938/1963. *Experience and education*. New York: Collier/Macmillan.

Di Liberto, T. 2020, October 16. "September 2020: Another record-setting month for global heat," NOAA.

Dodwell, D. 2020, April 4. "Relevant lessons from climate change and a global pandemic in the 19th century," *South China Morning Post*.

Dorsch, J. 2020, March 3. "Tech hedges its election donation bets," *EETAsia*.

Eavis, P. and Krauss, C. 2021, February 23. "What's really behind corporate promises on climate change?," *New York Times*.

Einhorn, C., Arréllaga, M., Migliozzi, B. and Reinhard, S. 2020, October 13. "The world's largest tropical wetland has become an inferno," *New York Times*.

Eisenhower, D. 1961, January 17. "President Dwight D. Eisenhower's farewell address." www.ourdocuments.gov.

Eldredge, N. and Gould, S. 1972. "Puncuated equilibria: An alternative phyletic gradualism," in Schopt, T., ed., *Models in paleobiology*. San Francisco CA: Freeman, 82–115.

Emmott, S. 2013, June 29. "Humans: The real threat to life on Earth," *The Guardian*.

Erdman, J. 2021, January 8. "America's most extreme weather cities 2020," *The Weather Channel*.

Ewing, J. and Boudette, N. 2021, April 24. "Chip shortage creates chaos for car makers," *New York Times*.

Fagan, B. 2000. *The little ice age: How climate made history, 1300–1850*. New York: Basic Books.

Falk, D. 1990, June. "Brain evolution in Homo: The 'radiator' theory," *Behavioral and Brain Sciences*, 1(2), 333–344.

Fausset, R., Rojas, R. and Fountain, H. 2020, September 16. "Emergency from climate change on two coasts," *New York Times*.

Fentress, E. and Fausset, R. 2021, March 13. "In Mississippi, failing water system is linked to a cascade of problems," *New York Times*.

Fernando, S., Wickremasinghe, R. and Wickremasinghe, R. 2012, April. "Climate change and Malaria: A complex relationship," *UN Chronicle*, 47(2), 21–25.

Feu-US. 2019, November. "The truth behind the climate pledges," The Universal Ecological Fund.

Fialkowski, K. 1986. "A mechanism for the origin of the human brain: A hypothesis," *Current Anthropology*, 27, 288–290.

Flavelle, C. 2020a, June 19. "Exposure to pollution and heat is tied to pregnancy risk," *New York Times.*

Flavelle, C. 2020b, July 15. "Data show an 'extraordinary' rise in coastal flooding," *New York Times.*

Flavelle, C. 2020c, October 29. "Pileup of climate calamities seeds a radical idea," *New York Times.*

Flavelle, C. 2021a, April 23. "Climate change could slash global wealth, an insurance giant warns," *New York Times.*

Flavelle, C. 2021b, May 4. "Blackouts are growing threat to U.S. cities," *New York Times.*

Flavelle, C. et al. 2020, June 29. "New data reveals hidden flood risk across America," *New York Times.*

Flavelle, C., Plumer, B. and Tabuchi, H. 2021, February 21. "Storms exposing a nation primed for catastrophe," *New York Times.*

Fountain, H. 2020, May 22. "'Expect more of these': Warmer climate raises risk of dam disasters," *New York Times.*

Fountain, H. 2020, December 9. "The Arctic is changing in ways 'scarcely imaginable even a generation ago'," *New York Times.*

Fox-Skelly, J. 2017, May 4. "There are diseases hidden in ice, and they are waking up," *BBC Earth.*

Freire, P. 2000. *Pedagogy of the oppressed*, 30th Anniversary edition. New York: Continuum.

Freire, P. 2004. *Pedagogy of indignation.* Boulder, CO: Paradigm Publishers.

Friedlingstein, P. et al. 2020, December 11. "Global carbon budget 2020," *Earth System Science Data*, 12, 3269–3340.

Friedman, L. 2019, February 21. "What is the Green New Deal? A climate proposal, explained," *New York Times.*

Friedman, L. 2021a, January 30. "Former climate leaders press U.S. on Amazon deforestation," *New York Times*, A10.

Friedman, L. 2021b, May 4. "Major greenhouse gases sharply cut by the E.P.A.," *New York Times*, A15.

Friedman, L., Sengupta, S. and Davenport, C. 2021, April 23. "Biden commits U.S. to emissions cuts as allies join vow," *New York Times.*

Frimpong, R. et al. 2021, March. "Pilot scale testing of an advanced solvent in a 0.7 MWe post-combustion CO2 capture unit," *International Journal of Greenhouse Gas Control*, 106.

Fuller, T. and Flavelle, C. 2020, September 11. "Disastrous wave of climate events slams California," *New York Times.*

Gardner, T. 2019, March 26. "Republicans defeat Green New Deal in senate vote democrats call a stunt," *Reuters.*

Goldstein, J. 2016, Spring. "Carbon bomb: Indonesia's failed mega rice project," *Arcadia*, 6.

Gore, A. 2006. *An inconvenient truth: The planetary emergency of global warming and what we can do about it.* Emmaus, PA: Rodale.

Gore, A. 2014, February 16. "Without a trace," *New York Times Book Review.* www.nytimes.com/2014/02/16/books/review/the-sixth-extinction-by-elizabeth-kolbert.html.

Gould, S. 1980. *The panda's thumb, more reflection in natural history.* New York: Norton.

Gould, S. 1989. *Wonderful life, the Burgess Shale and the nature of history.* New York: Norton.

Gould, S. 1997, June 26. "Evolution: The pleasures of pluralism," *The New York Review of Books*, 47–52.

Gramling, C. 2020, July 1. "4 ways to put the 100-degree Arctic heat record in context," *Science News*.

Gray, E. 2016, May 4. "Expanding tropics are pushing high altitude clouds towards poles," *NASA Earth Science News Team*.

Gray, E. and Merzdorf, J. 2019, June 13. "Earth's freshwater future: Extremes of flood and drought," *NASA Global Climate Change*.

Gray, J. 2014, September 2. "This changes everything: Capitalism vs the climate review: Naomi Klein's powerful and urgent polemic," *The Guardian*.

Gray, P. 1982. *The Irish famine*. New York: Harry N. Abrams.

Greenberg, J. 2021, April 5. "Fact-check: Is Biden's infrastructure plan the Green New Deal?," *Austin American-Statesman*.

Grier, P. 2005, September 12. "The great Katrina migration," *Christian Science Monitor*.

Gross, R. 2018, April 16. "Everything you ever wanted to know about earth's past climates," *Smithsonian*.

Gugliotta, G. 2001, November 5. "Anthrax has inspired dread and breakthroughs," *Washington Post*.

Hackley, R. 2018, July. "The world's natural aquifers at risk," *Stockholm Waterfront*, 2.

Hall, S. 2015, October 26. "Exxon knew about climate change almost 40 years ago," *Scientific American*.

Hall, S. 2020, June 16. "New suspect in cold case has long, deadly record," *New York Times*.

Hallock, B. 2014, January 27. "To make a burger, first you need 660 gallons of water," *Los Angeles Times*.

Hamburger, T. 2014, November 5. "Sen. Inhofe, denier of human role in climate change, likely to lead environment committee," *Washington Post*.

Hannah-Jones, N., ed. 2019, August 18. "The 1619 project," *New York Times Magazine*.

Hardenburg, W. 1912. *The Putumayo, The devil's paradise*. London, UK: T. Fisher Unwin.

Harris, M. 1990. *Our kind: Who we are, where we come from, where we are going*. New York: HarperCollins.

Hausfather, Z. 2018a, June 19. "How scientists estimate 'climate sensitivity'," *Carbon Brief*.

Hausfather, Z. 2018b, September 4. "Analysis: How much 'carbon budget' is left to limit global warming to 1.5C?," *Carbon Brief*.

Healthwise. 2020. "Hypothermia and cold temperature exposure," University of Michigan.

Herring, D. and Lindsey, R. 2020, October 29. "Hasn't Earth warmed and cooled naturally throughout history?," *NOAA Climate Watch*.

Hess, L. 2020, October 21. "World on fire 2020: Experts explain the global wildfire crisis," *Global Landscape Forum*.

Hickman, 2020, February 27. "NYC flood barrier project suspended by Trump administration," *The Architect's Newspaper*.

Hine, A., Boothroyd, J. and Nummedal, D. 2013, August 1. "Glacial outwash plain shoreline, South-central Iceland," *Coastal Care*.

Hoegh-Guldberg, O. et al. 2018. "Impacts of 1.5°C global warming on natural and human systems," Chapter 3 in *Global warming of 1.5°C*. Geneva, Switzerland: IPCC.

Holden, E. 2020, July 27. "What the US exiting the Paris climate agreement means," *The Guardian*.

Huxley, A. 1956, October. "A case of voluntary ignorance," *Esquire*.

ILO. 2019. *Working on a warmer planet: The impact of heat stress on labour productivity and decent work*. Geneva, Switzerland: International Labour Office.

Im, E., Pal, J. and Eltahir, A. 2017, August 2. "Deadly heat waves projected in the densely populated agricultural regions of South Asia," *Science Advances*, 3(8).

Ivanova, I. and Layne, R. 2020, June 30. "15 million U.S. homes are at risk of flooding: 70% higher than FEMA estimates," *CBS News*.

Jiang, Y. et al. 2021, March. "Techno-economic comparison of various process configurations for post-combustion carbon capture using a single-component water-lean solvent," *International Journal of Greenhouse Gas Control*, 106.

Johnson, G. 1996, August 20. "Social strife may have exiled ancient Indians," *New York Times*.

Kahle, T. 2015, December 11. "What comes after capitalism?," *Jacobin*.

Kaiser, A. 2019, August 27. "AP explains: Role of the Amazon in global climate change," *Associated Press*.

Kaneda, T. and Haub, C. 2020, January 23. "How many people have ever lived on Earth?," Population Reference Bureau.

Kelley, C. et al. 2015, March 17. "Climate change in the Fertile Crescent and implications of the recent Syrian drought," *PNAS*, 112(11), 3241–3246.

Kimmelman, M. 2017. "The Dutch have solutions to rising seas: The world is watching," *New York Times*.

King, M. 1967. *Where do we go from here: Chaos or community?* Boston, MA: Beacon Press.

Klein, N. 2009, April 16. "Hopebroken and hopesick, Obama fans need a new start," *The Guardian*.

Klein, N. 2011, November 9. "Capitalism vs. the climate," *The Nation*.

Klein, N. 2014. *This changes everything: Capitalism vs. the climate*. New York: Simon & Schuster.

Klein, N. 2017, May 31. "Economic pressure could jolt Trump into action on climate change," *New York Daily News*.

Klein, N. 2019. *On fire: The (burning) case for a Green New Deal*. New York: Simon & Schuster.

Knabb, R., Rhome, J. and Brown, D. 2005, December 20. "Tropical cyclone report Hurricane Katrina 23–30 August 2005," National Hurricane Center.

Kolbert, E. 2014. *The sixth extinction: An unnatural history*. New York: Henry Holt.

Kolbert, E. 2021, January 18. "Have we already been visited by aliens?," *The New Yorker*.

Kornei, K. 2020, June 30. "A far-off volcano and the Roman Republic's end," *New York Times*.

Krauss, C. 2019, April 8. "Big oil bets on carbon removal," *New York Times*, B1.

Krugman, P. 2010, April 11. "Building a green economy," *New York Times Magazine*.

Lakhani, N. 2020, January 13. "'Heat islands': Racist housing policies in US linked to deadly heatwave exposure," *The Guardian*.

Lau, T. 2019, December 12. "Citizens United explained," *Brennan Center for Justice*.

Lavelle, M. 2017, April 19. "Fossil fuel industries pumped millions into Trump's inauguration, filing shows," *Inside Climate News*.

Lawler, A. 2015, December. "Did Egypt's old Kingdom die: Or simply fade away?," *National Geographic*.

Lenton, T., Rockström, J., Gaffney, O. et al. 2019, November 27. "Climate tipping points: Too risky to be against," *Nature*.

Lepore, J. 2006. *New York burning: Liberty, slavery, and conspiracy in eighteenth-century*. New York: Vintage.

Lewandowsky, S. et al. 2013, March 26. "NASA faked the moon landing-therefore, (climate) science is a hoax: An anatomy of the motivated rejection of science," *Psychological Science*, 622–633.

Li, Q. 2018. *Forest bathing: How trees can help you find health and happiness*. New York: Viking.

Linden, E. 2006. *The winds of change: Climate, weather, and the destruction of civilizations*. New York: Simon & Schuster.

Lindsey, R. 2016, February 9. "Global impacts of El Niño and La Niña," *NOAA Climate.gov*.

Lipscy, P., Kushida, K. and Incerti, T. 2012, November 1. "Protecting nuclear plants from nature's worst," *Washington Post*.

Livingston, I. 2020, September 1. "Hottest season on record: Merciless Phoenix heat blasts by all-time monthly, summer milestones," *Washington Post*.

Lomborg, B. 2020a. *False Alarm: How climate change panic costs us trillions, hurts the poor, and fails to fix the planet*. New York: Basic Books.

Lomborg, B. 2020b, July 24. "We need free and honest debate on climate change policy," *Orange County Register*.

Londoño, E. and Casado, L. 2019, November 18. "In Brazil, Amazon deforestation has risen sharply on Bolsonaro's watch," *New York Times*, A4.

Lustgarten, A. 2020, July 26. "The great climate migration," *New York Times Magazine*.

Mandel, K. 2019, July 16. "Former Rick Perry staffer raises over $1 million for Trump's reelection campaign," *Think Progress*.

Marsooli, R. and Lin, N. 2020. "Impacts of climate change on hurricane flood hazards in Jamaica Bay, New York," *Climate Change*, 163, 2153–2171.

Marx, K. and Engels, F. 1848. *The communist manifesto*. London: Workers' Educational Association.

Mecklin, J. 2021, January 27. "It is 100 seconds to midnight," *Bulletin of the Atomic Scientists*, 2–11. https://thebulletin.org/wp-content/uploads/2021/01/2021-doomsday-clock-statement-1.pdf.

Mencimer, S. 2019, January 22. "Google, Facebook, and Microsoft sponsored a conference that promoted climate change denial," *Mother Jones*.

Mohajerani, A., Bakaric, J. and Jeffrey-Bailey, T. 2017, July 15. "The urban heat island effect, its causes, and mitigation, with reference to the thermal properties of asphalt concrete," *Journal of Environmental Management*, 197, 522–538.

Montaigne, F. 2019, September 4. "Will deforestation and warming push the Amazon to a tipping point?," *Yale Environment 360.*

Morris, S. 1998. *The crucible of creation: The Burgess Shale and the rise of animals.* Oxford: Oxford University Press.

Moynihan, C. 2020, September 21. "From time, to time remaining," *New York Times.*

Moynihan, C. 2021, April 20. "Union Square's climate clock is ticking with good news," *New York Times.*

Moynihan, D. 1969, September 19. "For John Ehrlichman," *Memorandum.* www. nixonlibrary.gov/sites/default/files/virtuallibrary/documents/jul10/56.pdf.

Muriel, P. and Singer, A. 2020. *Supporting civics education with student activism.* New York: Routledge.

Myers, S. 2020, August 22. "After virus, new hurdles for China from flooding," *New York Times.*

Myers, S. 2021, March 16. "Sandstorm in China wraps millions in dusty yellow haze," *New York Times.*

NASA. 2019, September 6. "What is the Sun's role in climate change?," *Global Climate Change.*

NASA. 2020, February 6. "Arctic ice melt is changing ocean currents," *Global Climate Change.*

NASA. 2021, February 1. "FAQ: How does the solar cycle affect Earth's climate?," *Global Climate Change.*

NASEM. 2004, February 11. "Report sets dietary intake levels for water, salt, and potassium to maintain health and reduce chronic disease risk," *National Academies of Sciences, Engineering, and Medicine.*

Nathanson, R. 2020, March 15. "Newark's lead crisis isn't over," *The Intercept.*

National Interagency Fire Center. www.nifc.gov/fireInfo/nfn.htm.

NOAA. n.d. "The coriolis effect," *National Oceanic and Atmospheric Administration.*

NOAA. "Hurricane damage potential," *National Weather Service.* www.weather. gov/jetstream/tc_potential.

NOAA. 2020, March 13. "Powerful 'Dragon' storm hits Egypt while Israel prepares for impact."

NOAA. 2021a. "U.S. billion-dollar weather and climate disasters," *NOAA National Centers for Environmental Information.*

NOAA. 2021b, March. "Climate at a glance: Regional time series," NOAA National Centers for Environmental Information.

NOAA. 2021c, April 7. "Despite pandemic shutdowns, carbon dioxide and methane surged in 2020," National Oceanic and Atmospheric Administration.

NOLA.com. 2015, August 27. "Hurricane Katrina migration: Where did people go? Where are they coming from now?," *Times-Picayune.*

Notaras, M. 2009, November 27. "Does climate change cause conflict?," *Our World.*

Nottingham, A. et al. 2020, August. "Soil carbon loss by experimental warming in a tropical forest," *Nature.*

Nuccitelli, D. 2015, November 5. "Scientists warned the US president about global warming 50 years ago today," *The Guardian.*

Nugent, C. 2021, April 20. "Biden wants a deal with Brazil's far-right president to protect the Amazon," *Time.*

Nuwer, R. 2020, June 1. "Extinctions are accelerating, threatening even human life," *New York Times.*

Ocko, I. et al. 2021. "Acting rapidly to deploy readily available methane mitigation measures by sector can immediately slow global warming," *Environmental Research Letters*, 16(5).

O'Neil, T. 2019, July 10. "Libertarian group demands NASA remove false '97 percent consensus' global warming claim," *PJ Media.*

Oskin, B. 2013, December 12. "Earth's greatest killer finally caught," *LiveScience.*

Oswald, A. 2013. *Wharram Percy: Deserted medieval village.* Swindon, UK: English Heritage.

Pachauri, R.K. and Meyer, L.A., eds. 2014. "Climate change 2014: Synthesis report," *IPCC.*

Pagano, A. 2017, November 3. "Massive 25-ton floodgates were installed in New York City: And it looks apocalyptic," *Business Insider.*

Patta, D. 2021, January 22. "COVID strain in South Africa shows huge resistance to antibodies from original virus," *CBS News.*

Penn, I. and Lipton, E. 2021, May 7. "Dispute exposes dirty secret about green cars," *New York Times.*

Penney, V. 2020, November 11. "5 Ways climate is changing hurricanes," *New York Times.*

Perkins-Kirkpatrick, S. and Lewis, S. 2020. "Increasing trends in regional heatwaves," *Nature Communications*, 11(1).

Pindyck, R. 2020, May 11. "What we know and don't know about climate change, and implications for policy," MIT Sloan School Working Paper 6114–20.

Plumer, B. 2021, February 17. "Frigid onslaught stretches limits of electric grids," *New York Times.*

Plumer, B. and Flavelle, C. 2021, January 19. "Businesses explore practical ways to pull greenhouse gasses from the air," *New York Times*, B5.

Plutarch. 1920. *The parallel lives*, vol. 9. Cambridge, MA: Loeb Classical Library.

Pope, K. 2019, April 10. "New research suggests climate change could enable mosquitoes to evolve more rapidly," *Yale Climate Connections.*

Popkin, G. 2020, August 18. "Hotter tropical soils emit more carbon dioxide," *The New York Times.*

Postel, S. 2015, February 12. "Love water for chocolate," *National Geographic.*

Potts, Richard. 2012. "Evolution and environmental change in early human prehistory," *Annual Review of Anthropology*, 41, 151–167.

President's Science Advisory Committee. 1965, November 5. "Restoring the quality of our environment," in *The White House.* Washington, DC: Government Printing Office.

Przywara, J. 2011. "Failure in structural steels and overview of I-35W bridge collapse," University of Notre Dame.

Public Health Law Center. 2019, January. "Master settlement agreement," *Mitchell Hamline School of Law.*

Pugh, B. 2021, March 16. "U.S. drought monitor," Center for Climate and Energy Solutions.

Readfearn, G. 2014, June 24. "The millions behind Bjorn Lomborg's Copenhagen Consensus Center US think tank," *Desmog.*

Reed, S. 2021, March 12. "Oil giants prepare to put carbon back in the ground," *New York Times.*

Revkin, A. and Mechaley, L. 2018. *Weather: An illustrated history*. New York: Sterling.

Rice, D. 2019, August 28. "What would the Earth be like without the Amazon rainforest?," *USA Today*.

Rigaud, K. et al. 2018. *Groundswell: Preparing for internal climate migration*. Washington, DC: World Bank Climate Change Group.

Robock. A. 2008, May/June. "20 reasons why geoengineering may be a bad idea," *Bulletin of the Atomic Scientists*.

Romero, R. and Emanuel, K. 2017, January. "Climate change and hurricane-like extratropical cyclones: Projections for North Atlantic polar lows and Medicanes based on CMIP5 models," *Journal of Climate*, 30(1).

Root, T., Freidman, L. and Tabuchi, H. 2019, July 10. "Following the money that undermines climate science," *New York Times*.

Sandy, M. 2019, December 6. "Amazon under Bolsonaro: 'Completely lawless'," *New York Times*, A12.

Sanger, D. 2001, June 12. "Bush will continue to Oppose Kyoto Pact on global warming," *New York Times*.

Schädel, C. 2020, December 2. "The irreversible emissions of a permafrost 'tipping point'," *Carbon Brief*.

Schiermeier, Q. 2012. "The Kyoto protocol: Hot air," *Nature*, 491(7426), 656–658.

Schwartz, I. 2020, September 12. "Tucker Carlson: Left uses fires for climate misinformation, see human suffering as a means to increase power," *Real Clear Politics*.

Scientific American. 2001, January 28. "Can somebody finally settle this question: Does water flowing down a drainspin in different directions depending on which hemisphere you're in? And if so, why?"

Seager, R. and Herweijer, C. 2010. *Causes and consequences of nineteenth century droughts in North America*. New York, NY: The Earth Institute at Columbia University.

Seager, R. et al. 2004. *Predicting Pacific decadal variability: Earth climate: The ocean-atmosphere interaction*. Washington, DC: American Geophysical Union.

Sengupta, S. 2020, August 8. "Here's what extreme heat looks like: Profoundly unequal," *New York Times*.

Sengupta, S. 2021a, February 27. "New targets for emissions fall far short of Paris goals," *New York Times*.

Sengupta, S. 2021b, April 8. "Global risks of climate and debt," *New York Times*.

Sengupta, S. 2021c, April 24. "As talks end, U.S. must sell climate goals," *New York Times*.

Sengupta, S. and Lawal, S. 2020, March 7. "To turn the tide, a Long Island tribe turns to nature," *New York Times*.

Servant, J. 2019, December 11. "China steps in as Zambia runs out of loan options," *The Guardian*.

Shabecoff, P. 1988, June 24. "Global warming has begun, expert tells senate," *New York Times*.

Sheridan, K. 2018, August 6. "Earth risks tipping into 'hothouse' state," *Phys.org*.

Shindell, D. et al. 2020, March 26. "The effects of heat exposure on human mortality throughout the United States," *GeoHealth*, 4(4).

Sinclair, U. 1935. *I, candidate for governor: And how I got licked.* New York: Farrar & Rinehart.

Singer, A. 2008. *New York and slavery: Time to teach the truth.* Albany, NY: SUNY.

Singer, A. 2018. *New York's grand emancipation jubilee.* Albany, NY: SUNY.

Singer, A. 2020, April 20. "Every day is Earth day: That's why I'm a Greta groupie," *Daily Kos.*

Singer, A. 2021, April 7. "Student climate activism and civics education," *Daily Kos.*

Skretteber, R. n.d. "Sahel: The world's most neglected and conflict-ridden region," *Norwegian Refugee Council.* www.nrc.no/shorthand/fr/sahel-the-worlds-most-neglected-and-conflict-ridden-region/index.html.

Smith, A. 2019, February 7. "2018's billion dollar disasters in context," *Climate.gov.*

Smith, A. 2020, January 8. "2010–2019: A landmark decade of U.S. billion-dollar weather and climate disasters," *NOAA Climate.gov.*

Smith, R. and Foster, J. 2017, May 4. "The significance of Naomi Klein: An eco-socialist exchange," *Climate & Capitalism.*

Smithsonian. 2020, September 1. "Climate effects on human evolution," Smithsonian National Museum of Natural History.

Sorkin, A. 2021, March 10. "It's not just Bitcoin that's huge: So is it's carbon footprint," *New York Times.*

Specia, M. 2020, September 19. "Rare, hurricane-strength storm batters western Greece's islands," *New York Times.*

Spilman, R. 2018, January 4. "Update: Looking back at when New York harbor froze," *The Old Salt Blog.*

Steffen, W. et al. 2018, August 6. "Trajectories of the Earth system in the Anthropocene," *Proceedings of the National Academy of Sciences (PNAS),* 115(33), 8252–8259.

Stein, R. and Hamilton, J. 2012, October 20. "The science of why Sandy is such a dangerous storm," *National Public Radio.*

Steinbeck, J. 1939. *The grapes of wrath.* New York: Viking Press.

Stevens, W. 1993, December 14. "Dust in sea mud may link human evolution to climate," *New York Times.*

Stiglitz, J. 2020, August 9. "Fog machine," *New York Times.*

Stokes, E. 2016, March 3. "The drought that preceded Syria's civil war was likely the worst in 900 years," *Vice News.*

Stone, A. 2020, July 6. "Heatwave trends accelerate worldwide," *Science Daily.*

Stone, B., Jr. et al. 2021, April 30. "Compound climate and infrastructure events: How electrical grid failure alters heat wave risk," *Environmental Science and Technology.*

Stone, P. 2020, August 9. "Big oil remembers 'friend' Trump with millions in campaign funds," *The Guardian.*

Struzik, E. 2020, September 17. "The age of megafires: The world hits a climate tipping point," *Yale Environment 360.*

Sullivan, W. 1965, May 1. "Jet trails' effect on climate studied," *New York Times.*

Szczepanski, M., Sedlar, F. and Shalant, J. 2018, September 13. "Bangladesh: A country underwater, a culture on the move," Natural Resources Defense Council.

Tabuchi, H. 2020, November 12. "Global firm casts big oil's messages as grassroots campaigns," *New York Times*.

Tabuchi, H. and Plumer, B. 2021, March 3. "No tailpipe doesn't mean no emissions," *New York Times*.

Tang, C., Davis, K., Delmer, C., Yang, D. and Wills, M. 2018. "Elevated atmospheric CO_2 promoted speciation in mosquitoes," *Communications Biology*, 1.

Thunberg, G. 2019. *No one is too small to make a difference*. New York: Penguin.

Thunberg, G. 2019, January 25. "Our house is on fire," *The Guardian*.

Tobacco Industry Research Committee. 1954, January. "A Frank statement to cigarette smokers," *The Tobacco Leaf*.

UNCC. 2021. "What is the Paris agreement?," United Nations Climate Change.

UNEP. 2012, November. "The emissions gap report 2021," United Nations Environment Programme.

United Nations. 2015, December 12. "Adoption of the Paris agreement." https://assets.documentcloud.org/documents/2646274/Updated-l09r01.pdf.

United Nations. 2019, June. "Growing at a slower pace, world population is expected to reach 9.7 billion in 2050 and could peak at nearly 11 billion around 2100," Department of Education and Social Affairs.

United Nations. 2021, February 26. "Nationally determined contributions under the Paris agreement," *United Nations Framework Convention on Climate Change*.

United States Geological Survey. n.d. "The water content of things," *United States Department of the Interior*.

United States State Department. n.d. "Leaders summit on climate: Schedule." www.state.gov/leaders-summit-on-climate/schedule/.

Unmüssig, B. 2017, October 12. "The geoengineering fallacy," *Project Syndicate*.

Uscinski, J., Douglas, K. and Lewandowsky, S. 2017, September 27. "Climate change conspiracy theories," *Oxford Research Encyclopedia, Climate Science*, Oxford University Press.

Van Doren, P. 2020, November 11. "What we do not know about climate change and why that matters," *Cato at Liberty*.

Van Doren, P. and Brannon, I. 2020–2021, Winter. "Climate change," *Regulation*.

Velasquez-Manoff, M. and White, J. 2021, March 2. "In the Atlantic Ocean, subtle shifts hint at dramatic dangers," *New York Times*.

Vidal, J. 2018, August 21. "Are coastal nuclear power plants ready for sea level rise?," *Hakai*.

Vrba, E. 1993. "Turnover-pulse, the red queen, and related topics," *American Journal of Science*, 293-A, 418–452.

Vrba, E. 1995. "The fossil record of African antelopes (Mammalia, Bovidae) in relation to human evolution and paleoclimate," in Vrba, E. et al., eds., *Paleoclimate and evolution with emphasis on human origins*. New Haven, CT: Yale University Press.

Walker, S. 2014, July 7. "Why your dog looks and acts like a puppy: The biology behind domestication," *American Society of Animal Science*.

Watts, J. 2017, November 28. "The Amazon effect: How deforestation is starving São Paulo of water," *The Guardian*.

Wayman, E. 2011, November 16. "What's in a name? Hominid versus hominin," *Smithsonian*.

Weisbrod, K. 2021, February 14. "Q&A: Is Elizabeth Kolbert's new book a hopeful look at the promise of technology, or a cautionary tale?," *Inside Climate News*.

Werrell, C., Femia, F. and Slaughter, A. 2013, February 28. "The Arab Spring and climate change: A climate and security correlations series," *Center for American Progress*.

WHO. 2018, July 20. "Zika virus key facts," *World Health Organization*. www. who.int/news-room/fact-sheets/detail/zika-virus.

Wiltgen, N. 2013, April 4. "Poll: 3 in 8 Americans believe global warming a hoax," The Heartland Institute.

Wire, S. and Phillips, A. 2021, April 28. "Senate votes to repeal a Trump-era methane rule," *Los Angeles Times*.

Witman, S. 2018, February 6. "Pinpointing effects of Hadley cell expansion," *Geophysical Research Letters*.

Witze, A. 2020, September 10. "The Arctic is burning like never before: And that's bad news for climate change," *Nature*.

WNA. 2021, March. "World nuclear power reactors & uranium requirements," World Nuclear Association.

Wood, G. 2015. *Tambora: The eruption that changed the world*. Princeton, NJ: Princeton University Press.

World Data Atlas. n.d. "Brazil/Amazonas." https://knoema.com/atlas/Brazil/ Amazonas.

WWF. "Amazon facts," *World Wildlife Federation*. www.worldwildlife.org/places/ amazon.

Xu, C., Kohler, T., Lenton, T. et al. 2020, May 4. "Future of the human climate niche," *PNAS*, 11350–11355.

Yee, V. and Goodman, P. 2021, March 25. "Traffic jam in Suez Canal as huge ship runs aground," *New York Times*.

Zafar, R. 2019, September 10. "Apple A13 for iPhone 11 has 8.5 billion transistors, quad-core GPU," *wccftech.com*.

Zimmer, C. 2018, December 11. "Earth's near-death experience," *New York Times*, D3.

Zimmermann, K. 2013, January 15. "What is the Gulf Stream?," *LiveScience*. www.livescience.com/26273-gulf-stream.html.

Zukerman, W. 2011, April 25. "Warmer oceans release CO_2 faster than thought," *New Scientist*.

Index